CONTEMPORARY ART
FROM CRESCENT MOON PUBLISHING

The Art of Andy Goldsworthy
by William Malpas

Andy Goldsworthy: Touching Nature
by William Malpas

Richard Long: Pocket Guide
by William Malpas

The Art of Richard Long
by William Malpas

Constantin Brancusi: Sculpting the Essence of Things
by James Pearson

Alison Wilding: The Embrace of Sculpture
by Susan Quinnell

Eric Gill: Nuptials of God
by Anthony Hoyland

The Erotic Object: Sexuality in Sculpture From Prehistory to the Present Day
by Susan Quinnell

Minimal Art and Artists In the 1960s and After
by Laura Garrard

Land Art, Earthworks, Installations, Environments, Sculpture
by William Malpas

*Land Art: A Complete Guide to Landscape, Environmental,
Earthworks, Nature, Sculpture and Installation Art*
by William Malpas

Andy Goldsworthy In Close-Up
by William Malpas

Land Art In Close-Up
by William Malpas

Mark Rothko: The Art of Transcendence
by Julia Davis

Jasper Johns
by L.M. Poole

Brice Marden
by Laura Garrard

Frank Stella: American Abstract Artist
by James Pearson

Maurice Sendak and the Art of Children's Book Illustration
by L.M. Poole

Sacred Gardens: The Garden in Myth, Religion and Art
by Jeremy Robinson

Sex in Art: Pornography and Pleasure in the History of Art
by Cassidy Hughes

Postwar Art
by George Knighton

Colorfield Painting

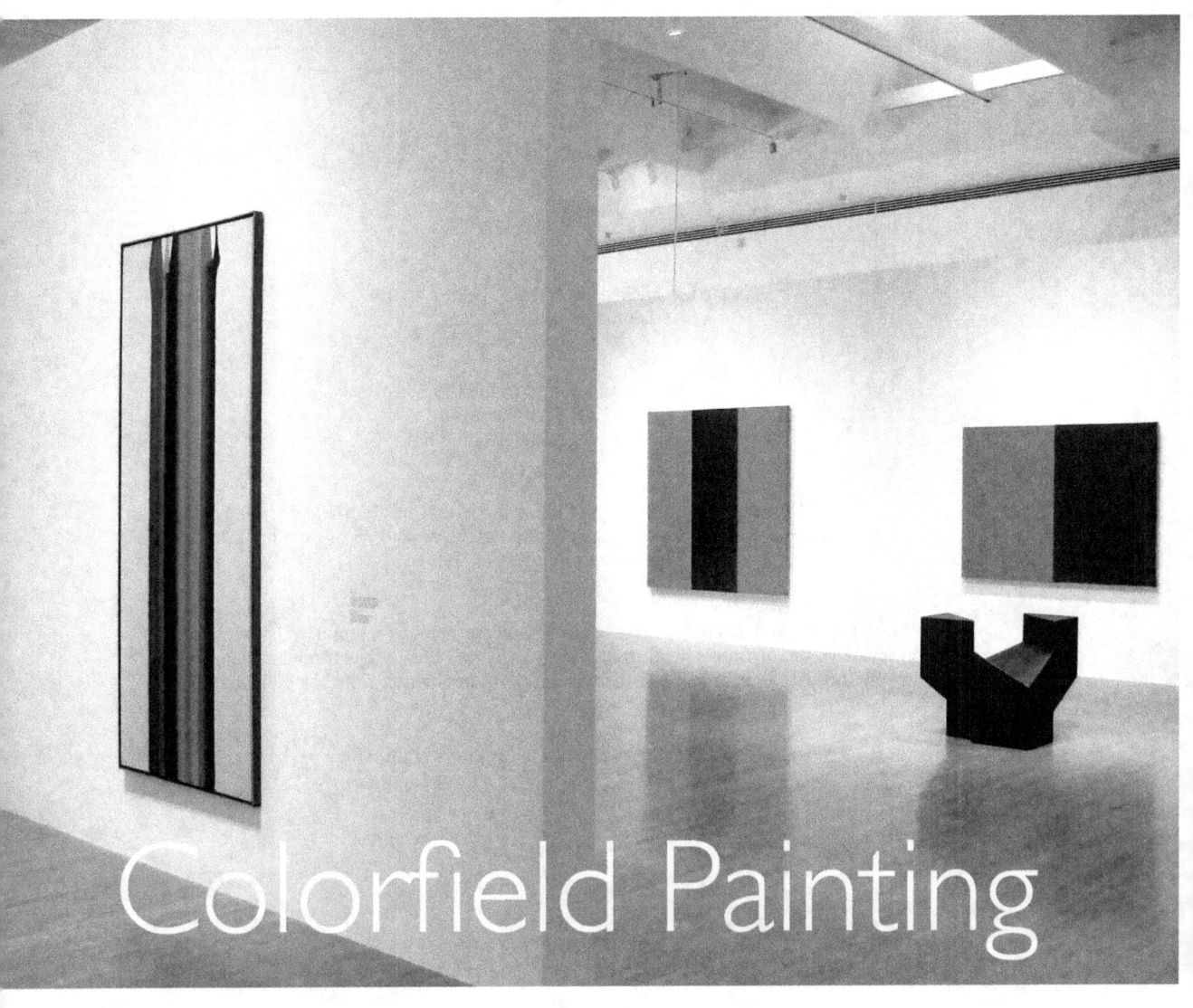

Colorfield Painting

Minimal, Cool, Hard Edge, Serial
and Post-Painterly Abstract Art
of the Sixties to the Present

Laura Garrard

CRESCENT MOON

First published 2007. Third edition, 2013.
© Laura Garrard 2007, 2013.

Printed and bound in the U.S.A.
Set in Rotis Serif 9 on 14pt.
Designed by Radiance Graphics.

British Library Cataloguing in Publication data

Garrard, Laura
Colorfield Painting
1. Minimal Art
I. Title
709'.04

ISBN 9781861714428 (Pbk)
ISBN 9781861713735 (Hbk)

CRESCENT MOON PUBLISHING
P.O. Box 1312,
Maidstone,
Kent, ME14 5XU,
United Kingdom
www.crmoon.com

Contents

Acknowledgements

Thanks to the authors quoted and their publishers.
Thanks to Mirabelle Marden.
To Ameringer & Yohe Fine Art, New York.
To Paula Cooper Gallery, New York.
To Matthew Marks Gallery, New York.
To Gagosian Gallery, New York.
To Kenneth Noland, Victoria Woodhull and the Kenneth Noland Studio.
To Susanne Singer, Inc.
To Dan Flavin, Ltd.

Illustrations © the artists and copyright holders.
Images are used for information and research purposes, with no infringement of copyright or rights intended.

Abbreviations

Colorfield Painting

Colors win you over more and more. A certain blue enters your soul. A certain red has an effect on your blood-pressure. A certain color tones you up. It's the concentration of timbres. A new era is opening.

Henri Matisse

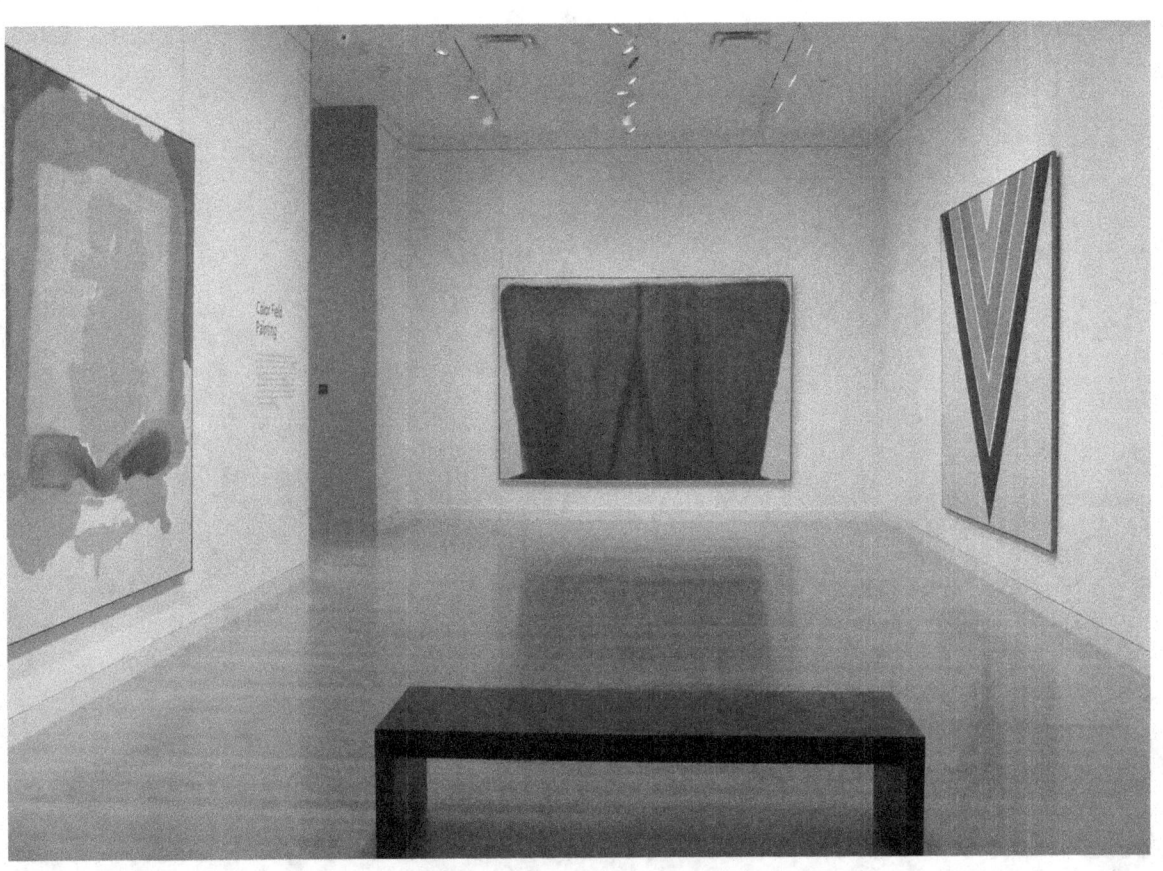

Helen Frankenthaler, Morris Louis and Kenneth Noland
at the wonderful Local Color show,
Smithsonian American Art Museum, Washington, DC, 2008

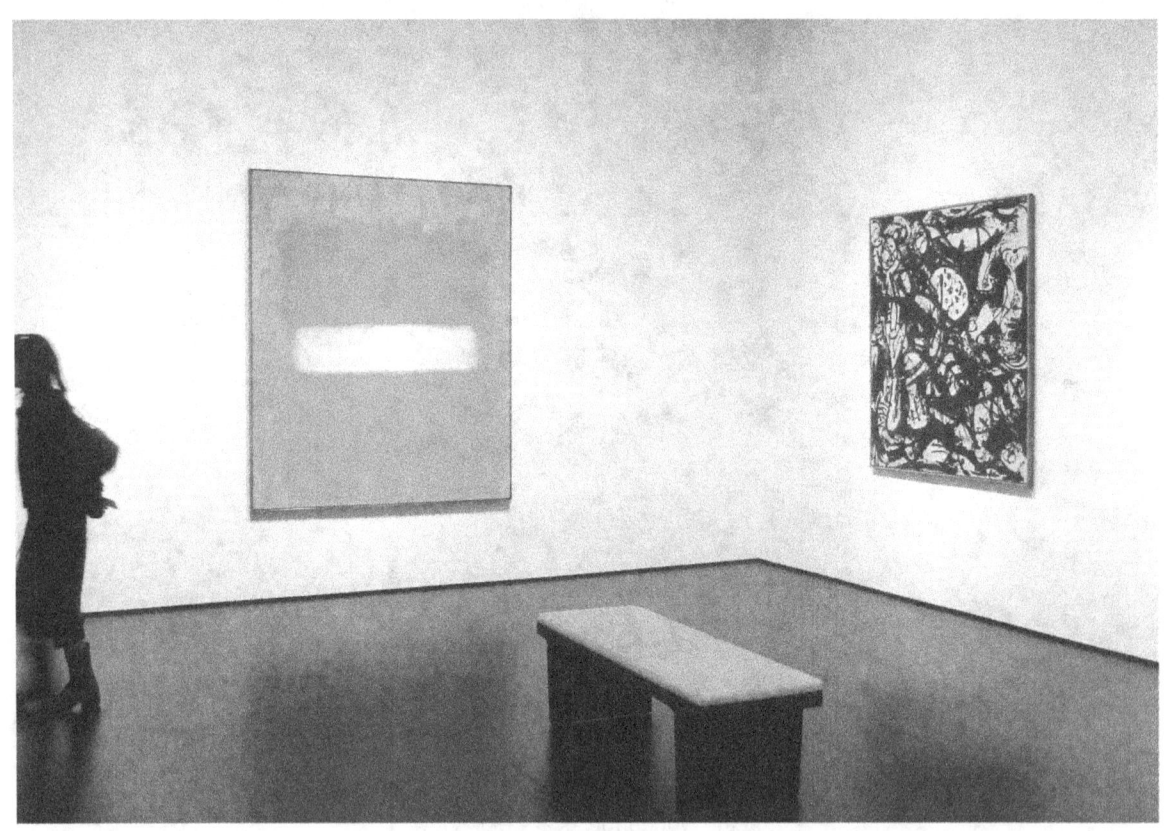

Mark Rothko in downtown L.A.

INTRODUCTION

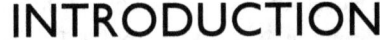

Sixties painting was variously termed Colorfield, Hard Edge, Minimal, Serial and Post-Painterly Abstraction, and was linked with Pop Art, Op (optical) Art, chromatic and kinetic abstraction, wholistic art, pure-painting, geometric abstraction, organic abstraction, ABC Art, Cool Art, Systematic Painting, Non-gestural Painting, Non-Relationalism, Abstract Mannerism and Abstract Sublime painting (I prefer the term 'Serial' to 'Systematic'). The 1960s period for Colorfield painting also meant the 1950s-1970s, and some Colorfield painters continued to make similar art way into the 1980s and beyond (Helen Frankenthaler, for example, has produced similar art into the 2010s).

According to critic Lawrence Alloway in his influential essay "Systematic Painting" (for the 1966 show of the same name), the term 'Post-Painterly Abstraction' comes via Roger Fry's coining of the term Post-Impressionist to cover Paul Cézanne, Georges Seurat, Vincent van Gogh and Paul Gauguin. For Alloway, the 'core of Post-Painterly Abstraction' was a technical procedure, the

> staining of canvas to obtain color uninterrupted by pressures of the hand or the operational limits of brush work. Poured paint exists purely as color, "freed" of drawing and modelling. (1966)

The term 'Cool Art' derived from Irving Sandler in the exhibition catalogue to *Concrete Expressionism* (1965), meaning mechanistic, impersonal and boring art.

Terms such as Post-Painterly Abstraction (from Clement Greenberg) seem unwieldy. New hyphenations and conjunctions had to be invented to describe the new painting. Ad Reinhardt, for example, might be described as a post-painterly, meta-structural, non-objective, post-religious, Minimal abstractionist.

The painters linked in this study with 'Colorfield', 'Hard Edge' 'Minimal', 'Cool', 'Serial' and 'Post-Painterly Abstraction' painting include Minimal artists such as Brice Marden, Sol LeWitt, Agnes Martin, Ad Reinhardt and Robert Ryman; Colorfield painters such as Helen Frankenthaler, Kenneth Noland, Sam Gilliam and Morris Louis; Post-Painterly Abstractionists such as Frank Stella, David Novros, Richard Diebenkorn, Al Held, Jo Baer and Jules Olitski; and Hard Edge painters such as Ellsworth Kelly, Robert Mangold, Joseph Albers and Elisabeth Murray.

Definitions are always in flux, however, because Frank Stella could be classed as a Minimal and a Hard Edge abstractionist, while Brice Marden's seemingly austere monochrome Minimal works of the 1960s could also be seen as lushly Colorfield. Further, the works of Sol LeWitt (the wall drawings), could be seen as more sculptural than painterly; while Stella's later works moved into three dimensions with a vengeance. The shaped canvases of Robert Mangold and Elisabeth Murray also possess many sculptural qualities. However one wishes to define them, these are the painters that will be central to this study: Brice Marden, Frank Stella, Morris Louis, Helen Frankenthaler, Kenneth Noland, Agnes Martin, Robert Ryman, Ad Reinhardt and Richard Diebenkorn.

Other painters associated with the Colorfield or Post-Painterly Abstraction type of Sixties painting include Jasper Johns and Robert Rauschenberg, two hugely influential artists whose works re-defined painting; Barnett Newman, the 'father' of Minimal painting (and, to a lesser extent, Mark Rothko, Jackson Pollock, Robert Motherwell and Franz Kline); and figures such as Andy Warhol, Yves Klein and Bruce Nauman.

Other painters contemporary with the ten or so painters studied here include Jo Baer, Jules Olitski, David Novros, Larry Poons, Dan Christensen, Robert Mangold, Robert Indiana, Elisabeth Murray, Sam Francis, Sam Gilliam, Cy Twombly, James Rosenquist, Josef Albers, Gillian Ayres, Al Held, William Turnbull, Ludwig Sandler, Jack Youngerman, Jack Tworkov, Dorothea Rockbourne, Jack Bush, Ron Davis, Victor Passmore, Georges Mathieu, Pierre Soulages, and Blinky Palermo. Later painters who developed some of the ideas of Post-Painterly Abstraction will also be noted: Gerhard Richter, Ian Daven-port, Callum Innes, Gotthard Graubner, Jennifer Bartlett, Julian Schnabel, Anselm Keifer, Thérèse Oulton, Herbert Brandal, Helmut Middendorf, Helmut Federle, Tom Downing, Gene Davis, Howard Mehring and Alma

Thomas. (I wish there were space and time to discuss all of them, but there isn't. I highly recommend the documerntary *Painters Painting* from the early 1970s, available on DVD, which has interviews with many of the artists studied here).

Some of the key exhibitions of the era included Lawrence Alloway's *Systematic Painting* (1967), Kynaston McShine's *Primary Structures* (1966) at the Jewish Museum, *Towards a New Abstraction* (1963), *Sixteen Americans* (1959), Michael Fried's *Three American Painters* (1965), *Unitary Forms* (San Francisco Museum of Modern Art, 1970), *Washington Color Painters* (Washington, 1965), and Clement Greenberg's *Post-Painterly Abstraction* (1964).

Important Minimal shows included: *Primary Structures*, *Sculpture of the Sixties* (curated by Maurice Tuchman in 1967), *9 in a Warehouse*, which featured Eva Hesse, Bruce Nauman and Richard Serra, and *Anti-Illusion*, at the Whitney Museum of American Art, which featured Lynda Benglis, Hesse, Nauman, Robert Ryman, Richard Serra, Joel Shapiro and Tuttle), *Live in Your Head* and *Square Pegs* (1969), *Information* (MOMA, 1970), and *Documenta 5* (which included Joseph Beuys, Daniel Buren, Christo, Gilbert & George, Eva Hesse, Jannis Kounellis, Sol LeWitt, Richard Long, Bruce Nauman, Dennis Oppenheim, Robert Ryman, Rich-ard Serra and Robert Smithson.)

Colorfield, Minimal, Serial, Hard Edge and Post-Painterly Abstract painting had a definite American (and New York) flavour to it, even if it was not produced in America or by American artists. In Bruce Glaser's "Questions to Stella and Judd", Donald Judd continually stressed the point that the new (Minimal) art is definitely American and non-European. Time and again Judd insisted that the new art was trying to get away from the European tradition. 'It suits me fine if that's all down the drain', Judd said. 'I'm totally uninterested in European art and I think it's over with'.[1] Kenneth Noland commented:

> The scene then as now was centered in New York. For the most part, I've kept a bit apart from that attractive and seductive city. I've done it by living in the country within commuting distance.

Robert Hughes remarked that the Colorfield paintings of Kenneth Noland, Jules Olitski, Morris Louis and Helen Frankenthaler was 'the most openly decorative, anxiety-free, socially indifferent canvases in the history of American art'.[2] After Louis, Hughes said in *American Visions*, Colorfield and abstract painting became Mannerist and lightweight: it became

> more and more a matter of cuisine, and timid cuisine at that. Declining into mannerism, it had taken belief in abstraction with it; American abstract art was now in the unenviably depleted condition of most Italian painting after the death of Titian. (1997, 549)

Colorfield painting was not confined to New York, however: Washington, DC was also a key centre: the so-called 'Washington Color School' included artists such as Morris Louis, Kenneth Noland, Helen Frankenthaler, Howard Mehring, Gene Davis, Paul Read, Anne Truitt, Tom Downing, Sam Gilliam and Alma Thomas. There was a famous show of Washington Colorfield art in 1965 (and, more recently, an exhibit in Washington in 2008, called *Local Color*, was absolutely stunning, and featured many of the famous names of Colofield painting).

Visiting DIA in Beacon in upstate New York is highly recommended – it houses one of the great collections of Minimal art in the world, as well as among the largest collections of contemporary art (and includes painters such as Agnes Martin, Robert Ryman, Gerhard Richter and Andy Warhol).

Many of the Colorfield and Sixties painters made extremely brilliantly colorful works in the 1960s then turned back to the sombre colors of gray and black in the late 1980s and 1990s. Painters such as Brice Marden, Frank Stella, Jasper Johns and Jules Olitski were ambiguous about saturated color: they moved back and forth from monochrome grays and blacks to full color. In the late 1980s and 1990s painters such as Stella, Olitski, Ellsworth Kelly and Larry Poons moved from bright color to muted monochrome.[3] Mid-1990s works by Stella were unpainted, using instead the natural colors of metal and wood; Marden turned from his luscious monochromes of the 1970s and 1980s to the black-and-white of Chinese calligraphy in the *Cold Mountain* series and other works.

An interesting sidelight on Colorfield and Sixties painters is that their works are not lasting very well. As Charles Riley notes, works by Mark Rothko, Frank Stella Kenneth Noland, Willem de Kooning, Robert Motherwell, Helen Frankenthaler, Hans Hofmann, Barnett Newman, Ad Reinhardt, Franz Kline and Morris Louis are 'falling to bits' (1995, 12), because they used mediums and solvents that only loosely bound the pigment to the canvas. Though painters such as Stella and Rothko knew about the traditional methods of painting, they often went out and bought cheap housepaint instead (proving a nightmare for museum and picture restorers of later generations).

I

THE AESTHETICS OF COLORFIELD, MINIMAL, HARD EDGE, SERIAL AND POST-PAINTERLY ABSTRACT PAINTING

PRESENCE

Post-painterly abstract paintings, like all paintings, demand that one see them in the flesh, so to speak. The colors, shapes, patterns, forms, canvases, stretchers and scale of the paintings are crucial; one has to see them close up. The shaped canvases of the Sixties usually had thick, solid stretchers; and thus a definite volume and mass; they were environmental as well as painterly; they combined painting, sculpture and even carpentry.¹ Post-painterly abstract paintings are very physical paintings, but this is true also of Berthe Morisot, Artemisa Gentileschi, Diego Velásquez, Mark Rothko, Giotto, or any painter one cares to name. Although Colorfield/ Hard Edge/ Post-Painterly Abstract paintings emphasize the frontal aspect, one can walk around the sides and look at them from other directions. Frank Stella's copper and aluminium metallic paint canvases, though apparently 'flat', are complex spatially and physically.

> People say that the paintings are always big because they're striving for effect [Stella said], but they're also big so that I don't trip over myself, so that I have room to work, and people can come in and be comfortable.

Some of Frank Stella's 1960s copper and aluminium stripe paintings are vast, zigzagging down gallery walls. Paintings such as Stella's *D* are a seven-foot polygon which, because of its scale, as with Mark Rothko, Morris Louis, Barnett Newman, Franz Kline or William de Kooning, towers over the spectator. Even so, Post-Painterly Abstract and Colorfield paintings are not domineering in the way that the canvases of Mark Rothko or Robert Motherwell can be. The very lightness and bright colors of Colorfield paintings dispel the sense of being overwhelmed by the paintings. Some Colorfield art – by Kenneth Noland, Frank Stella, Helen Frankenthaler and Morris Louis, for example – is not oppressive or gloomy at all, but is vivacious, muscular, positive and sometimes joyous.

COLOR

The paintings of Post-Painterly Abstract/ Colorfield/ Hard Edge/ Cool art are among the brightest and most lushly colorful in the history of art. Color was the one element of painting that Sixties art was incredibly successful at exploring. The painters whose exuberant colors were the ancestors and influences of Sixties Post-Painterly Abstraction include Vincent van Gogh, Henri Matisse, Pierre Bonnard, Emil Nolde and Mark Rothko. It was Matisse who embodied in his paintings many of the æsthetics of color which subsequent 20th century painters took on board. Matisse had a reverence for color, like van Gogh's, which was mystical.

Colors win you over more and more [Matisse wrote]. A certain blue enters your soul. A certain red has an effect on your blood-pressure. A certain color tones you up. It's the concentration of timbres. A new era is opening. (H. Matisse, 143)

However, Henri Matisse was far less reluctant than the Colorfield and Sixties painters to admit to the affectivity, the emotion of painting. Matisse wrote:

My purpose is to render my emotion. This state of soul is created by the objects which surround me and which react in me: from the horizon to myself, myself included. For very often I put myself in my pictures, and I am aware of what exists behind me'.[3]

If one looks closer at painters such as Brice Marden, Robert Ryman and Frank Stella, one finds Romantic views, and admissions of the subjective, emotional aspects of painting. 'I would say that the poetry of painting has to do with feeling. It should be a kind of revelation, even a reverent experience', said Robert Ryman, seen by some as a severe, restrained Minimal artist.

You come away feeling delight. You feel sustained, and it can last for several days. It's a feeling of well-being. Poetry does it, music does it, painting does it. (R. Ryman, 1983)

In a 1948 interview, Jackson Pollock spoke of the significance of the subjective response; he said that what interested him was that modern subject matter could be found inside the artist. Modern painters 'work from within', Pollock noted.[2]

For Ellsworth Kelly, everything was all already there. There was no need to invent:

Everything that I saw became something to be made, and it had to be exactly as it was, with nothing added. It was a new freedom: there was no longer the need to compose. The subject was there already made, and I could take from everything. It all belonged to me: a glass roof of a factory, with its broken and patched panels, lines on a road map, a corner of a Braques painting, paper fragments in the street. It was all the same: anything goes.

Color has been central to postwar and contemporary artists such as Barnett Newman, Clyfford Still, Christopher Le Brun, Gillian Ayres, Howard Hodgkin, Kenneth Noland, Jules Olitski, Joseph Albers and others. Albers made a thorough exploration of color in his *Homage to the Square* series. Painters such as Helen Frankenthaler rejoice in the exuberance of pure color. See, for example, her *Movable Blue* (1973, Citizens Fidelity Bank and Trust Company, Louisville) and *Nature Abhors a Vacuum* (1973, Andre Emmerich Gallery, New York).

The Sixties was an era which drew attention to the *physicality* of artworks. Color was another element in the physicality of an art object. Color was treated in the same physical way as the other formal aspects of the artwork (size, shape, texture, weight, and so on). For the Post-Painterly Abstract painters (such as Morris Louis, Jules Olitski, Ellsworth Kelly, Richard Diebenkorn and Marcia Hafif), color has a direct sensual effect. The symbolic and iconological aspects of color were seen as not as important as haptic physicality.

WHAT YOU SEE IS WHAT YOU GET

The holistic quality of Abstract Expressionism was crucial – the instantaneous Zen-like 'all-over effect', as Barnett Newman described it. The repeated single form might be called One Image art, Lawrence Alloway suggested. Donald Judd said that this holistic approach was the legacy of Jackson Pollock: this unification was 'the paramount quality and scheme of Abstract Expressionism', and it is central to the art of Frank Stella, Kenneth Noland, John Chamberlain, Mark Rothko and Barnett Newman (1964, 28). In "Specific Objects", Donald Judd wrote that

> it isn't necessary for a work to have a lot of things to look at, to compare, to analyze one by one, to contemplate. The thing as a whole, its qualities as a whole, is what is interesting. (1965)

For Judd, 'most of the best new work is intended to have much more impact at once'. Jackson Pollock and Abstract Expressionism had to come first before Frank Stella's paintings could blossom. Stella makes many references to Jackson Pollock in *Working Space*:

> we need to use Pollock. We see the potential: in the speed of the moving line, in the encapsulation and entanglement of shallow space, and in the sheer beauty of the painting's literalness, what amounts to the embodiment of its abstraction... We should be able to expand Pollock's pictorial space and to follow the lead of his paint skeins. Painting desperately needs the literalness, immediacy, freedom, and clarity of the drip paintings. (60)

FLATNESS

Clement Greenberg had noted that any painterly mark alters the state of the canvas: '[t]he first mark made on a canvas destroys the literal and utter flatness', he wrote (1961, 106). Jackson Pollock had moved in this direction with his 'non-figurative' skeins of color.[4] But when one comes to Brice Marden, Kenneth Noland, Jo Baer and Morris Louis, one sees the paint straight on the canvas, with no attempts at the usual forms of traditional Renaissance illusion, other than a simple pattern. When one first confronts a Post-Painterly Abstract painting, and sees the bare canvas, it stops the viewer up short. Something is different about Colorfield paintings. One doesn't at first notice what it is. One looks closer: yes, one can see raw canvas. This bare canvas is not a sly reference on the painter's part to the manufacture of the painting (though it is that too). S/he are not showing the canvas to show the viewer how the painting is made, much as a movie camera can pull back from a scene to show the lights, crew, director and people standing around smoking. Marden, Noland, Louis and Stella reveal the canvas for different reasons. The paint on their canvases is not 'representational', in the usual sense. It is not paintwork referring to something outside of itself. It is there, it partakes of *thereness* or *dasein*, to use the terms of Zen Buddhism and Existentialism, two important influences on contemporary American art.

The link between American abstract painting and Eastern mysticism can be extended to the practice of Zen meditation. This comparison will seem far-fetched until one recalls the ways in which many Minimal and Colorfield artists spoke of their work and the reactions they hoped to induce in the spectator. Many artists sink into a light trance or muse state when they create. In Zen Buddhist mysticism, it is called 'vertical meditation', a going-down and a breaking-through.[5] The huge fields of saturated colors of Mark Rothko, Barnett Newman, Morris Louis and Helen Frankenthaler may promote an intro-spection similar to Zen contemplation. The upright zips, stripes and canvases of Rothko, Louis, Stella and Newman may correspond to 'vertical meditation'. After Zen meditation comes Zen *satori* or *samadhi*, the ecstatic shock. From the empty spaces a 'marvellous Void' may appear.[6] Painters such as Jackson Pollock, Franz Kline, Morris Louis and Jules Olitski use Zen Buddhist methods of spontaneity and asymmetry.[7] The concept of formlessness is found in painters such as Rothko, Louis, Newman and Frank-enthaler, but Ad Reinhardt was more concerned with delimitation than trying to paint emptiness.

BARE CANVAS

Frank Stella encourages the viewer to confront the paint stuck on the bare canvas. A new sort of painting is created. For Sheldon Nodelman, Stella and Kenneth Noland created a new fusion of paint and canvas, so that 'no contrast' will be 'set up between the image-content and the picture-object' (1967, 75). Finally, a painting will become an object, as Jo Baer writes:

> The last radical paintings to attend figure-ground problems were Kenneth Noland's circle paintings of about 1960. Painters discarded ground altogether, and paintings became objects altogether. (1967, 6)

For Donald Judd, simply working in three dimensions cuts out one of the recurring problems of Sixties art – that of illusion:

> Three dimensions are real space. That gets rid of the problem of illusionism and of literal space, space in and around marks and colors – which is riddance of one of the salient and most objectionable relics of European art. The several limits of painting are no longer present. A work can be as powerful as it can be thought to be. Actual space is intrinsically more powerful and specific than paint on a flat surface. (1965)

2

ABSTRACT EXPRESSIONISM AND SIXTIES COLORFIELD PAINTING

ABSTRACT EXPRESSIONIST PAINTING

For Hilton Kramer, Abstract Expressionism was all about painting, about reducing painting to nothing more than painting that referred to its manufacture, to its essence, as a material object (E. De Antonio, 143). It was this materiality that Robert Rauschenberg liked about the Abstract Expressionists: 'they let their brushstrokes show', Rauschenberg said, there was a sense of materiality about their works (ib., 87). The Post-Painterly, post-Abstract Expressionist painters – Brice Marden, Ellsworth Kelly, Jo Baer, Kenneth Noland, Richard Diebenkorn, Morris Louis and Ad Reinhardt – are regarded by some critics as having squeezed out the emotion from painting: they took the Abstract Expressionist forms and made them unexpressive. Lawrence Alloway writes in "Residual Sign Systems in Abstract Expressionism":

> If we compare paintings by Frank Stella and Ellsworth Kelly with those of the Abstract Expressionists, it becomes evident that a dime of allusion, an aura of content, has been denied by the later artists. They certainly take off from positions given by Newman, Rothko, but the field of color, the holistic imagery, and the expanded scale of the canvas no longer imply momentous content. The allusions of older artists' feelings compared to the reduced passion of the younger generation... (1973)

Flatness in painting is necessary, Helen Frankenthaler said, if one wanted to have an artwork clear of connotations.

> Sentiment and nuance are being squeezed out so that if something is not altogether flatly painted then there might be a hint of edge, chiaroscuro, shadow and if one wants just that pure thing these associations get in the way. (1965, 38)

The Minimal and Colorfield painters (such as Kenneth Noland, Frank Stella, Jo Baer, Brice Marden, Jules Olitski and Morris Louis), seem closer to Barnett Newman than Mark Rothko. One can see a direct strand of painting moving from Newman's 'all-over' paintings to Brice Marden's or Jo Baer's monochrome panels. Newman's form of Abstract Expressionism is an obvious precursor of Minimalism and of Sixties one-color paintings. Newman said: 'I was concerned constantly in doing a painting that would move in its totality as you see it. You look at it and you see it' (E. De Antonio, 70). Clement Greenberg's definition of the 'all-over' painting applies to Minimal form, including sculpture, as well as Sixties abstract painting.

> The all-over, 'decentralized', 'polyphonic' picture... relies on a surface knit together of identical or closely similar elements which repeat themselves without marked variation from one edge of the picture to the other.[1]

For Peter Fuller, Brice Marden and the Minimal artists did not produce a positive æsthetic emptiness, but one which was spiritually bankrupt. Referring to Rudolf Otto's influential book *The Idea of the Holy,* Fuller wrote:

> It seems to me that there is every difference

in the world between this spiritually replete emptiness and the numbing vacuity of works by artists such as Carl Andre, Agnes Martin, Ellsworth Kelly or Brice Marden. (1993, xxxv)

Fuller was wrong, however.

Frank Stella regards 1970 as a key moment in the history of abstract painting, for here Post-Painterly Abstraction had run its course, had 'turned to ashes' (1986, 1). And in that year, Barnett Newman and Mark Rothko died. For Frank Stella, post-1970 abstract painting was/ is full of dull, flat, shallow acrylic surfaces: 'unbearably thin and shallow' (ib., 42-43). Worse, abstract painting, Stella maintains, 'has always been flawed by spatial conservatism' (ib., 43). This statement seems odd, when so many people seem to have problems even now with abstract painting, as if abstract painting were too 'avant garde', too 'mod', too 'difficult'. No, says, Stella, abstraction is not avant garde, it is conservative. For Stella, abstract art 'has rendered itself space-blind' in order to survive, because to survive art must become literary (ib., 46). Certainly, if Stella's view of post-1970 painting is applied to Brice Marden, it does ring true. Marden's work is 'literary', in its mythic allusions, for instance; Marden's work is 'flat, dull, inert', to use Stella's terms (criticisms which are often levelled against Marden).

BARNETT NEWMAN

The two key painters of the 'Abstract Sublime' were Barnett Newman and Mark Rothko. Barnett Newman (1905-70) was a canny theoretician,[1] as his writings demonstrate. While Clyfford Still despised the authority of tradition, Newman and Rothko revelled in it. While Newman and others denied the rhetoric of exultation in their theoretical writings, their paintings shouted it. Newman's canvases usually had religious, symbolic, metaphysical or cosmic titles and projects: there were paintings of creation, singularity, totality and unity: the *Onement* series, *Day Before One* (Kunstmuseum, Basle), *The Beginning* (Chicago), *Day One* (Whitney Museum), the *Be* series (*Be I*, Detroit); many paintings were concerned with a cosmic light: *Primordial Light* (Houston), *Anna's Light* (1968, Kawamura Memorial Museum of Art, Japan), *Black Fire* (Philadelphia), *Noon-Light* (Houston), *White Fire* (Kunstmuseum, Basel), *Voice of Fire* (Ottawa); other works referred to Biblical, Judæo-Christian and Creation/ *Genesis* themes: *The Word, Abraham* (MOMA, New York), *The Stations of the Cross* (Washington), *Jericho* (Paris), *Covenant* (Washington), *Cathedra* (Amsterdam), *Chartres* (private collection), and the *Canto* lithographs (Fogg Art Museum); there were also paintings that referred to mythic or religious personalities: *Vir Heroicus Sublimis* (MOMA, New York), *The Queen of the Night* (Osaka, Japan), *Joshua* (Chicago), *Adam* (Tate Modern, London), *Dionysius*

(Washington), *Ulysses* (Houston), *Uriel* (private collection) and *Achilles* (Washington).

☆

Donald Judd said that paintings are rarely, if ever, totally 'flat'. 'Two colors on the same surface almost always lie on different depths', reckoned Judd in his article "Specific Objects", '[a]n even color, especially in oil paint, covering all or much of a painting is almost always both flat and infinitely spatial' (1965). This certainly applies to Barnett Newman's monochrome paintings, which appear 'both flat and infinitely spatial'. Judd continues:

> Rothko's space is shallow and the soft rectangles are parallel to the plane, but the space is almost traditionally illusionistic. In Reinhardt's paintings, just back from the plane of the canvas, there is a flat plane and this seems in turn indefinitely deep. Pollock's paint is obviously on the canvas, and the space is mainly that made by any marks on a surface, so that it is not very descriptive and illusionistic. Noland's concentric bands are not as specifically paint-on-a-surface as Pollock's paint, but the bands flatten the literal space more. (1965)

Newman's paintings emphasized verticality, frontality, flatness, single-color, all-overness, unified space, and grand scale. Newman developed his first stripe/ zip paintings in the late 1940s: *Onement I* (1948, MOMA, New York) was the breakthrough painting: it was not a conscious, deliberate decision, Newman said, to make the zip: it happened (Newman preferred the term 'zip' to

'stripe'). What he was doing, he said, was 'emptying the canvas by assuming the thing empty, and suddenly in this particular painting, *Onement*, I realized that I had filled the surface' (E. De Antonio, 67). The formal invention, the 'zip', divides immense horizontal areas of color. The zip as a pictorial device has obvious affinities with Frank Stella's stripes. Sometimes Newman's zip is meticulously painted, with smooth, unbroken edges, as in *Who's Afraid of Red, Yellow and Blue II* and *Now I* (Madrid). At other times it is distinctly ragged and unpolished, as in *Right Here* (1954, Amsterdam) and *The Promise* (1949, New York), in which two white 'zips', one smooth and one rough, stand side by side in an area of black. In some paintings (*Treble*, 1960, New York, and *The Stations of the Cross*), the Newman zip is defined 'negatively', by the brushmarks on each side of the zip, which is left blank: it is defined by an absence. In *Tertia* (1964, Stockholm) and *The Third* (1962, Walker Art Center), the orange background to the left of the yellow zip is left unpainted and ragged.

Sometimes the large areas of color are relatively uniform, as in *Onement no. 6* (1953, Wisman Family Collection), while in other paintings, such as *Cathedra* (1951, Stedelijk Museum, Amsterdam), the color is broken up in lights and darks, though it never loses its sense of being a single color. In some paintings color is applied meticulously and unbroken, as in *The Gate* (1954, Amsterdam) or *The Voice*

(1950, MOMA, New York). Sometimes the fields of color are deliberately mixed with darker tones – this often occurs in the blue canvases, where ultramarines mix with prussian blues: *Onement V* (1952, private collection), *L'Errance* (1953, New York), and *Ulysses*.

Barnett Newman's *Anna's Light* (1968, Kawamura Memorial Museum of Art, Japan) uses one of the most radiant reds in painting, like the equally incandescent red in Newman's *Vir Heroicus Sublimis*. The zip breaks up the areas of color. Newman considered his sense of drawing and planning an important part of his art. But it is the vastness of the areas of color in Newman's paintings that is so striking. In *Vir Heroicus Sublimis* there are four zips, which create five rectangles: the central rectangular area is by far the largest: the zips are placed in the left- and right-hand thirds of the painting, as often in a Newman work. The central expanse of color is what strikes one first in *Vir Heroicus Sublimis*, as in *Anna's Light*.

In "The Plasmic Image", Barnett Newman wrote:

> The present painter can be said to work with chaos not only in the sense that he is handling the chaos of the blank picture plane but also in that he is handling the chaos of form. In trying to go beyond the visible and the known world he is working with forms that are unknown even to him. He is therefore engaged in a true act of discovery in the creation of new forms and symbols that will have the living quality of creation.[2]

Barnett Newman affirmed the openness of his paintings. They were not so much about objects, or spaces, or graphic elements: they were open paintings (E. De Antonio, 159). In *Cathedra* the sense of carefully controlled architectonics is apparent: the whitish zip is nearly central, dividing the painting into huge zones of blue: the off-centre geometry of the white zip is balanced by the second, pale blue zip on the right-hand side of the canvas. In *Anna's Light*, when the glow of the mid-red has softened and been absorbed by the viewer, one becomes aware of the sense of proportion and scale: there are two bands of white, one very thin band on the left hand edge, and a larger band on the right-hand edge. Clement Greenberg, in a 1955 article, "'American-Type' Painting", said that Newman's 'huge, calmly and evenly burning canvases' amounted to an art which was 'deep and honest, and carries a feeling for color without its like in recent painting'.[3]

In the *Who's Afraid of Red, Yellow and Blue* series of the mid/ late 1960s, Barnett Newman showed that he could take colors as apparently simple and direct as the three primary colors and make them submit to his æsthetic project of meta-physical totality.[4] Like Mark Rothko with his late gray, brown and black paintings and the bright red works, Newman's *Who's Afraid of Red, Yellow and Blue* series was influenced by the younger Colorfield, Hard Edge and Post-Painterly Abstractionist painters. The *Who's Afraid of Red, Yellow and Blue* paintings recall

Hard Edge painting and artists such as Ellsworth Kelly, Kenneth Noland, and Al Held as well as Frank Stella. *Who's Afraid of Red, Yellow and Blue I* (1966, private collection) pushed the blue and yellow to the edges of the vertical format painting, so that the red was dominant. *Who's Afraid of Red, Yellow and Blue II* (1967, Stuttgart) again used red as the main ingredient: the blue and yellow were as before confined to narrow zips in the centre and edges of the composition. *Who's Afraid of Red, Yellow and Blue III* (1966-67, Stedelijk Museum, Amsterdam) took the color format of the first *Who's Afraid of Red, Yellow and Blue,* and applied it to one of Newman's distinctive vast horizontal paintings. The immense expanse of scarlet recalls *Vir Heroicus Sublimis* and *Anna's Light. Who's Afraid of Red, Yellow and Blue IV* (1969-70, Berlin) squashed the dark blue in between two enormous planes of red and yellow.

Not a few art critics have seen correspondences with Barnett Newman's *Stations of the Cross* series of paintings and Mark Rothko's Houston murals: both were New York School abstract meditations on emotions and themes some of which corresponded to or alluded to the Christian Passion. Although Newman and Rothko are different artists, Newman is probably the artist closest to Rothko in many ways. However, Newman's *Stations of the Cross* paintings are different in some key formal respects from Rothko's Houston Chapel and mural series: the reference to the Christian Stations, for example, was only one of many allusions Newman wanted to make (he also used the *Old Testament,* Greek mythology, the *Qabbalah* and Jewish religion). Each of Newman's *Stations of the Cross* uses the same format (6.5 by 5 foot canvases, with the bands and zips in the same place, painted mainly in black, with some white paint), while Rothko's are determinedly sombre and dark, without any lighter tones, and in a variety of sizes and proportions.

Even within his tight set of formal components, Barnett Newman works out many variants: in *The First Station,* a black zip on the left is disturbed by a roughly daubed zip on the right. The loose brushmarks of the right-hand zip upset the steady equilibrium of the area of black and white paint on the left-hand side of the painting. In subsequent *Stations of the Cross* this right-hand zip settles down somewhat, to become a very narrow black zip in *The Fifth Station.* At this point, though, the left-hand black zip, which has been in a state of passivity up 'til now, suddenly deliquesces, its edge becoming fractured. By *The Twelfth* and *Thirteenth Station,* the black has enveloped most of the canvas, so that, in the penultimate *Station,* the configuration of white and black of the first *Stations of the Cross* has been reversed.

Although Barnett Newman employed the potent phrase *lema sabachthani,* the allusions to the Christian Passion are much stronger in Rothko's mural series and chapels than in Newman's *Stations of the Cross.* Both Rothko's and Newman's series of paintings, though, were about the importance of (religious) faith, of the subjectivity and intensity of being a pilgrim, someone on a quest for something transcendent, something beyond, timeless, unknown, eternal. The cry *lema sabachthani* was the 'question that has no answer', said Newman, a cry of despair (and also exaltation) that is uttered outwards, into the darkness (of ignorance, alienation, Godlessness) that surrounds the modern soul.

QUOTES BY BARNETT NEWMAN

Any art worthy of its name should address 'life', 'man', 'nature', 'death' and 'tragedy'.

•

I hope that my painting has the impact of giving someone, as it did me, the feeling of his own totality, of his own separateness, of his own individuality.

•

I prefer to leave the paintings to speak for themselves.

MARK ROTHKO

The art of Mark Rothko (1903-70) has been described by critics as 'transcendent' (Dore Ashton, Bryan Robertson), 'a sort of spiritual Stonehenge' (Anita Brookner), 'lavish self-indulgence' (Max Kozloff), 'Dionysian' (Robert Hobbs), 'sensuous and spiritual' (Diane Waldman), 'enormous, beautiful, opaque surfaces' (Peter Selz), 'enigmatic, gripping presence' (Robert Goldwater), 'emotionally charged' (Harold Rosenberg), 'incandescent color' (Clement Greenberg), 'haunting' (David Sylvester), 'visionary simplicity' (Irving Sandler) and 'tinted hallucinatory cloth' (Willem de Kooning).[1] Greenberg wrote:

> Rothko's big vertical pictures, with their incandescent color and their bold and simple sensuousness – or rather than *firm* sensuousness – are among the largest gems of abstract expressionism.[2]

For John Ashbery, Rothko 'seems to eliminate criticism'.[3] The archetypal response to Mark Rothko's art is that it is a 'heroic', 'transcendent', 'spiritual', and 'tragic' art. These are four of the most commonly deployed adjectives in Rothko art criticism (others include 'Buddhist', 'Faustian' and 'death-conscious'). Rothko's painting is seen as 'heroic' because it attempts to achieve something great in a world of Existential suffering. Out of the slime and the pain rise Rothko's heroic canvases. (Robert Motherwell calls large paintings 'heroic' [E. De Antonio, 65]). 'Around the hero everything becomes a tragedy', Friedrich Nietzsche wrote in *Beyond Good and Evil* (97). It is Existential because Rothko manages to create something from the Heideggerian state of being 'thrown into the world'. It is 'transcendent' because it aims to go beyond the usual realms of art, in terms of content and form. It is also religiously transcendent, pointing towards the sort of transcendence that mystics speak of, an ontological and metaphysical going beyond of earthly states.[4]

Mark Rothko's art is deeply 'spiritual' simply because he deals with spiritual matters. Rothko's sense of the spirit and the spiritual dimension informs all of his painting. Art critics emphasize the religious dimension in his art: Harold Rosenberg likened the dark slabs in the multiform paintings to stone tablets (1972); Rothko is naturally a spiritual or religious painter, like Duccio, Giotto or Fra Angelico. Robert Hughes reckoned Rothko may have been a religious painter, but in another era.[5]

Once Mark Rothko had established some structures and rules for his mature art, around 1949, he explored the possibilities that large oil on canvas paintings offered. Some of the paintings used a blanched palette, such as *Number 11* (1949, Washington), with cream and white painted over watery blue, to pull it back to a very light tone. In another painting from the same year, though, Rothko began to delve into large areas of black, like so many other American postwar painters.

Untitled (1949, Metropolitan Museum, New York) layers black or a very dark blue over reds, yellows and whites.

One could extract from Mark Rothko's *œuvre* a group of paintings which might support a reading of Rothko as a dark, tragic painter of dark, tragic paintings.6 There are works such as the mural commissions, the maroon paintings of the late 1950s or the black and gray pieces from the late 1960s, which would support a gloomy, introspective reading of Rothko's art. It's true, some of his painting are like this. From the middle period of the 1950s there are works such as *Earth and Green* (1955, Museum Ludwig, Cologne), which is a sombre composition of three colors, an earthy dark brown rectangle above a larger dark viridian rectangle against a prussian blue background. The *Untitled* painting of 1953 (Washington), has a large dark blue rectangle dominating the painting, but it is capped by an expanse of lipstick pink. The radiant colors at their best, Max Kozloff wrote, effect an

> ignition that results from the impact of a fierce palette upon an aloof and fastidious temperament [which] flusters exhaustion and begins to hold the haunted spectator longer than he intended. (1961)

Dore Ashton said that Mark Rothko's black was 'never black but a seething mass of deep, rich hues' (1958). Rothko's light was likened to a Biblical opening of the heavens by another critic, a light of annunciation and revelation.3

The sombre interpretation of Mark Rothko is knocked away by a survey of the paintings from the 1950s onwards. There are many, many more brightly colored paintings than dark, brooding ones. *Orange, Red and Red* (1962, Dallas Museum of Art), for example, is excessively hotly colored, with an enormous rosy orange rectangle above a darker red rectangle, backed by red. These radiant reds did not cease with the darkening into maroon of the Houston, Harvard and Seagram mural series either: Rothko continued to employ incandescent crimsons up until his death. The reds persist through the 'depressed' black and gray period of the late 1960s: two works, both called *Untitled* (both Washington), are supremely, unashamedly, victoriously *red*. Not only red, but *red on red*.

In canvas after canvas one finds sonorous yellows above equally sonorous yellows (*Untitled*, 1952, Tate Gallery); radiant orange rectangles rising above carmine pink forms (*Number 12*, 1951, private collection); brilliant lemon hues above oranges and below soft lilacs (*Number 7*, 1951, Sarah Campbell Blaffer Foundation); buttercup yellow forms above wine red and gray over dark red (*Orange, Wine, Gray on Plum*, 1961, Estate of Mark Rothko); in *Number 16* (1958, Estate of Mary Alice Rothko), a large tangerine form is a solid base to a strip of white across the central zone and a drab light chocolate upper form.4

The sheer abundance of incandescent

color of mid-period Mark Rothko is striking. There is a long series of paintings, for example, which are founded on the most positive, brightest colors of the spectrum – yellow and orange – often modulated by another hot color, red: *Number 7* (noted above); *Untitled* (1954, Yale University Art Gallery, New Haven) is a mainly yellow canvas, with a rectangle of lilac layered over a deep orange rectangle; another *Untitled* (1954, Estate of Mark Rothko), echoes the format of the previous *Untitled*, but leaves the dark orange to shine on its own; the 1955 *Untitled* (Estate of Mark Rothko) divides two huge fields of corn yellow with a broad band of white; *Orange and Yellow* (1954, Albright-Knox Art Gallery, Buffalo), *Yellow and Gold* (1956, MOMA, New York) and *Untitled* (1956, Estate of Mark Rothko), are three of Rothko's most vibrant paintings: the predominant color is orange, the phosphorescence of which is emphasized by being paired not with a complimentary, but with yellow. As with some of Vincent van Gogh's wheatfields and sunflowers, this combination of orange and yellow is really intense. One could anchor these paintings to a tragic interpretation if one wished: one could see them as the final conflagration before the final apocalypse. Alternatively, one could see these six by seven foot yellow and orange canvases as life-affirming statements.

Towards the end of the Fifties, when Mark Rothko started working on his mural commissions, there are a number of paintings which mix red and black, but not as severely or as closely as the murals. Paintings such as *Light Red Over Black* (1957, Tate Gallery), *Brown and Black in Reds* (1958, private collection), *Grayed Olive Green, on Maroon* (1961, Washington), *Orange, Red and Red* (1962, Dallas Museum of Art, Texas), and *Untitled* (1963, Estate of Mark Rothko), are distinctly darker than paintings of the early 1950s. Even as he mixed in more and more black into his color patterns, Rothko kept his colors vibrant. *Light Red Over Black*, for example, depicts two large rectangular forms of black, but the scarlet that is brushed in around the black shapes is so radiant, it cancels any melancholy or 'negative' connotations the blacks might generate. *Brown and Black in Reds* consists of two dark forms, the upper narrow rectangle in mid-brown, and the large rectangle in near-black, but these are overwhelmed by a swamp of red, scarlet at the centre, and a deeper alizarin crimson towards the base of the painting.

Even the dimmest of Mark Rothko's 1950s paintings, such as *Grayed Olive Green, on Maroon*, are set alive by Rothko's careful arrangements of a variety of reds. *Black, Ochre, Red Over Red* (1957, collection: Panza di Biumo), is structured around the dramatic form of three of Rothko's 'things' which are weighted down by the solid black form at the top. The dark tone so high up in the vertical format painting gives the work an unusual sense of being top-heavy. The reds underneath it, however, are larger and quite adequate to support the black rectangle. A comparable work, of a year before (*White Cloud,* 1956), which is the reverse of *Black, Ochre, Red Over Red* (a smaller white rectangle over a huge red ground), shows how powerful the color red can be, how it can carry any other colors with it, if there is enough of it. Within the color red, Rothko showed that he could use slightly lighter and slightly darker tones of the same red and make a painting work. *Four Reds* (1957, collection: Daniel Schwarz) is one of those paintings which demonstrates Rothko's mastery of lighting and darkening a single color.

Mark Rothko's Houston Chapel murals are the tightest and most carefully controlled of the murals series. The colors are extremely close. Rothko meticulously adjusted the amount of light the murals emitted, and the amount of light they would absorb. It is easy to understand how viewers speak of the 'subliminal' or 'transcendent' qualities of the Houston Chapel murals. There seems to be hardly anything in them, to grasp onto. At least in Claude Monet's *Waterlilies* the viewer can always return to nature, to the shapes of the lilies and the reflections on the water. In Monet's art, one can find the way back to nature and the world. Rothko's Houston Chapel paintings invite a different sort of participation. His murals invite the viewer to lose themselves in the paintings, thereby losing themselves

to themselves, in themselves. That is, the paintings are not the final stage in the participants' (religious) project. They can't be. Art in churches, religious art in general, is not the endpoint. One must not get stuck on the art object, but on what the art object is trying to evoke, or point towards. In the case of Rothko's murals, which is church art like Renaissance altarpieces were church art, the viewer is invited to go beyond the paintings and ponder on holiness within and without the self.

Many (most) of Mark Rothko's late paintings are entitled *Untitled.* While in the late 1940s and subsequent works *Untitled* did not seem so threatening a title, with the late 1960s paintings it acquires a new foreboding connotation, with Rothko's illness in 1967, his subsequent depression, and death looming at the end of the decade. The last works are a series of mainly two color paintings, many of them acrylic on paper. Typically, the upper color is black, brown or dark gray; the lower is usually a mid to light gray. In the late gray/ brown/ black paintings, the 'dark is always at the top', Rothko said.[7]

The stereotypical interpretation is that these are depressing works which presage Mark Rothko's death by his own hand. Surveying the black-and-gray paintings cursorily, one can see how they can appear melancholy. There is not much to look at, for a start: the grays and browns are applied in a seemingly uncaring fashion. There is not much that is immediately 'sensuous' about these late paintings, to an eye looking for visual pleasure. If one recalls that in the Houston Chapel murals Rothko said he was concerned not so much with color but with *proportion* and the relationship between shapes, then the black-and-gray paintings become much clearer. The closer one looks at the late works, the more one sees that Rothko was exploring the same formal aspects that have always concerned painters: the relation between color and size, scale and shape; the relation between tone and luminosity; the relation between proportion and color; the relation between surface texture and inner luminescence, and so on.

The duality or tension between the black and the gray rectangles can be interpreted any which way one chooses: between spirit and matter, spirituality and physicality, mind and body, soul and God, masculine and feminine, past and present, past and future, eternity and now, inner and outer, life and death, and so on. Certainly there is something deeply obsessive about these late works, as with the late works of Vincent van Gogh or J.M.W. Turner, as if there was something Mark Rothko felt he had to get at, somehow, and so he kept working over the form until it offered up its secret knowledge. In this respect, as an alchemical quest, Rothko's late black-brown-gray paper works recall the seven-year project of Ad Reinhardt, obsessively turning out

those square black paintings, in the hope of reaching some sublime point, some absolute, some infinity or end zone. 'All painters enjoy a certain advantage in treating the sublime,' wrote Cliff Mc-Mahon,

> since rejecting natural forms in favour of abstract ones supplies an immediate ascent towards the spiritual, intellectual, and ineffable. To abstract is in a sense to elevate, and there is an inherent grandeur in the abstract mode.[8]

Mark Rothko's melancholy interpretation is further debunked by the fact that not all the late works consist of black, brown and gray. There are, for example, light pink paintings, such as *Untitled* (1969, Estate of Mark Rothko, 2069.69). Now this really is a surprise, especially after the previous decade, since the late 1950s, when Rothko's palette (or, more correctly, his bench of tins) darkened. This pink is exceptionally light – it is not the radiant pink of the 1950s works (such as *Number 12*). It is a large expanse of shell pink, framed with sky blue behind white. Other paintings include soft gray-pinks below white-grays. Another late acrylic on paper, *Untitled* (1968) is a vertical format work in the old multiform manner, depicting three white rectangles on a brilliant cardinal ground. The white forms are a return to the 'clouds' of the 1950s. And then, in *Untitled* (1967), an oil on canvas painting (private collection), there is an incredibly bright dark rose form underneath a sonorous mid-red. The

painting vies with the Colorfield and
Post-Painterly Abstractionists (Olitski,
Kelly, Noland, Stella, Louis) at their most
colorful.

3

'MONOCHROME AND MONOTONOUS': COLORFIELD PAINTING AS 'BORING ART'

Monochrome painting was variously known as 'opaque painting', 'silent painting', 'cool painting', 'fundamental painting' and 'essential painting'. Frank Stella's paintings are lean, but leanness does not necessarily mean unfeelingness. This is the problem that monochrome painting creates, and Minimal art in general. People think Minimal art is boring. In Minimal painting and sculpture, surfaces are, typically, smooth, utterly smooth and 'pure'. ('I wanted everything to be on the surface', said Stella [1986, 155]). Andy Warhol remarked: 'I like boring things. I like to be exactly the same over and over again', a classic Warholian statement (K. Stiles, 340).

Minimal art seems to have no hidden depths, therefore no subtlety. Simplicity is exalted, as is repetition, seriality, process, and flatness as well as volume and space. The many materials are flattened out and depersonalized, and gestures, so important to certain kinds of painting and sculpture (such as that of Pablo Picasso or Michelangelo Buonarroti), are suppressed. Indeed, the flatness of the surfaces, whether in the art of Brice Marden, Agnes Martin, Jo Baer or Jack Bush, is crucial. The urge to the 'non-gestural', to eradicate the human touch, was central to Sixties high art æsthetics. Yves Klein famously 'exhibited' an empty gallery (*Le Vide*, 1958). He 'sold' air. There was nothing in the gallery to show, but bare walls. The result was interpreted by critics as a conceit, an in-joke, a gesture of ironic non-participation. But the alleged 'boringness' of Post-Painterly Abstract art becomes a part of the metaphysics of 1960s art.[1] Lucy Lippard wrote in the mid-Sixties:

> The exciting thing about...the "cool" artists is their daring challenge of the concepts of boredom, monotony and repetition... their demonstration that intensity does not have to be melodramatic. (1966)

'Any incentive to paint is as good as any other', said Robert Rauschenberg in 1959, playful as ever (K. Stiles, 321). Boring art for some is exquisite art for others (just as erotic art for some can be pornography for others). Thus, James Mellow wrote that one of Donald Judd's shows was 'one of the most provocative of the season' (1966, 89), while many other spectators wouldn't agree. Irving Sandler reckoned that the very 'boringness' of art could be its most interesting aspect. Sandler said that

> in its boredom, Stella's painting has affinities to Reinhardt's, but... Stella appears to have made it the content of his art – a content so novel and perverse as to be interesting.[2]

Donald Judd answered the charge, often levelled against Minimal art, of reductionism:

> If my work is reductionist it's because it doesn't have the elements that people thought should be there. But it has other elements that I like.[3]

On 'boringness', Robert Morris commented that art is found 'boring' by those who desire 'specialness':

Such work which has the feel and look of openness, extendibility, accessibility, publicness, repeatability, equanimity, directness, immediacy, and has been formed by clear decision rather than groping craft, would seem to have a few social implications, none of which are negative. Such work would undoubtedly be boring to those who long for access to an exclusive specialness, the experience of which reassures their superior perception. (1967, 29)

Minimal art, said John Perreault, 'in spite of the polemics, is emotional, but the emotions and the experiences involved are new and unexpected'. As it's made by humans, Minimal art is not robotic and cold, but always human. It is just as human as 'Egyptian architecture, Tibetan banners, or Sung paintings'.4

Minimal artists such as Donald Judd, Robert Mangold, Sol LeWitt and Morris explored the notions of 'boringness' and 'interestingness'. 'Boring art is interesting art', writes Frances Colpitt in her book on Minimalism (121). Donald Judd, the chief explicator of Minimal æsthetics, wrote: 'I can't see how any good work can be boring or monotonous in the usual sense of those words', adding: '[a]nd no one has developed an unusual sense of them'.5 Clearly, the Minimal artists thought they were making 'interesting' art. Or at least, *they* were interested in it. If art's good, it can't be 'boring', said Judd, claiming that 'a work needs only to be interesting'.

In "Specific Objects", Donald Judd described his vision of a 'minimal' art, one reduced to its interesting essentials:

A work needs only to be interesting. Most works finally have one quality. In earlier art the complexity was displayed and built the quality. In recent painting the complexity was in the format and the few main shapes... The thing as a whole, its quality as a whole, is what is interesting. The main things are alone and are more intense, clear and powerful. (1965)

The discussion of 'interesting', 'boring' and 'value' becomes a quagmire of semantics and the metaphysics of meaning. Language soon fails to describe the kinds of intentions that artists have, and the kind of responses that critics have to works. For painters, talking about art is not art. Only art is art, or as Ad Reinhardt put it, '[a]rt is the only valid criticism of art' (1991, 74).

Making art has first of all to do with honesty [commented Ellsworth Kelly]. My first lesson was to see objectively, to erase all 'meaning' of the thing seen. Then only, could the real meaning of it be understood and felt.

Robert Mangold said: 'I certainly know whether I'm interested in the work or whether I'm not interested in the work'.6 Sol LeWitt explained his view thus:

I wouldn't say that I wanted to like uninteresting things or to dislike interesting things. I think that's one way that you measure your response, if it interests you. 'Interests' means that it somehow makes a bridge between you and it, you and the object, you and the art object. If it hits home, it means that it's of interest.7

One might see Robert Ryman's white-on-white paintings as unsensual, flat, 'boring'. In fact, Ryman's paintings are very powerful. The surfaces themselves are highly poetic, but Ryman also moves towards the state of sculpture, like Frank Stella, with his use of many different materials, from wood to steel, from fibreglass to Plexiglass, from cardboard to copper. It would be hard to see Sol LeWitt's cuboid, mathematical, conceptual sculpture as sensual. LeWitt's angular objects – the frames of cubes painted white – seem to be the antithesis of sensual art.[8] His art is all about ideas: the initial idea, the conception, is everything. As LeWitt said:

> all of the planning and decisions are made beforehand and the execution is a perfunctory affair. The idea becomes a machine that makes the art.[9]

Much of contemporary sculpture consists of hard-edged cubes or rectangular slabs. Whether this use of such stark mathematical forms as cubes is rational or intuitive, it takes a scientific, numerical approach to art to extremes. The idea, Donald Judd wrote, is to simply do 'the next thing': 'one thing after another'. It is a strategy that is not called a strategy, a systemless system. One of Jasper Johns' key statements was:

> *Take an object*
> *Do something to it*
> *Do something else to it*
> " " " " [10]

The Colorfield, Minimal and Post-Painterly Abstract painters took up the notion of seriality and repetition and explored it. Painters such as Frank Stella and Kenneth Noland employed simple geometric shapes in the 1960s upon which they painted complex sequences of colors. These paintings, such as Stella's *Protractor* series, used the simple form in order to explore other aspects of painting. Donald Judd pointed that although the new art can seem 'simple' at first, it isn't:

> Usually when someone says a thing is too simple, they're saying that certain familiar things aren't there, and they're seeing a couple maybe that are left, which they count as a couple, that's all. But actually there may be those couple of things and several new things to which they aren't paying attention. These may be quite complex.

Ellsworth Kelly prefer to use the term 'easy' rather than 'simple':

> Simple, I don't like the word simple. I like easy better. I want to forget about the technique. I sweat and worry but I don't want it look like that; but you can't separate the artist and his technique.

For Jasper Johns the aim was to create 'things which are seen and not looked at', and explained further:

> Using the design of the American flag took care of a great deal for me because I didn't have to design it. So I went on to similar things like the targets – things the mind already knows. That gave me room to work on other levels.[11]

For Michael Fried, the concept of endlessness, of going on, or of having to go on, was central to the notions of interest and objecthood in 1960s literalist art. Endlessness might be be 'the experience that most deeply excites literalist sensibility', Fried claimed (1967). For Lawrence Alloway, what made form in Sixties art meaningful was not 'ingenuity or surprise' but 'repetition and extension'.12 Alloway's view applies equally to painting as well as sculpture.

'After all, the work isn't the point; the piece is', insisted Donald Judd. Of Frank Stella's paintings, Judd wrote in "Specific Objects" that the 'order is not rationalistic and underlying, but is simply order, like that of continuity, one thing after another'.13 The notions of Sixties art (or 'ABC', 'Cool', Colorfield or Minimal art) – seriality, succession, progression, repetition, permutation – have been around for a long time. Leonardo da Vinci, one might say, painted the same picture in different ways, often abandoning projects before completion. But, whether the 'system' is serial or modular, whether there is progression or simply repetition, the notion of Donald Judd's, 'doing the next thing', 'one thing after another', explains so much of Sixties art. It explains so much of Judd's work, for instance, his 'ladders' of forms ascending to the ceiling in bronze or plastic, and those long lines of curved shapes set on a wall. It also describes how artists simply go on making work, as variations, or repetitions, or progressions, like Brice Marden with his many monochrome canvases that explore different combin-ations of gray, black or white, or Ad Reinhardt's seemingly repetitious but actually methodical explorations of five-foot square black canvases. In a 1977 interview, Robert Rauschenberg said:

I don't think any honest artist sets out to make art. You love art. You live art. You are art. But you're just doing something. You're just doing what no one can stop you from doing.14

For some, Brice Marden's abstract paintings created a response of 'so what?' His paintings were beautiful and sensual (a 'beautiful presence and another and another and another', as one critic put it), but to what end?15 But beyond the difficulty and restraint of Marden's paintings, there was quite a bit going on. It's the same with other Minimal and Post-Painterly and Serial art. The closer one looks, the busier and more complex and sensual these works become.

A cursory glance at Robert Ryman's paintings, for example, would see nothing but white squares of different sizes (typically 60 or 72 inches square). Looking closer, however, one saw that Ryman was meticulously and vigorously exploring the relationships between color and support, between shape and color, between object-ification and illusion, and between abstraction and figuration. Far from being all the same monotonous white-on-white, Ryman's paintings were all individual. Each one had its own specifications of frame size, support (aluminium, canvas, plastic, wood, fibreglass). There were clips around the edge of some paintings, while others were bolted to the wall.

Another white-on-white Minimalist, Agnes Martin, also seemed to have little of interest happening in her paintings. When one looked closer, one saw different grids, different ways of marking the grid (gold leaf, pencil, ink). Sometimes the grid was very tight and compact, with a tiny rectangle being described; sometimes there was a web of horizontal lines, widely spaced; sometimes the white was attenuated by a faint pink or gray or cream between each set of horizontal bands.

Then take Donald Judd. His works seem to be firmly fixed in a monotonous, rect-angular view of the world. It seemed to be an arid, vacuous world of boxes and more boxes. Looking closer, one saw that there was a great sense of play and humour at work in the choice of materials (sometimes wood, sometimes steel, or glass, or copper, or lacquer, or Plexiglas). Sometimes Judd's serial boxes were open, and one could see inside them; at other times, Judd placed colored Plexiglas over the end, and the interior was hidden or vaguely discern-ible; sometimes the boxes were sprayed with Harley Davidson motorbike lacquer and enamel, so they'd be bright green, or red. Seemingly hollow and fragile, with their thin walls, Judd's boxes were also constructed from strong materials, and were fixed, immobile, to the wall.

There was in fact a lot going in Donald Judd's works, What appeared from a distance to be a uniform set of paintings or sculptures turned out to be a collection of individual works, each created with its own set of æsthetic considerations. What Marden, Agnes Martin, Robert Ryman, Donald Judd and Sol LeWitt were doing was exploring art with an apparently narrow or 'minimal' set of æsthetic constraints. When one looked closer, the sense of narrowness and limitation dis-appeared. The feeling of openness and play blossomed.

4

SIXTIES COLORFIELD, MINIMAL, SERIAL AND POST-PAINTERLY ABSTRACT PAINTERS

FRANK STELLA

FRANK STELLA

Frank Stella (b. 1936) knows where he fits into the history of contemporary art: he comes after Barnett Newman and is contemporary with Jasper Johns (b. 1930), Jim Dine (b. 1935) and Sol LeWitt (b. 1928). Stella was happy to be slotted into a post-Mondrian tradition of painting by a critic:

> Take, as an example, the first printed criticism of my work, which appeared in the *New Yorker* in 1960. There Robert Coates lamented "how sad it was to see the 23-year-old Frank Stella right back where Mondrian was twenty-five years ago." I realized that this remark was a polite put-down; nevertheless, the thrill it gave me was overpowering. It would have been an honour to be right back where Mondrian was twenty-five years ago, if that had been the case; but even without that possibility, the fact that my name appeared in print in the same sentence with Mondrian's seemed to be an incredible affirmation of personality and ability. It actually took me a while to get over the shock of publicity, the quick glare of history passing over me. (1986, 146)

Frank Stella's paintings command relatively high prices in the art market, though perhaps not as high as Jasper Johns' works. In Stella's 1987 show at Knoedler Gallery in London's Cork Street, the larger pieces were selling for 260,000 dollars. His art was derisorily called 'bank art', the sort big companies buy. Stella has always been successful and popular, it seems. He has not gone out of fashion: his works have been a part of group shows and one-person shows ever since the late Fifties/ early Sixties. His Charles Eliot

Norton lectures in 1983-4 were very popular with students.

Frank Stella has carved out a niche in the art world for himself. There are no works quite like Stella's around. There are similar pieces, but Stella's works remain instantly recognisable as Stella's works. The same cannot be said for any number of other artists.

Frank Stella wrote of contemporaries he admired, Barnett Newman and Morris Louis in *Working Space*:

> The strength of his [Newman's] painting comes from the ability of the stripes (or, as he liked to call them, "zips") to attach themselves to and into the background. They fit beautifully, zipping the space together. Newman sets up the motion of his figuration counter to the motion of the space supporting it... It may be that what makes Morris Louis's late paintings so appealing is their peculiar Kandinsky-like understanding of Newman. Louis brought a determined looseness to Newman's abstraction that Kandinsky would have applauded. Louis had the opportune sense of contiguous touch that is so necessary to link the moving elements of abstraction. This touch enabled him to exploit separation in a way that modern painting admires but cannot seem to imitate. (1986, 123-125)

At the same time, Frank Stella's art broke with earlier art, as Mel Bochner noted:

> Stella's work neatly bypassed most of the traits common to the painting that preceded him. Subsequent art, therefore, did not have to be the same as previous art. (1966, 40)

In *Working Space*, Frank Stella nostalgically recalled his early days in

New York, where he arrived as a young would-be artist.

> Exciting abstract expressionist painting seemed to be everywhere. I went from gallery to gallery, museum to museum, opening to opening, and then back to my studio to look at my own painting... The painting activity surrounding me held me up physically and emotionally. The painting activity that was flowering everywhere was very open and available... (1986, 153)

Donald Judd often praised Frank Stella. Getting rid of illusion in painting, Judd said, was one of the 'decisive advances' made by Stella and Kenneth Noland.[1] In 1980 Judd said that Stella's painting had been important in the 1960s because it was non-relational and non-anthropomorphic (F. Colpitt, 69). Stella's new sense of space, Judd argued,

> makes Abstract Expressionism seem now an inadequate style, makes it appear a compromise with representational art and its meaning. (1964, 28)

For Donald Judd, a Stella painting (referring to one of the aluminium series) was 'something of an object, it is a single thing, not a field with something in it, and it has almost no space' (1963). Sheldon Nodelman concurred with Judd, claiming that Stella and Noland had finally done away with illusionism.[2] Willis Domingo said that Stella solved

> the contradiction in a spatial ambiguity whereby literal and illusionistic space become indistinguishable from one another.[3]

When one looks at Frank Stella's paintings, the intention is that all of the painting is glimpsed all at once. The effect really is like that of Zen Buddhism, and the references to Zen of course were occurring in places such as the Beat poets in New York in the late 1950s, when Stella was starting out as a painter. The Beat poets – Allen Ginsburg, Jack Kerouac, William Burroughs, *et al*, appropriated Oriental philosophy for their own ends. They Americanized it, one might say.

Frank Stella steers clear of such philosophizing, but the all-over, instantaneous effect he desired in painting has much in common with the 'timeless now' of Taoist and Zen philosophy. It is other American painters who theorized in the grand fashion, bringing in Oriental mysticism – such as Robert Motherwell and Barnett Newman. In *Working Space*, Stella sticks to theorizing in the Western tradition about æsthetics, making references to the 'great' names of Western painting: Titian, Michelangelo Merisi da Caravaggio, Pablo Picasso, Peter Rubens.

Frank Stella relates to the Old Masters and historical tradition. Just as Kasimir Malevich made references to the Byzantine ikon tradition and Brice Marden acknowledges Old Masters such as the Spanish painters Francisco de Zurbarán, Diego Velásquez, Édouard Manet and Paul Cézanne, so Stella refers consciously to many former artists. Michael Fried, in a "New York Letter" of 1964, writes that F Stella and Barnett Newman are 'historically self-aware' (1964). Stella's acute (art) historical self-awareness came out very clearly in his book *Working Space*.

Frank Stella often talked about the uncertain reaction to the new painting:

> I always get into arguments with people who want to retain the old values in painting – the humanistic values that they… find on the canvas. If you pin them down, they always end up asserting that there is something there besides the paint on the canvas. My painting is based on the fact that only what can be seen there is there… What you see is what you get.
>
> ☆

Frank Stella was certainly influenced by Jasper Johns, as William Rubin noted:

> Frank was, I think, very interested in Johns' work in his last months at Princeton and immediately after he graduated. Johns' flags would be the pictures we'd have to look to in that sense, because they provided a concept of a picture that would be striped, as these pictures are, and also where the stars are a kind of box, which is not unrelated to the box in the center of *Coney Island*. Johns' pictures interested Frank because of certain repetition, repetition of numbers or letters or stripes of the flag, and Frank saw possibilities in this repetition which Johns himself was not to see.[4]

Jasper Johns' ideas on painting are much more romantic than Stella's: Johns writes of his desires for painting:

> I think that one wants from a painting a sense of life. The final suggestion, the final statement, has to be not a deliberate statement but a helpless statement. It has to be what you can't avoid saying.[5]

The power of Jasper Johns' works comes partly from his incredible surfaces, which are made of oil and wax or encaustic, spread thickly on the canvas. Paintings such as *White Flag* (1955, collection: the artist), *Highway* (1959, collection: Mrs Leo Castelli, New York), *Scent* (1973-74, collection: Ludwig Aachen) and *Canvas* (1956, collection: the artist) are really exquisite works, so intensely tactile and sumptuous. In Frank Stella's art the sense of surface is not as stridently sensual as in Johns' art. Stella is interested in different things.

Frank Stella was relatively successful early on in his career, like his contemporaries Jasper Johns and Robert Rauschenberg. Of Johns' career, which parallels that of Stella, Peter Fuller wrote:

> In 1958, Alfred Barr cooled his support of Abstract Expressionism, and urged artists to rebel against their elders. Significantly, Barr, too, was involved in the manufacture of Jasper Johns. Until 1958, Johns was an obscure artist who had inserted certain Dadaesque representational components into what was essentially a modified Abstract Expressionist style. That year, he was given a one-man show by Castelli; before it opened, the decision had been taken to put him on the front cover of *Art News* (hitherto a partisan Abstract Expressionist publication). MOMA immediately purchased examples of his work.[6]

William Rubin discussed the relation between Jasper Johns and Frank Stella, and the influence it had on Stella:

> there's a vast difference in sensibilities and in aims, so I don't want to make this relationship too close, but I think Johns also had

one other importance. That is, his flag pictures and some of the other images he made were the first paintings in which the field of the pictures is absolutely identical with the motif of the picture: the boundaries of the pictures are identical with the boundaries of the flag. The flag is laid out as a flat pattern on the surface, and although Johns is a representational painter in that sense and Frank became an abstract painter, I think the notion of making the motif identical with the shape of the field, even though that shape remains rectangular in Johns' flag, lurks somewhere behind what would become the principle of Frank's shaped canvas. And that principle is, if I can define it in its simplest way, essentially that the boundary of the picture is going to be determined by the governing pattern of the surface, and that there will be an absolute reciprocity between the outer shape of the picture, which might be considered simply the outside line of a pattern that operates over the entire surface.[7]

Marcel Duchamp and Kurt Schwitters are usually cited as precursors of Robert Rauschenberg's and Jasper Johns' mixed media explorations. Rauschenberg and Johns rewrote the notion of painting-as-object by sticking objects onto it. Schwitters is often cited as a major exponent of multi-media formalism. Schwitters explained how he came to do it:

> I simply could not see any reason why old streetcar tickets, driftwood, coat checks, wire and wheel parts, buttons, junk from the attic and heaps of refuse should not be used as material for paintings, any less than colors made in a factory.[8]

Frank Stella moved into three dimensions in the 1970s, building his paintings out from the wall, with paintings such as *Warka III* and *Leblon II.*

There are many other contemporary artists who have developed out of Jasper Johns' and Frank Stella's post-Abstract Expressionist painting: among the more successful are painters such as Christopher Le Brun, Thérèse Oulton, Lance Smith, Hughie O'Donoghue, R. B. Kitaj, Jim Dine, Richard Diebenkorn and Anselm Keifer (such as in his *Wayland's Song* (1982), which uses oil, emulsion, straw on photo, on canvas with lead). Painters who seem to have a direct Stellan component include Brice Marden, Sean Scully, Howard Hodgkin and Gerard Richter. The Minimal sculptors – Donald Judd, Robert Morris, Carl Andre – have acknowledged Stella's importance.

Frank Stella employed hard-edged, angular motifs, shapes such as Vs, Zs, Xs, Hs, Ls, Ts, Us, 'notched Vs', polygons, squares and rectangles. He also used symmetry, an exact symmetry made explicit and bold by his stripes and the shaped stretchers, so that the stripe pattern, writes John Coplans, 'begins at the center and spreads outward by his use of various kinds of symmetry'.[9] For Stella, the new sense of symmetry was not sited within an illusionistic space; rather, the use of hard edges, symmetry and the monochrome bands helped to push away illusionistic space:

> A symmetrical image or configuration placed on an open ground is not balanced out in the illusionistic space. The solution I arrived at – and there are probably others although I know of only one, color density – forces illusionistic space out of the painting

at a constant rate by using a regulated pattern.[10]

Frank Stella's symmetry, then, is not concerned with 'illusionistic space', as he calls it, the space of traditional Western post-Renaissance art, but with a new flatness. Stella said:

> I had to do something about relational painting, i.e. the balancing of the various parts of the painting with and against each other. The obvious answer was symmetry – make it the same all over.[11]

While painters such as Frank Stella and Kenneth Noland stressed the flatness of Sixties painting, Helen Frankenthaler said that

> all totally abstract pictures – the best ones that really come off – Newman, Pollock, Noland – have tremendous space; perspective space despite the emphasis on flat surface. (1965, 36)

Even when the stretchers are not shaped, as in with the *Black Paintings*, which were (usually) rectangular, the V-shapes still deny illusionistic space. At first, the *Black Paintings* seem to be somewhat 'traditional', as they employ the rectangular shape. Inside the field of the rectangle, though, Stella paints, directly onto the canvas, stripes of black, in V-shapes and rectangles, as in *Tomlinson Court Park* and *Point of Pines*.

In 1962, Max Kozloff wrote of Jasper Johns' motifs, the flags and targets saying they were

merely so many abstract forms upon which social usage has conferred meaning, but which now, displaced into their new context, cease to function socially. From this tremendous insight alone have sprung the momentum of Pop Art and the huge quantities of abstraction that is emblematic in character.[12]

The key to Jasper Johns' reworking of formalism and abstraction in the flags, targets, numbers and alphabets was precisely the sensuality of his art. It was the way he so powerfully employed the techniques of the Old Masters, of 'great art', that made his flags and targets so successful. For critics could not see Johns' banal signs culled from popular culture as trivial art, because Johns used one of the key elements in high art, the sensual, heavily impastoed surface. Johns' art could not be dismissed by critics, then as now, because its surface is as sensual and painterly as Rembrandt van Rijn, Diego Velásquez, Édouard Manet or Titian. In *Working Space*, Stella discusses Michelangelo Merisi da Caravaggio's art:

> The second miracle of Caravaggio is the miracle of surface. Skin, flesh, and pigment blend into reality. Painting is acknowledged as an act and as a physical fact, but immediately afterward, almost simultaneously, the presence of the human figure is felt as real, touchably there. (1986, 11)

Frank Stella, though he would deny it, also created sensual art objects. Stella often denies any 'emotion' or 'feeling' in his art. It is not about that, he says. For some people, he knows, his art comes across as cold. Brian O'Doherty called

Stella 'the Cézanne of nihilism, the master of *ennui*'.[13] Donald Kuspit called his art 'authoritarian' and mechanistic (1977, 25).

It is not Frank Stella's intention to be 'cold' or 'unfeeling'. Stella reckons his *Black Paintings* were as emotional as Mark Rothko's tragic canvases:

> Certainly no one would see the black paintings now as cold and calculating or very logical, but they seemed to seem that way in the context of '59 and '60. They were lean compared with some paintings, but the general look of them, if you really looked, seemed to me to have an awful lot to do with somebody like Rothko in feeling – and no one accused Rothko of being cold and intellectual. [14]

For Donald Judd, 'painterly feeling' was not valid anymore. Painterly feeling did not have to be the only element in art, Judd said. 'It's been fully exploited and I don't see why the painterly relationship exclusively should stand for art'.[15] There does not seem to be much going on in Frank Stella's paintings, as in many Post-Painterly Abstract paintings. But there is, in fact, a lot going on. Stella limits himself to a narrow set of rules. Like Brice Marden, Kenneth Noland, Barnett Newman, Morris Louis and Mark Rothko, Stella sets himself to explore a few configurations of painting. But these things – shape of the canvas, internal organization of the stripes, color of the bands – offer up endless permutations. Painters go over the same simple patterns and set-ups again and again. J.M.W. Turner painted thousands of seascapes –

the same basic ocean, framed in the same lower third of the picture, the same mixture of clouds and sun in the sky, and so on, attacking it from thousands of different viewpoints and different locations, from every shoreline of Britain, to France, Switzerland, Italy and Germany. Similarly, Monet painted the same basic picture of a sunlit river time after time.

Like other Sixties artists, Frank Stella explored the endless permutations that a few very simple elements offered up. The results seem to be 'lean', but even in the most minimal of Minimalist works there is sensuality and presence. Samuel Wagstaff notes that the Minimal painting asserts the painting above the painter: the author slips into the background: '[t]here is an attempt to suggest the presence of paint rather than the presence of the painter' (1964, 62). Michael Fried remarked that 'the vital presence of Stella's paintings cannot be understood'. Stella said that he didn't want the heroic gestures and detail of traditional or Abstract Expressionist painting:

> One could stand in front of any Abstract Expressionist work for a long time, and walk back and forth, and inspect the details of the pigment and the inflection and all the painterly brushwork for hours. But I wouldn't particularly want to do that and I also wouldn't ask anyone to do that in front of my paintings.[16]

Certainly Frank Stella's art is intense: his *Black Stripe Paintings*, his *Protractor* series, his copper paintings, and his *India*

Birds, are intense examples of art. Works such as *Quath-lamba* (1964), *D* (1963) and *Avicenna* (1960), are very powerful paintings. *D*, in particular, is impressive: one of the *Purple Polygons* series, it is a huge (7 feet high and wide) ten-sided polygon, with the centre left empty, as so often in Stella's paintings. This exhibition of *Purple Polygons* was called 'boring' and 'monotonous' by some critics[17] but how could paintings such as *D* be termed 'boring'? Just the opposite of boring, one could say.

On Frank Stella's stripe, Kenneth Noland commented:

> It's as if Frank works from the outside of the picture in. I'd always felt myself like I was working from the inside of the picture out, and that the shape was a resulting factor rather than a determining factor.[18]

Carl Andre commented on Frank Stella's stripe thus:

> Frank Stella has found it necessary to paint stripes. There is nothing else in his painting. Symbols are counters passed among people. Frank Stella's painting is not symbolic. His stripes are the paths of brush on canvas. These paths lead only into painting. (1959, 76)

'I lose sight of the fact that my paintings are on canvas, even though I know I'm painting on canvas, and I just see my paintings', said Frank Stella.[19] In the *Black Stripe Paintings* the space between each stripe is smudged; in the *Dartmouth* and later in the *Protractor* paintings, the bands became more and more clearly defined, so that Stella ended up with a clear width between each area of paint. As with David Hockney, Morris Louis and other painters who worked directly onto canvas, Stella's colors fuse with the support and canvas. The realization that the painting is an object in its own right developed in Stella's æsthetics, until the movement into painting-reliefs and then into sculptural paintings, or painterly sculptures, was quite natural. 'A sculpture is just a painting cut out and stood up somewhere', said Stella.

Frank Stella's stripes or bands are a powerful visual element which firmly anchor his paintings. The relation between the shaped canvas and the stripes makes sure that the painting remains intense. In *Chocorua III* (1966), a bright yellow stripe follows the edge of a complexly shaped canvas, creating a luminous zigzag which partially enclosed an equilateral canvas, which is slotted into the larger canvas. This bold conception is made powerful by Stella's use of the yellow stripe abutting a gray stripe, which encloses the pink centre of the triangle. Stripe and shaped paintings such as *Valpariso Flesh and Green* (1963), are typical of Stella's boldness and simplicity: two triangular stretchers are slotted together: one is orange, the other is green, both triangles are painted in stripes.

In many Frank Stella paintings, the stripes 'radiate out from the center of the canvas towards the edge', wrote William Rubin (1970, 65). Paintings such as *Gur*

(1968) are powerful, relying on a simple geometry – a circle dissected into colored segments – coupled with blinding colors: pink, yellow, light white, orange, black, purple, blue. Stella is very dexterous at handling colors, at putting colors beside each other. His colors are so exuberant partly because of his handling of complimentary colors, the way he sets yellow next to black, or green next to orange.

The all-over evenness of his paintwork enhances the power of his paintings. As he wrote: 'I tried for an evenness, a kind of all-overness, where the intensity remained regular over the entire surface'.[20] But Frank Stella did not want people to stand in front of his admiring his dexterous skill in painting. He was not 'showing off' gesturally. He didn't want attention drawn to the marks he made, but to the painting as a whole. Stella changed his mind, though: in the late 'maximalist' works there is a huge emphasis on gesture and brushwork. Paint is daubed in all manner of gestures on the huge aluminium and steel reliefs. Glitter is stuck onto the surfaces, the paintings beg for a sensual response. 'I don't know how I got into sculpture. I liked its physicality, that's the only reason'.

Frank Stella's supports in the 1980s became increasingly complex, and huge. The Vs, Zs, Xs, Hs, Ls, Ts, Us and polygons of the Sixties dazzle with their simple geometry. Like the Pyramids in Egypt, they are simple shapes, but given a bombastic, decisive, rigorously methodical treatment.

The use of monochrome helped to give the huge paintings a pictorial unity. Some of the metallic paintings are vast. The *Protractor* paintings combined circles and rectangles, but it is the colors which one notices first, the complex interlocking arches and circles of colors, reds interweaving and overlapping with yellow, pink, blue, purple, amber, green, black. Incredible colors, in Stella's *Protractor* series, utterly distinctive, visible from a great distance.

Frank Stella's paintings are full of confidence and assertiveness. They are paintings that know exactly what they are doing. They are full of a drive that one might see as ruthlessness, but is in fact the Sixties ethic of taking an idea to its logical conclusion. Stella loves method, like so many artists. One can follow his thinking as he moves from pattern to pattern, from each configuration of color, shape, support, scale, stripes and space. 'The paintings got sculptural because the forms got more complicated. I've learned to weave in and out'.

In Frank Stella's post-1970s paintings, there is no attempt to smooth over the edges, or to provide a smooth surface to the paint, as with the Sixties *Protractor* paintings. Rather, Stella draws attention to the expressive qualities of his brushwork, as with William de Kooning or Julian Schnabel. The expressiveness of Stella's gestures becomes an important element in the painting. The brushstrokes are not hidden as in Barnett Newman's art, who painted with a small brush in small strokes, building up his layers of paint carefully, so that no brushstrokes showed. Stella, rather, constantly draws attention to his brushstrokes, to the very manufacture of his paintings. Works such as *La Vecchia dell'orto* (1986), *Guadalupe Island* (1979), *Shards II* (1983), *Steller's Albatross* (1976) and *Shama* (1979), open out to reveal their manufacture.

In the 1960s, Frank Stella used bright colors, like Morris Louis, but kept them neatly bounded within their stripe patterns. The late maximalist works continually refer to the making of paintings. For Stella, the artist is a privileged participant in the making of art: the 'audience' or viewer is always one step away, is always 'after the fact': '[t]he sensation is one that the artist experiences as the first and only necessary viewer' (1986, 127).

QUOTES BY FRANK STELLA

You see what you know!

•

When I'm painting the picture, I'm really painting a picture. I may have a flat-footed technique, or something like that, but still, to me, the thrill, or the meat of the thing, is the actual painting. I don't get any thrill out of laying it out.

•

No art is any good unless you can feel how it's put together. By and large it's the eye, the hand and if it's any good, you feel the body. Most of the best stuff seems to be a complete gesture, the totality of the artist's body; you can really lean on it.

•

Remember that the 60s was up against the best American art that anyone had produced, and probably the best international art of the 20th century, minus Picasso and Matisse. But who was going to be as good as Barnett Newman and Clyfford Still? Maybe we weren't, but there was a lot of variety and a lot of trying.

•

What you see is what you see.

•

You can't shake your own sensibility. No matter what the concept is, the artist's eye decides when it's right... which is a notion of sensibility.

•

The whole idea of making art is to be open, to be generous, and absorb the viewer and absorb yourself, to let them go into it. I have to go into all those places in order to make it work.

•

Time is what you have left.. you just
march with it and use it the best you can.

MORRIS LOUIS

MORRIS LOUIS

Morris Louis (1912-1962) was a Colorfield painter, who died of lung cancer age 49 in 1962. Louis studied at the Maryland Institute of Fine and Applied Arts, between 1929 and 1933. In the late 1930s, he lived in New York City for four years, and met artists such as Arshile Gorky, Jack Tworkov, and David Alfaro Siqueiros. He worked for the Works Progress Administration Federal Art Project. He taught in Baltimore (privately) between 1940 and 1948. In 1947 he married Marcella Siegel. By 1952, Louis was living in Washington, D.C., where the art scene included artists such as Anne Truitt, Kenneth Noland, Gene Davis, Tom Downing and Howard Mehring. In the late 1950s (between 1955 and 1957), Louis destroyed many of his paintings.

Among the important exhibitions of Morris Louis' work were the retrospectives in 1986 at New York's MOMA and a touring show at the Hirshhorn in D.C. in 2007-08. Also, shows in Washington in 1976, Boston in 1967, and the Guggenheim in 1963.

Unlike some of the other Sixties and Colorfield painters, Morris Louis sometimes used titles for his paintings which recalled the mythic subjects favoured by the Abstract Expressionists.

Morris Louis's guru was the critic Clement Greenberg. According to Robert Hughes, Louis's paintings were selected and altered by Greenberg; the critic decided 'where to cut off the stripes'.[1] Apart from Greenberg, influences on the development of Louis's art included the intense coloration of Pierre Bonnard and Henri Matisse. Painters such as Matisse and Pablo Picasso are cited time after time in discussions of Colorfield and Post-Painterly Abstraction, as well as Abstract Expressionism. The other important presence in painting for the Sixties Colorfield painters was Jackson Pollock (and also Mark Rothko and Willem de Kooning). One can see how Pollock's way of approaching the canvas directly inspired Louis.

The other significant presence in Morris Louis's career was Helen Frankenthaler. It was seeing one of Frankenthaler's huge stained canvases (*Mountains and Sea*, 1952 and later paintings) that supposedly inspired Louis (and Kenneth Noland), when the artists visited Frankenthaler in Gotham in 1953. He called Frankenthaler's method of stained painting a 'bridge between Pollock and what was possible'.[2] For Clement Greenberg, Louis was reacting against his former Cubism. 'The crucial revelation he got from Pollock and Frankenthaler had to do with facture as much as anything else', Greenberg remarked.[3]

In Morris Louis's works, John Elderfield noted in his 1986 monograph on the artist, color was freed up from 'sculptural modelling', 'but not entirely, because in such a white-infused, close-valued style, shifts of color tend also to read as shifts of tone'.[4] The problem for Louis was that when color is used in abstract painting without any visual motifs it can lose the 'traditional stability and gravity' of painting, can be descriptive more of dusky atmosphere than clean open air'.5 In his 1987 essay on Jackson Pollock and Louis, Andrew Kagan claimed that Louis learnt from Pollock about 'æsthetic morality, about the necessity of risk, about greatness, seriousness, absoluteness, bigness, and individualism'.6

Morris Louis advocated the direct contact with the canvas that characterizes much of Post-Painterly Abstraction. Louis poured paint onto the canvas in creases and twists and folds, to produce deeply saturated furls, blotches and curtains of color, in paintings such as *Alpha-Delta* (1961, Everson Museum of Art, New York), *Saraband* (1959, Guggenheim Museum, New York), *Vav* (1960, Tate Gallery), and *Aleph* (1960, collection: del Amo, Madrid).

Morris Louis did not want the process of making the painting to be apparent: he did not want brushstrokes to be seen. Instead, he folded the canvas and used gravity to stain the canvas. Robert Morris and the Process artists later reversed this tendency, by making the process of making the work one of its most prominent features. Louis wanted the paint to fuse with canvas, so that all sense of illusionism would be avoided. Louis's stained paint was semi-transparent, so the veils of color seemed to float apart from the cotton duck canvas. Louis's aim, according to Clement Greenberg, was to keep the

pigment thin enough to prevent a sense of the tactile, so that when the canvas was soaked with paint it becomes 'paint in itself, color in itself'.7 Louis's veils were held back, color-wise, at the edges: he overlaid gray and brown on his veils of bright color.

Cloaking them outwardly in dignified reserve, he allowed only precisely measured, tantalizing glimpses of the passionate intensity within. He created images not only of great beauty but also of monumental power

wrote Andrew Kagan (139).

Morris Louis's method of pouring paint onto canvas was kept a secret, and, because there is not very much documentation, it is not certain exactly what his methods were. Louis worked in a small room, and it is thought that the fumes from his solvents contributed towards the lung cancer he died from at 49 years old.

Part of Morris Louis's staining technique derived from the particular kind of paint he used: Magna was a synthetic medium (oil-miscible acrylic resin paint) which could be thinned to the consistency of watercolor. Also the Magna paint dried quickly, so that Louis could pour the paint in layers, on top of each other.8 Paint manufacturer Leonard Bocour supplied Louis with his new acrylic polymer emulsion, in gallon cans ('big tubes for big paintings'). Louis told Bocour that 'part of my thesis is that materials influence form' (ibid.). Louis controlled the absorbency of the paint using thinners, adding turps and resins thinner; later, he abandoned sizing the canvas, so the color could penetrate the weave deeper.

The 'Veils' and 'Unfurleds' were made by attaching the canvas to some scaffolding: Morris Louis poured the paint down the canvas, putting one color on top of another. Some of the overlapping areas produced stunning color effects (as in *Saraband, Beth Chaf, Atomic Crest* or *Longitude*). The floral motifs were achieved by pouring the paint onto the cotton duck from a few different points towards the centre (as in *Point of Tranquillity, Number 99, Spawn* and *Aleph*). The staining technique (in the *Floral* series, for example) related also to Renaissance fresco painting, as well as Impressionism's open color and the example of Henri Matisse's open color (J. Elderfield, 1986).

In paintings such as *Beth* (1959-60, Philadelphia Museum of Art), *Point of Tranquility* (1959-60), and *Aleph Series V* (collection: H. Frankenthaler), Morris Louis produced some enormous, incredibly luminous, and very memorable works. *Point of Tranquility, Spawn* (1959-60, London) and *Number 99* (1959-60, Cleveland) were riots of rainbow hues: bright yellows, oranges, reds, greens, and blues, all exploding outwards from the centre of the huge canvas (*Point of Tranquility* is 2.58 by 3.43 yards).

Beth is one of Morris Louis's most radiant paintings, being predominantly red (the vibrancy of the scarlet is only slightly modulated by the introduction of smaller patches of green and blue). *Beth Chaf* (1959, collection: M.L. Brenner) was similarly warm-hued, with only a thick stripe of dark green countering the reds, oranges and browns. In *Aleph Series V* the color saturation reaches a new intensity, with the explosion of rainbow colors being overlaid with layer upon layer of pigment, so that the main central area is stained dark brown by the sheer force of one color on top of another.

In the 'Veils' series, Morris Louis's paintings layered and mixed colors, sometimes not always successfully. The 'Veil' paintings could be overwhelming, being walls of color. In the *Gamma, Sigma, Alpha* and *Omega* paintings of the early Sixties, Louis kept the colors more separated. The centre of the canvas was often left unpainted, resulting in more open and relaxed forms. In *Gamma Iota* (1960, private collection), *Gamma Pu* (1960, private collection), and *Alpha Alpha* (1960, collection: W. Ehrlich), there are fewer stripes of color than usual (4 on each side), green, blue and black on the right, red, purple and black on the left. In *Alpha Beta* (1960, collection: I.M. Pei), there are only three bands of colors on each side, and the whole color scheme only consists of two hues: green and yellow (thus, on the left and right, the diagonal rivers of color are yellow-green-yellow). In *Alpha Tau* (St Louis Art Museum), Louis left a very wide gap of bare canvas between the diagonal stripes (eleven on each side). *Alpha Lambda* (1961, collect-ion: C. Hendrickson), *Beta Kappa* (1961, National Gallery of Art, Washington), *Beta Lambada* (1960, MOMA, New York) and *Sigma* (1961, private collection) were more typical, employing a bunch of some 13 or 14 diagonal bands, with hot and cool colors complementing each other. Generally, in these *Alpha* diagonal paint-ings, the colors on each side reflect each other. Not in a simple symmetry; but the orange stripe on the left would be picked up on the right, tho' in a different place.

Pillars of Hercules (1960, Thyssen-Bornemisza Collection) was part of Morris Louis's 'Column' series, made before he started on his 'Unfurleds' series. The strips of Magna paint are vertical, three or four on each side of the canvas: yellow, violet and two reds on the left, two reds on the right. Other paintings in the 'Column' series, all featuring narrow bands of color grouped together to form a single column, included *Number 11* (1961, private collection), a tight mesh of overlapping colors; *Burning Stain* (1961, University of Nebraska, Lincoln), much softer/ lighter hues; *Number 9* (1961, collection: L. & G. de Menil), closely-packed brightly-hued stripes (greens, yellows, oranges); *Third Element* (1961, MOMA, NY), where blues and greens alternate with reds, yellows and oranges; *Number 33* (1962, private collection) and *Biplane* (1962, collection: T. Wiesel), in which the column is separ-ated by a single band of bare canvas; *Number 2-64* (1962, collection: A. Rock),

a simple group of six colors; *Number 19* (1962, collection: D. Mirvish), a narrow group of 8 hues; and *Castor and Pollux* (1962, the Eli and Edythe L. Broad collection), 9 bands of bright colors, framed by an orange stripe each side. Then there were one or two of the 'Columns' series which featured more than one column, such as *Number 1-99* (1962, collection: L. Brenner), which had three columns.

Omega IV (1959-60, private collection) was unusual in Morris Louis's *œuvre*: it had two series of rivers of color interweaving from opposite directions on the canvas; in *Delta Upsilon* (1960, private collection), the group of colors on the right is joined by another group, breaking the usual Louisian sense of symmetry. In *Alpha Eta* (1960, private collection) and *Alpha Epsilon* (1960, Museum of Contemporary Art, Los Angeles), the rivers of color were joined together over a strip of bare canvas.

Morris Louis's *Blue Veil* (1958-59, Fogg Art Museum) was a vast area of mainly blue paint. The edge of the paint stain could be clearly seen around the edge of most of the canvas. Underneath the blue paint Louis had poured variations of violet and green, both colors linked with blue in the traditional color wheel. Yellow was also employed (on the right-hand side) as an under-color The effect was a curtain of blue modulated by green, violets and yellows, which moved in and out of the dominant hue. *Blue Veil* was in musical terms a variation on blue, using the colors that harmonized with blue. The effect recalled the layering technique of Mark Rothko's paintings. In *Blue Veil* the facture of the work is plainly visible: the viewer can take apart the process of making the artwork, so that Louis can almost be glimpsed pouring the acrylics, folding the canvas, manipulating the paint using gravity, allowing one layer to dry, but ensuring another layer is poured on top of one that's still wet.

Blue Veil is one of Morris Louis's most appealing, most mesmeric canvases, in the way that the hues of the pigment shifts as they travel across the picture, the selection of voluptuous colors, the way some colors melt into others, and some retain their form, with harder edges, the balancing of hues (for example, pale blues on the extreme right and left), and the sheer scale of the painting. *Blue Veil* celebrates the act of painting, so that there's no way it could be said that Painting Was Dead by 1960.

In its way, Morris Louis's *Blue Veil* is as vivacious and subtle a celebration of the art of painting as any of the Old Masters. Certainly Louis's method of layering pigment is as technically dazzling as the films of oil paint the Early Netherlandish painters (Jan van Eyck, Rogier van der Weyden, Hans Memling *et al*), where paintings were created by building up successive layers of oil, to produce that glowing inner light. Louis's light may be much more on the surface than Early Flemish art, but just because it doesn't

enshrine depth doesn't mean it's no less valuable (Louis's canvases look towards the flatness and surface of postmodern art, where everything happens on the surface, where everything is brought to the front, *à la* Jean Baudrillard and Frederic Jameson).

Another curtain work, *Number 1-89* (1959, Des Moines Art Center), was unusual, in being a light-toned and largely monochromatic work, this time in yellow and ochre. *Verdicchio* (1959, collection: J.D. Murchison) was a similarly single-color curtain of paint (light green). *Mem* (1959, collection: B. Wright) was in the more familiar Louis hue of orange/ gold.

Tet (1958, Whitney Museum of American Art) was another large *Unfurled* canvas (twelve feet nine inches wide), comprising curtains of blue and green superimposed on yellows and golds. It achieved an impressive wash of pure color, with the canvas cut around the sides just above and around the points where the synthetic polymer soaked into the canvas. In *Untitled* (1959), an unfurled painting, swathes of blended acrylic create a curtain of color in this portrait-format picture. In between the large areas of pigment, Morris Louis had left bare canvas.

Kaf (1959-60, collection: Kimiko & John G. Powers, New York) is one of Morris Louis's most fabulous canvases, an 8' 4" by 12' painting in rich, warm reds, oranges, yellows, greens, blues and purples. The unrestrained, opulent colors spread over the surface of the canvas in irregular patterns, outward from the centre, as in other *Unfurleds*, but with darker areas of red and blue in the middle vaguely reminiscent of the vertical stripes.

A series of veils or curtains of the mid-Fifties (*Iris, Salient, Pendulum, Longitude, Atomic Crest, Intrigue*) were much paler, with more of the translucent effects of watercolor technique. These paintings employed washes of pastel hues – pinks, purples, blues, greens – recalling Helen Frankenthaler's paintings. *Intrigue* (1954, collection: J. Slifka, New York) used mainly purples and pinks and reds; *Atomic Crest* (1954, Lannan Foundation) merged similar hues with more blues and grays; in *Salient* (1954, collection: D. Zucker), Louis thinned the pigment considerably, so that towards the base of the canvas the colors were faded; *Longitude* (1954, collection: M.L. Brenner) veered towards the warmer end of the color spectrum, with an irregularly-patterned staining composition; *Iris* (1954, collection: E. Schwartz) and *Pendulum* (1954, collection: H.W. Anderson) moved into the more familiar, darker tones of the later Louis paintings, with a more complex and multi-layered structure.

The 'Bronze Veils' series were large horizontal canvases with swathes of stained paint merging together: *Beth Anin, Earth, Beth Gimel, Beth Kuf, Curtain, Beth Rash, Beth Heh, Beth Nun, Beth Samach, Beth Peh* and *Spark*. They were all in gold, bronze, brown, yellow and ochre colors, with all the color values relatively close, like the tones. Yellow under-painting is allowed to burst out from underneath, to the right, in the otherwise sombre all-over brown of *Beth Gimel* (1958, collection: R. Rowan). In *Beth Samach* (7 ft 5 in x 11 ft 5 in) the greeny-gold on the left merges into orangey-gold, then reddish-gold; then greenish-gold on the right. In *Beth Heh* (collection: G. Gund), there is brown on the left, ochre in the centre and right, with red stains in the middle. In *Beth Ayin*, swathes of brown frame gold and red in the centre. 1959's *Golden Age* (Ulster Museum) was a curtain of dark ochre and gold, with yellow, blue and green under-painting. *Loam* (1958, Houston) was a much darker canvas, with a similar interior composition to *Golden Age*.

Bower (1958, Nationalgalerie, Berlin) was another bronze/brown painting, but with the luminous reds and greens of the under-staining showing in patches over the surface. In *Beth Rash* (1958-59, collection: J. Lebron), the palette moves towards dark blues and purples, but caught in the same vertically symmetrical composition, with the colors being poured from the top downwards. In *Beth Rash*, some of the colors underneath can be glimpsed in rows at the top of the canvas: purple, orange, turquoise, red, yellow. *Italian Bronze* (1959, collection: S. Hahn) had fused stains bleeding into each other: green, blue, brown, damson, and black.

Where (1960, Smithsonian Institute) was

another large (3.33 yards wide) landscape format 'curtain' of color, but this time with no layering or under-painting; each stripe of color was kept separate, with a few inches of bare canvas in between. The stripes ran vertically across the whole of the canvas, from top to bottom. The color choices combined to create an ecstatic piece: yellow, orange, green, blue, lemon, khaki, brown, red, turquoise. *While Series II* (1959-60) was similar to *Where*, but had the vertical stains overlapping in groups. *While Series II* was also framed each side by a very dark blue and black stripe. In *Moving In* (1961, André Emmerich Gallery, NYC), narrow bands of acrylic run in vertical stripes from roughly the same point in this portait-format canvas. Warm hues predominate: reds, oranges, yellows.

Later, Morris Louis produced a series of paintings consisting of stripes in groups. Louis mounted these either vertically or horizontally. *Horizontal I* (1962, collection: M. Cogan) was a simple group of colors (beige, orange, red, brown, blue, and yellow), clustered in the lower half of the nearly three-yard-wide canvas. *Horizontal III* was a landscape-format painting (1962, private collection) consisting of two groups of bands of colors (yellow, red, green, purple and black). *Horizontal VIII* (1962, private collection) also featured two groups of horizontal bands of color, four above and four below, separated by a layer of empty canvas.

Morris Louis's *Omicron* (1961, private collection) has a large empty V-shaped space at its centre, with the familiar Louis stripes each side, running diagonally from the sides of the canvas to the base. The colors of the right-hand group of diagonals – red and purple – are picked up in the left-hand group. While the 'Columns' inevitably recalled Barnett Newman and his famous zip or stripe, some of Louis's last works evoked the art of Kenneth Noland and Ellsworth Kelly: these pieces (such as *Hot Half*, 1962, private collection and *Equator*, 1962, private collection), featured a band of stripes moving across the canvas diagonally. However, the edge of each band of color was straight, recalling Hard Edge and Colorfield painting.

In *Working Space* Frank Stella wrote of this new painterly/ Post-Painterly/ Colorfield/ Hard Edge abstraction:

> The free-unfettered access to abstraction's early roots had a wonderful and powerful effect: close attention to the early masters coupled with a natural, relaxed attitude toward enlarged pictorial scale and gesture made exciting painting. Jack Youngerman, Ellsworth Kelly, and Sam Francis took off in what seemed like a marvellous, yet familiar, vector. Helen Frankenthaler and Friedel Dzubas were reaching new, relaxed, lyrical heights. Morris Louis, Kenneth Noland, and Jules Olitski undertook an exotic trip in search of firstness, while Donald Judd, Larry (now Lawrence) Poons, and I laid the track to literalism. (160)

Here one senses Frank Stella's pride in being a part of 1960s painterly abstraction. With Stella's *Black-Stripe Paintings*, one is really surprised by their size. In this they take much from Abstraction Expressionism, but the contact between paint and canvas is new. There is no attempt at tonal, sculptural painting in the art of Morris Louis and Frank Stella. The paint touches the canvas in one flood of color. Stella's paintings are not aiming at illusionistic space. In contrast, though, Stella moved towards the notion of an illusionistic 'working space' in his later painting, those 'maximalist' paintings/ 'reliefs'. Louis, Stella reckons, suggested a new form of pictorial space in painting:

> What is needed is a serious effort at structural inventiveness. What Morris Louis did for a while twenty years ago, following the lead of Barnett Newman, remains more of a promise than a fulfilment. But if his promise were read rightly – if the structural potential of his spatial dynamics were understood and the disjunctive intensity of his color appreciated – his painting could lead to a new beginning... Morris Louis was nearly the last abstract painter to hint at the potential that abstraction might have for creating a full and expansive pictorial space like that of Rubens. (66)

Morris Louis exploded color, developing it from Wassily Kandinsky and Henri Matisse. Robert Hughes called Louis's paintings 'among the most purely optical ever made in America'.9 Critics spoke about Louis's art in terms of 'optical', 'retinal', 'opulence', and 'hedonism'. Daniel Wheeler wrote of a 'new retinal beauty of Matissean hedonism and opulence, but pure, luminous, fluid, and incorporeal as never before' (191).

Morris Louis focussed the viewer on his colors: there was simply the color on the canvas, with no references to other things. Yet, of course, Louis's furls, like Frank Stella's black stripes, were also æsthetic structures, which spoke of pictorial illusion. There was a structure to Stella's *Black Stripe Paintings*, as there was to Louis's 'Unfurleds' and curtains of color.

Morris Louis's paintings were not simply paint thrown at a canvas. Similarly, Jackson Pollock's painting were not the result of random splashes, as if someone had set off some grenades in a row of tins of paint on 25 square yards of canvas. Frank Stella liked to use paint 'as good as it was in the can'.10 Pollock, Louis and Stella planned their paintings carefully. The paintings were imaginative, artistic works, each speaking of the personal touch and gesture of the artist. Although Louis did not use a paintbrush, his gestures were unmistakable. Stella's marks were apparent more in the later works. In Stella's Sixties *Protractor* series, the paint was applied smoothly, as in Brice Marden's monochrome panels. Yet one can see the personal touch in Marden's paintings: he left a gap at the base of his paintings, and allowed drips to form there.

Frank Stella changed his mind about Morris Louis, Kenneth Noland and Helen Frankenthaler, painters with whom he felt were his contemporaries. In 1972, for instance, he said:

> What I felt at the time – and I don't feel this now – I felt very strongly that Morris Louis, for example, and Ken Noland and particularly Helen Frankenthaler, in their use of

the staining technique, there was identific-
ation with the facture and weave and all
that, but it still seemed to me basically those
stains read quite illusionistically.[11]

Morris Louis's paintings, with their huge
splotches of color, are, as Frank Stella
says, loose, open works. Louis's paintings
are free of figurative imagery and illus-
ions, even though the stripes, furls, columns and curtains and star shapes are all
æsthetic constructs. A.J. Carmean
commented: '[f]or Morris Louis the
staining technique was such a breakthrough'.[12] Like Helen Frankenthaler's
paintings, Louis's staining technique
allows for an æsthetic freedom which is
refreshing after so much tight, close, dry
paintwork, as found in, say, the art of
Nicolas Poussin and René Magritte. Frank
Stella wrote:

> It may be that what makes Morris Louis's
> late paintings so appealing is their peculiar
> Kandinsky-like understanding of Newman.
> Louis brought a determined looseness to
> Newman's abstraction that Kandinsky
> would have applauded. (125)

It's true, Wassily Kandinsky would have
enjoyed Morris Louis's multicolored
explosions, for example, *Point of Tranquillity* (1958, Hirshhorn and Sculpture
Garden, Washington DC), where yellows
and oranges predominate, anchored by
deep blues and a vivacious green. Frank
Stella and Louis are the product of a long
tradition in art of broken color: Titian
broke up color in his late works; J.M.W.
Turner did too; the Impressionists broke

up color further; Georges Seurat turned it
into dots.

Some critics regarded Morris Louis's
paintings are the first properly abstract
paintings, because they did not relate to a
theme or subject, but existed as themselves.
In this sense, Louis went further than
Wassily Kandinsky, Kasimir Malevich,
Piet Mondrian, Jackson Pollock or
Barnett Newman (D. Wheeler, 193). Louis
influenced painters such as Frank Stella,
Richard Diebenkorn, Jules Olitski, Sam
Francis, Sandro Chia, Sigmar Polke, David
Salle and Arnulf Rainer (C. Riley, 167).

Critic Peter Fuller, in his grumpy,
eccentric way, reckoned that the New York
School did not 'influence' British painters
in a one-way flow of æsthetic information. After 1958, Fuller said, American
painting no longer triumphed over the
rest the world.[13] Fuller thought that Patrick
Heron influenced the American painters:
'I believe not only that Heron's stripe
paintings preceded those of Morris Louis,
but also that they are better, much better,
in æsthetic terms'.[14] Compared with
Heron's late 1950s work, Fuller claims,

> there is a dowdy and depressing feel about
> even the best Morris Louis canvases. With
> few exceptions, Louis's paintings, today,
> have the look of last season's used and
> abused fashions. (ib., 218)

Peter Fuller's negative appraisal of
Morris Louis's art is part of his basic,
lame anti-American, pro-British philosophy. Instead of spending idiot amounts
of money on Louis's canvases, Fuller said,

collectors would be better off buying
Patrick Herons.

Peter Fuller may be right about the
influence of Patrick Heron on Morris
Louis, with regard to the colored stripe
motif of the latter. But Heron's own stripe
paintings – the stripes moving horizontally across a portrait format canvas –
look suspiciously like Mark Rothko's late
1940s and early 1950s paintings. Rothko's
paintings of the late 1940s, such as
Number 11 (1949, Washington) and
Number 17 (1947, New York), are clearly
the ancestors of Heron's late 1950s
paintings (such as the Tate Gallery's
Horizontal Stripe Painting by Heron). And
Louis's stripe paintings are far superior to
those of Heron.

HELEN
FRANKENTHALER

HELEN FRANKENTHALER

There is a sense of openness and relax-
ation in Helen Frankenthaler's (b. 1928)
and Morris Louis's huge cotton duck
canvases stained with colors. The new
synthetic paints and the new household
paints produced brilliant colors. Louis's
and Frankenthaler's paintings are
overwhelming when viewed up close. In
reproductions so much is lost. It's the same
with Mark Rothko, Barnett Newman,
Jackson Pollock, Frank Stella and Robert
Motherwell: the scale is crucial. Lucy
Lippard writes:

> a sense of scale is also a *sense* proper. Scale
> is *felt* and cannot be communicated either
> by photographic reproduction or by
> description. (1968)

Helen Frankenthaler's *Movable Blue*
(1973, Louisville) is really huge, a long
horizontal-shaped canvas, twenty feet
wide, recalling Claude Monet's *Waterlilies*.
Morris Louis's *Saraband* is smaller – 8.5
by 12.5 feet – but the curtain-like flood of
colors – blue, white, orange, yellow, lilac –
is spectacular, and consuming.

Helen Frankenthaler said, like so many
Sixties painters, that she didn't want the
manufacture of the painting to be
apparent:

> I poured the paint and used relatively few
> brushstrokes. I didn't want the sign of the
> brush or how the picture was made to
> appear.[1]

Helen Frankenthaler spoke of the way a
really good picture looks 'as if it all
happened or was made in one stroke at
once'.[2] This compares with Barnett Newman's sense of all-overness and Zen
Buddhist totality, but Frankenthaler's
sense of instantaneousness was intended
to hide the manufacture of the painting,
something earlier Abstract Expressionists
– Jackson Pollock, Adolph Gottlieb,
Clyfford Still – were keen to keep
prominent.

When it comes to titling paintings,
Frankenthaler doesn't like numbers.
Naming a painting is a way of referring
to it, in order to remember it, not for a
sentimental reason. Thus, Frankenthaler
names pictures *Blue Territory* or *Scattered
Shapes* because of what she sees in the
painting (1965, 37).

QUOTES BY HELEN FRANKENTHALER

There are no rules. That is how art is born, how breakthroughs happen. Go against the rules or ignore the rules. That is what invention is about.

•

A really good picture looks as if it's happened at once. It's an immediate image.

•

One really beautiful wrist motion, that is synchronised with your head and heart, and you have it. It looks as if it were born in a minute.

•

I wanted things that I couldn't at times articulate.

•

We would sift through every inch of what it was that worked, or if it didn't, and wonder what was effective in it, in terms of paint, the subject matter, the size, the drawing.

•

Whatever the medium, there is the difficulty, challenge, fascination and often productive clumsiness of learning a new method: the wonderful puzzles and problems of translating with new materials.

•

How did we do it? How did we get it? It is one thing for the artist to have a certain magic and produce a certain magic, but for the technicians and the press to get it...

KENNETH NOLAND

KENNETH NOLAND

Kenneth Noland (1924-2010) was Morris
Louis's associate in Washington D.C.
Noland's æsthetics concerned
concentrating solely on painting, on the
problems painting produces, and on color.
Noland's precursors were Paul Klee and
Henri Matisse, and also Ilya Bolotowsky
and Josef Albers, who taught at Black
Mountain College. Like Louis, Noland
developed a technique of directly applying
Magna paint onto canvas, inspired partly
by their visit to Helen Frankenthaler's
studio. In a 1977 interview, Noland
described how in the 1960s he and other
painters like him wanted to try other
kinds of paint and canvas; they wanted to
experiment with putting paint directly
onto unstretched or unsized canvas, to
treat the canvas more as a fabric than as
a stretched surface. Noland explained:

> To use paint thinner and more economically,
> to find new paints, from the industrial
> system, like plastics. This is something that
> artists have always done. They've always
> used a minimum of the means of technology
> in any period.[1]

Kenneth Noland concentrated on
making hard-edged geometric shapes (like
Frank Stella) with brilliant colors (like
Morris Louis). Noland's instantly recognizable motifs include chevrons (such as
in *Every Third*, 1963, private collection),
inverted chevrons (*Tropical Zone*, 1964),
bull's eyes and horizontal stripes (such as
in *Via Mojave*, 1968, collection: the

artist). Frank Stella wrote:

> Ken Noland has put things in the center and
> I'll use a symmetrical pattern, but we use
> symmetry in a different way. It's non-
> relational. In the newer American paintings
> we strive to get the thing in the middle, and
> symmetrical but just to get a kind of force,
> just to get the thing on the canvas. The
> balance factor isn't important. We're not
> trying to jockey everything around.[2]

Like Morris Louis, Kenneth Noland
wanted to make the pigment so thin it
would fuse entirely with the canvas.
Noland spoke of the physicality of color:

> One thing that people don't generally talk
> about is the fact that the experience of color
> is tactile. We talk about the relative cool-
> ness and warmness of color, or transparency
> or opacity, and really all those descriptive
> terms are tactile descriptions rather than to
> do with the redness of red. (E. De Antonio,
> 84)

In 1969, Kenneth Noland said he
wanted 'to have color be the origin of the
painting'.[3] One of Noland's most famous
paintings is *Via Blues* (1967, collection:
R.A. Rowan, Pasadena). This is a huge (22
feet wide) horizontal-format canvas with
the familiar Noland stripes traversing the
entire width of the painting. There was no
fussing for Noland at the edges of the
painting: the stripes are painted right up
to the edge of the painting then they stop.
As with Morris Louis's stripes, it was the
grouping of particular colors and the
width of the bands that made Noland's
Via Blues so successful. In *Erin* (1970,
Paris) nearly all of the area of the
painting is taken up with a solid green

band, with the different colored stripes pushed to the top and bottom edges of this huge canvas (some three and a half yards long). In *Navajo* (1971, Paris), the stripes are much more balanced, more in proportion to each other, and in a variety of sizes, with wider bands alternating with narrow bands. The colors deployed too (purple, blue, green, red, pink, orange) are more vibrant than in the more austere *Erin*.

In Ken Noland's *17th Stage* (1964, Virginia Museum of Fine Arts), an imposing chevron, composed of blue, green and red acrylic stripes, descends boldly as if from above. *Grave Light* (1965, collection: Robert A. Rowan) is a wide, shallow trapeze shaped canvas, whose colors (yellow, green, and dark blue) are thick bands of plastic paint which are controlled by the internal geometry of the shape of the stretcher.

Using the kind of color æsthetics developed by Josef Albers and Victor Vassarely, Kenneth Noland set closely-toned but differently-hued colors next to each other. Like Frank Stella and Ad Reinhardt, Noland aimed for an art which eradicated many of the concerns of traditional æsthetics. 'No graphs, no systems, no modules,' Noland said in 1968.

No shaped canvases [an obvious reference to Stella]. Above all, no *thingness*, no *objectiveness*. The thing is to get that color down on the thinnest conceivable surface, a surface sliced into the air as if by a razor. And surface. That's all.[4]

It is interesting to compare Frank Stella's painterly technique with his contemporary, Kenneth Noland:

Sometimes I apply the paint with brushes, sometimes with rollers... any way that I can get it on where the tactile result is compatible with the nature of the color I'm going to use there... When the color is first laid down, it doesn't have anything to do with the resulting size or shape really. Once you lay it down, you can choose by sight how to bring the total color into a certain quantity... For instance, I could make that picture more square, and if I made it more square, then it would become denser and the color would have movement in it. If I extended it longer, you would have a faster kind of movement. You have a way of getting the color to take on a different degree of speed, translucence, transparency, opacity, density, even to the warmth or coolness for that matter. (E. de Antonio, 84)

QUOTES BY KENNETH NOLAND

Because of this the representation I'm interested in is of those things only the eye can touch.

•

For me context is the key – from that comes the understanding of everything.

•

I paint my paintings directly. I almost never paint over. This maintains the attention of the picture for me, my contact with what I am doing. I think of painting without subject matter as music without words.

•

Earlier on I had taken Morris to New York to meet the critic, Clement Greenberg. He was a catalyst because he'd written about and pointed toward the best artists, past and present.

•

I've followed other artists gratefully and I hope I've also followed my own path… sometimes along side other artists.

•

On the other hand, purely formal characteristics exercise the senses as do string quartets, piano concertos, Dixieland.

ROBERT RYMAN

ROBERT RYMAN

*As I worked and developed the painting, I
found that I was eliminating a lot. I would
put the color down, then paint over the
color, trying to get down to a few crucial
elements. It was like erasing something to
put white over it.*

Robert Ryman[1]

Ad Reinhardt painted black-on-black
squares (though Robert Rauschenberg had
painted all-black paintings before
Reinhardt). Jasper Johns' use of gray, and
Reinhardt's and Rauschenberg's use of
black influenced other monochrome
painters, such as Brice Marden, Frank
Stella and Robert Ryman.[2] Ryman (b.
1930) explored the sensuality of surfaces
via really sumptuous white squares.
Ryman delved into the mysticality of
white-on-white, as Kasimir Malevich had
done.[3]

I would say that Rothko had an important
influence on me [acknowledged Ryman].
There was also Matisse, particularly, and
Cézanne. What interested me in Matisse was
not so much what he was painting but how
he was doing it. It was his sureness, the way
he put the paint down... He was so sure, it
was so immediate. (R. Ryman, 1983)

Robert Ryman said that Mark Rothko
was the first artist to see the painting as
an æsthetic object; Ryman said he wanted
to emphasize the objecthood of a painting
by using paint: 'I wanted to make a
painting getting the paint across. That's
really what a painting is basically about'
(1971).

A cursory glance at Robert Ryman's
paintings would see nothing but white
squares of different sizes (typically 60 or
72 inches square). Looking closer, however, one saw that Ryman was meticulously and vigorously exploring the relationships between color and support,
between shape and color, between object-
ification and illusion, between abstraction
and figuration. Far from being all the
same monotonous white-on-white,
Ryman's paintings were all individual.
Each one had its own specifications of
frame size, support (aluminium, canvas,
plastic, wood, fibreglass). There were clips
around the edge of some paintings, while
others were bolted to the wall.

Paintings of Robert Ryman's such as
Department (1981, oil on aluminium, 60 x
60 in, collection: Rhona J. Hoffman,
Chicago), *Untitled,* a small painting by
postwar standards (53.5 inches square), or
the very small *Untitled* of 1961 (12 inches
square), display a sense of the tactile to
rival Jasper Johns. Ryman's art, like
Johns' art, is founded largely on the
sensuality of paint, of surfaces, of the
eroticism of texture. One comes back to
this again and again in art criticism, this
sensualism of surface. As Lynda Nead
writes of Kenneth Clark: 'Clark reads
brush marks and lines as though they are
part of a symbolic language of sensual
impulses, telling traces of sexual desire'.[4]

Robert Ryman's use of white was not to
hide the painting's manufacture under a
cloak of blankness. The white, rather,

emphasized the painting's structure and sensuality. Ryman used white 'in order to make other things in the painting visible, color for instance'.5 The use of white unified the formal aspects of the painting, so the artwork was read as a whole. Aspects of the piece, from surface texture to the support, became interpreted as a totality. White was useful in painting, Ryman explained, because it didn't 'interfere.' It was a

> neutral color that allows for a clarification in painting. It makes other aspects of painting visible that would not be so clear with the use of other colors. (ib., 16)

By limiting himself to one color, Robert Ryman, like Brice Marden and Ad Reinhardt, freed himself up for an exploration of different formal aspects. There was nothing limiting about Ryman's concentration on the color white (which is all colors, optically). In Ryman's case, the formal exploration included moving through a range of media, for Ryman painted in white on many kinds of material: canvas, linen, cotton, wood, paper, steel, copper, aluminium, mylar, fibreglass, Plexiglass, cardboard. He painted with different sorts of media: oil, baked enamel, paper, vinyl acetate emulsion, and so on. As Ryman said, typically of so many contemporary artists: '[t]here is never a question of what to paint, but only how to paint'.6

It didn't matter that most of Ryman's paintings were white. A Robert Ryman exhibition, too, was not at all 'boring'.

Indeed, there was a sense of greatness in his painting to rival the masters of contemporary art, such as Mark Rothko. Ryman demonstrated that by limiting oneself in one respect, an unlimited realm would be opened up for exploration. A Robert Ryman show is thus also a display of how to paint, how paint can be used on a variety of media. Different sorts of paint – oil, enamel, emulsion – produce different sorts of effects. Go into any household superstore these days and one can see just how many subtle variations there are of white and cream. Ryman showed that even when one limits art to a very narrow set of attributes, infinite variations are still possible. Ryman showed that there isn't just one kind of white. Painters have always known this, but Ryman's concentration on white made it obvious.

Instead of being cool, detached or unemotional (which one might expect from such a Minimal project of painting nothing but white paintings), Robert Ryman's art was highly emotive. 'What is interesting about his work,' wrote Arthur Danto in "The Historical Museum of Monochrome Art", 'is the degree to which, for all its blank whiteness, it reflects the times through which the artist lived' (1997, 169). In the Fifties, Ryman's work reflected the gestural, pigment-rich of Abstract Expressionism; in the Sixties, Ryman became a Minimalist and materialist, and the paintings become 'surface, support, and pigment and nothing more' (ib., 169). In the Eighties and Nineties the works become sculptural, incorporating plastic, waxpaper, bolts and fasteners.

Some of Robert Ryman's white paintings of 1960-61 fill the entire surface with scumbled and impastoed white oil paint. Though severe they are also beautiful, and, in a way, traditional. The white paintings of the late 1970s and 1980s introduced add-ons such as aluminium clips of fasteners which became part of the painting. Attention was thus drawn to the borders of the work, as with the Hard Edge painters, and artists such as Frank Stella, Morris Louis and Jo Baer. The aluminium fasteners drew attention to the painting as object, as something physical to be attached to a gallery wall. The primacy of illusion inside the painting was shattered. The painting had to be considered in its entirety, not simply as something upon which paint was arranged to suggest something outside of itself (a painting of a sky, a tree, a person). Paintings such as *Dominion* (1979), *Courier* (1982), *Director* (1983) and *Report* (1983, all Saatchi Collection, London), were internally smoothly painted in all-over white. The interesting things seemed to be happening around the edges: prominent aluminium clips in *Dominion*; large fasteners in *Courier* as well as the use of oil and enamelac on fibreglass; the same media in *Director*, but with a narrow stripe of a cream hue across the centre of the painting; and a square of fibreglass with the mount being visible in *Report*.

Art critics wondered whether Robert Ryman's all-white squares represented the 'end of painting', as with Ad Reinhardt's black squares.[7] Arthur Danto mused whether Ryman's white squares could been seen as the beginning something new in art, in the way that Giotto stood at the beginning of the Renaissance (1997, 155). Ryman's work can be seen as the end of narrative, modernist art, or as part of a postmodern, pluralist art, where painting is one element in amongst installation art, photography, video art, earthworks, performances and so on (ib., 171).

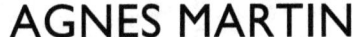

AGNES MARTIN

AGNES MARTIN

Agnes Martin (1912-2004) is an archetypal Minimalist, 'Cool' or Post-Painterly Abstract painter. Her paintings, in which 'nothing seems to happen', to use a Samuel Beckettian phrase, are deeply poetic. As with Robert Ryman's white paintings (which are more like Martin's than most), there was a lot happening in Martin's paintings. From a distance, Martin's works looked like off-white squares with hardly anything done to them. When one looked closer, one saw different grids, and different ways of marking the grid (gold leaf, pencil, ink). Sometimes the grid was very tight and compact, with a tiny rectangle being described; sometimes there was a web of horizontal lines, widely spaced; sometimes the white was attenuated by a faint pink or gray or cream between each set of horizontal bands.

Agnes Martin's paintings are, like Robert Ryman's and Ad Reinhardt's paintings, flat squares in a human-scale (often five or six foot square, for instance). They have poetic titles: *Mountain II* (1966, collection: R. Solomon, New York), *Drift of Summer* (1965, Saatchi Collection, London), *Graystone* (1981), *Song* (1982) and *Night Sea* (1963, Saatchi Collection, London).

Agnes Martin's white paintings are not all they seem at first, as with Frank Stella's *Black Stripe Paintings* and Robert Ryman's work. *Night Sea* is, unusually in Martin's œuvre, a light blue, hinting at nature, at skies and seas. It is painted in oil and gold leaf. The variations that Martin makes within her basic format are many: sometimes the grid is packed tightly, as in *Drift of Summer* and *Stone*, but lightly drawn, so the painting remains mainly white all over. In *Night Sea* the rectangles are much larger, so that the spaces between the blue paint is visible from a distance. In *Untitled No. 8* (private collection) the grid becomes vertical stripes forming a salmon-pink row of bands. In *Untitled No. 12* (1977, Pace Gallery), the pencil and india ink lines define small vertical rectangles on a six-foot square canvas. In the series of paintings entitled *Untitled* (*Untitled I, Untitled II, Untitled II* and so on up to *Untitled XII* and beyond [made in 1979, Saatchi Collection, London]), the graphite marks (on linen) do not describe rectangles but bands of horizontal lines. *Untitled No. 9* (1980) is a series of repeating vertical bands of pale, nearly ephemeral colors (pink, yellow and blue).

> Beauty and happiness and life are all the same and they are pervasive, unattached and abstract and they are our only concern. They are immeasurable, completely lacking in substance. They are perfect and sublime. This is the subject matter of art.

Agnes Martin's painterly reductionism seems austere, but in fact poeticizes the world, as with the art of Robert Ryman or Brice Marden. Martin's paintings, according to Barbara Rose,

> require a degree of concentration so intense from the viewer that, like Ad Reinhardt's

black paintings, they are oases of quiet in a tumultuous, over-stimulated environment.[1]

Rather than being aligned with the polemical Minimal artists, such as Donald Judd and Robert Morris, Agnes Martin is more usefully associated with the Abstract Expressionist painters most often linked with the Colorfield and Minimal painters (that is, Barnett Newman and Mark Rothko).

In Agnes Martin's art, subject matter was crucial. This alone distances her work from painters such as Morris Louis and Frank Stella, who insisted on the thing-in-itself, the ubiquitous 'what you see is what you get' principle of much of Minimal (and 1960s) art. Martin's art, meanwhile, emphasized poetry and evoked nature.

In "The Untroubled Mind", Agnes Martin wrote

My work is anti-nature
The four storey mountain
You will not think form, space, line, contour
Just a suggestion of nature gives weight
light and heavy
light like a feather
you get light enough and you levitate.
When I say it's alive, it's inspired
alive
inspiration and life are equivalents and they come from outside (1973, 17)

Agnes Martin says that inspiration is 'moments of happiness', which are always around us. 'Inspiration is there all the time for everyone whose mind is not clouded over with thoughts whether they realize it or not'.[2] Martin's inspiration is

thus an æsthetic and ontological openness, a state of awareness which some artists cultivate or hope to induce in others. Inspiration, Martin says, is always waiting for the untroubled mind. As children seem to be more untroubled than adults, they have more inspiration, and thus sensibility, says Martin. Instead of parents trying to 'educate' their children in social issues or traditional education, Martin reckons that 'the awakening to their sensibility is the most important thing' (1973, 24).

My paintings are not about what is seen. They are about what is known forever in the mind.

Once she had discovered the basic format of her work – the white square canvas upon which a screen of small rectangular shapes were drawn – Agnes Martin proceeded to explore, as with Robert Ryman, the possibilities of such a reduced configuration. The use of small rectangles or the grid was distinctly Minimalist, but the use Martin made of it pointed towards a lyricism and spirituality Minimalism seldom consciously courted. Critics such as Thomas Hess and Daniel Wheeler could not help associating Martin's art with the New Mexico desert where she lived – linking the sparseness and grandeur of the desert with Martin's ascetic, pared-away but often beautiful art. Oh, and the famous and exquisite New Mexico light: if you've been in New Mexico (or Colorado or Arizona or

California), you'll appreciate the quality of light there, and the Big Skies.

QUOTES BY AGNES MARTIN

Art is the concrete representation of our most subtle feelings.

•

My paintings are not about what is seen. They are about what is known forever in the mind.

•

Happiness is being on the beam with life – to feel the pull of life.

•

Any material may be used but the theme is the same and the response is the same for all artwork... we all have the same concern, but the artist must know exactly what the experience is. He must pursue the truth relentlessly.

•

To progress in life you must give up the things you do not like. Give up doing the things that you do not like to do. You must find the things that you do like. The things that are acceptable to your mind.

•

When I think of art I think of beauty. Beauty is the mystery of life. It is not in the eye it is in the mind. In our minds there is awareness of perfection.

AD REINHARDT

AD REINHARDT

Ad Reinhardt was born in Buffalo, New York, December 24, 1913, and died August 13, 1967 in New York City. Reinhardt was an Abstract Expressionist whose characteristic works were the five-foot square black canvases with their dim cruciform shapes he made late in his career. Reinhardt was probably the most polemical of the American abstract painters of the 1960s. This extract from one of his "Art-as-Art" pieces is typical:

> No lines or imaginings, no shapes or composings or representings, no visions or sensations or impulses, no symbols or signs or impastos, no decoratings or colorings or picturings, no pleasures or pains, no accidents or readymades, no things, no ideas, no relations, no attributes, no qualities – nothing that is not of 'essence'.[1]

This extract from Ad Reinhardt's unpublished notes is typical, and defines not only his own form of painting, but also that of other 'Northern' painters such as Mark Rothko, Barnett Newman, Christopher Le Brun, Thérèse Oulton, Brice Marden and Anselm Keifer:

> "Northern" preferences for black medium
> "Black," medium of the mind
> Puritan, self-righteous, self-criticism
> Conscience of a bad conscience
> Luminous darkness, true light, evanescence
> "Him that has made the dark his hiding place"
> "Flight of the lone to the alone"
> Perfection, central, cohesive, purifying principle
> Polemic, dogmatic, scriptural (1991, 90)

Ad Reinhardt's writings are sometimes pretentious and portentous, quite different from Barnett Newman's matter-of-fact statements, or Joseph Cornell's wistful, dreamy diaries. Reinhardt's written statements are sometimes brilliantly argumentative, so much so that his art seldom seemed to live up to his polemics. On the other hand, if Reinhardt's black paintings had not been powerful on their own, they would have severely weakened his artistic statements.

Ad Reinhardt advocated a violent break with everything that had gone on before in the history of art. Reinhardt proposed in "Twelve Rules For a New Academy" (1957) that the modern artist use no texture, no brushwork, no sketching, no forms, no design, no colors, no light, no space, no time, no size, no movement and no object.[2] Reinhardt discarded the 'religious' monicker, and disliked the allusions viewers made to Islam, Christianity, Buddhism and Hinduism when discussing his paintings (even though he wrote about religion more than almost any other contemporary painter). Reinhardt even stated that 'painting really has no relation to any of the religions nor ever has' (1991, 14). This is an extraordinary statement from a well-read artist, for art since earliest times has been associated deeply with religion, and much of the greatest art made in the last hundred thousand years has been in the service of religion.

Before he embarked upon his arduous

quest for the Ultimate Black Painting, Ad Reinhardt made some rather mundane abstract art, such as *Abstract Painting, Blue* (1953, Connecticut), *Abstract Painting, White* (1955, private collection), and *Abstract Painting, Red* (1953, Washington). In these paintings, blocks of slightly different hues of one color – red in some, blue in others, then lastly black – made rectilinear shapes. Before the paintings of the 1950s, Reinhardt had produced political cartoons and journalistic sketches aligned with Communist politics. He also participated in demonstrations. marches and picket lines. Robert Hughes called him a '[g]adfly, fanatic, and dandy', who though he was of the same generation as the Abstract Expressionists, he 'had nothing in common with their spirit. He was an aphoristic preacher and a deadly parodist'.[3]

By the late 1950s, Ad Reinhardt developed his art to the reductionist point of no return: the series of black paintings. Reinhardt's black paintings were all called *Abstract Painting, Black.* He dubbed them '[c]lassical black-square uniform five-foot timeless trisected evanescences of the sixties' (1991, 10). Examples of the *Abstract Painting, Black* include *Abstract Painting, Black* (1960-66, National Gallery of Australia, Canberra), *Abstract Painting, Black* (1960-66, Marlborough Gallery, New York), *Abstract Painting, Black* (1960, collection: Arnold Glimcher, New York), and *Abstract Painting, Black* (1960-66, Gilman Paper Company). Each one is different but all are united by the same philosophy. On the back of the Tate Modern, London's *Abstract Painting, Black (no. 5),* Reinhardt wrote 'Reinhardt/ 732 Broadway/ NYC 3' and a plan of the painting, indicating in capitals the red, blue and green colors that were mixed with matt black.

Ad Reinhardt defined the *Abstract Paintings, Black* like this:

> A square (*neutral, shapeless*) canvas, five feet wide, five feet high, as high as a man, as wide as a man's outstretched arms (*not large, not small, sizeless*), trisected (*no composition*), one horizontal form negating one vertical form (*formless, no top, no bottom, directionless*), three (*more or less*) dark (*lightless*) no-contrasting (*colorless*) colors, brushwork brushed out to remove brushwork, a matte, flat, free-hand painted surface (*glossless, textureless, non-linear, no hard edge, no soft edge*)... a pure, abstract, non-objective, timeless, spaceless, changeless, relationless, disinterested painting (1991, 82-83)

They were meant to be formless (but they weren't), lightless (they couldn't be), spaceless (not possible), changeless (they were not) and relationless (they were full of relations, internally, and were related to countless other works of art). Ad Reinhardt's paintings were sensual where he wanted them to be beyond sensuality; they were never completely imageless because Reinhardt insisted on the cruciform shape. Richard Stankiewicz wrote of them: '[t]he extraordinary object, the one with presence, is one which is subjectively and tyrannically there... It is the ultimate realism, this presence'.[4]

I've taken on all the bad terms of the '30s [Reinhardt said]. Like meaningless, useless, imageless - those kinds of words. Words like inhuman, sterile, cold-they became cool.

For all his exaltation of Oriental mystical precepts, his insistence on the radical reductionism of his art, his belief in black as negation ('pure non-being'), his desire to 'push painting beyond its thinkable, seeable, feelable limits', Ad Reinhardt's abstract black paintings were not the last paintings to be made, or that could be made. In his quest for an image-less, relationless, timeless art, Reinhardt was doomed to failure, for despite his insistence on the immateriality of his quest, the painter is always deeply entrenched in the materiality of painting. The difficulty was evoking the void using physical objects. As Barnett Newman said: '[e]mptiness is not that easy. The point is to produce it with paint'.5 Yves Klein had experimented with notions of emptiness; his exhibition *The Void* was also known as *The Specialization of Sensibility from the State of Prime Matter to the State of Stabilized Pictorial Sensibility*. So that his aura could impregnate the gallery space Klein had the walls whitewashed.

Ad Reinhardt's task of describing the indescribable with the halfway decent means of paint was bound to fail. The quest for delimitation and non-representation was much stronger in Reinhardt than in the art of Mark Rothko or Barnett Newman: Reinhardt kept up with the *Abstract Paintings, Black* for some seven years, from the end of the

1950s to his death in 1967. As David Sylvester put it in a review of Reinhardt's 1964 ICA (London) show:

> The extreme thing about Ad Reinhardt, by twentieth-century standards, is not that he's done paintings which are black all over; it's that for ten years all his paintings have been black all over. (1996, 68)

Ad Reinhardt's art did not offer the same pleasures as Abstract Expressionists such as Mark Rothko, Michael Benedikt suggested: no sensuality, no 'sheer puls-ation' in Reinhardt's art; instead, Rein-hardt's paintings offered a pleasure that was architectural rather than painterly.6 Instead of offering traditional notions of 'beauty', Reinhardt should be admired as a 'spiritual worker', Benedikt suggested, someone who changed how attitudes are used in art, not just producing a different painterly style (ibid.). Clement Greenberg was dismissive:

> Reinhardt has a genuine if small gift for color, but none at all for design or placing. I can see why he let Newman, Rothko, and Still influence him toward close and dark values, but he lost more than he gained by the desperate extreme to which he went, changing from a nice into a trite artist.7

For Harold Rosenberg, Ad Reinhardt was 'a drier logician than Rothko', and Rothko would not follow Reinhardt's reductionism to its radical finality (1972). Mark Rothko commented on Reinhardt thus:

> The difference between me and Reinhardt is

that he's a mystic. By that I mean that his paintings are immaterial. Mine are *here*. Materially. The surfaces, the work of the brush and so on. His are untouchable.[8]

The ironic thing is that Ad Reinhardt's paintings were no more immaterial or 'untouchable' than those of Mark Rothko or Barnett Newman. Furthermore, what people think of Reinhardt also applies to Colorfield and Minimal painting. What is said by critics of Reinhardt's art can apply to Colorfield and Minimal art, and vice versa.

Ad Reinhardt's lifelong friend, the mystic Thomas Merton, wrote of the disappearance of the self in God, which could apply equally to Reinhardt's black square paintings as a project: '[s]o it is with one who has vanished into God by pure contemplation. God alone is left'.[9] The theologian Paul Tillich said of Reinhardt's work that it depicts the 'non-representational expression of mystic depths of experience.'[10]

Ad Reinhardt's black paintings do mark the end of a certain strain of painting, which might be said to go back to Matthias Grünewald and Early Netherlandish painters such as Rogier van der Weyden. It is a bein of Northern European painting which descends into the shadows (Rembrandt van Rijn, Georges de La Tour, Frans Hals), of which Mark Rothko and Reinhardt can be seen as the last flowering. Other painters did not agree that 'painting was dead', that there was nothing else to do. Jasper Johns remarked that painters continue to work,

while Helen Frankenthaler said in 1970: 'I think there's still a lot more to do in abstract painting'.[11]

'The one direction in fine art or abstract art today is in the painting of the same form over and over again', affirmed Ad Reinhardt, justifying making his series of black paintings.[12] There is something deeply obsessive about Reinhardt's late works, as with the late works of Vincent van Gogh or J.M.W. Turner, as if there was something Reinhardt felt he had to get at, somehow, and so he kept working over the form until it offered up its secret knowledge. In this respect, as an alchemical, shamanic quest, Reinhardt's seven-year project of obsessively turning out the square black paintings seemed to be in the hope of reaching some sublime point, some absolute, some infinity or end zone. Reinhardt pursued his ritualistic journey with utter ruthlessness, aided by reams of æsthetic dogma. Art is useless, Reinhardt declared, and 'can only be defined as exclusive, negative, absolute, and timeless'.[13] Reinhardt went further than most by going over the same problem again and again. His passion for pure painting was daunting, but not heroic, nor laudable necessarily.

Making itself is a gesture: thus Ad Reinhardt's painting, like other Minimal works, could not be totally 'non-gestural'. The human touch could not be utterly erased. Reinhardt's paintings aimed at a nothingness that could only ever be conceptual. Franz Kline had made paintings of black brushstrokes on white (such as *Wotan, Untitled* and *Elisabeth*) which looked like Chinese ideograms. Kline's world of giant Chinese signs recalled Zen Buddhist art, in which the concept of nothingness is embodied in the term *mu* (in Japanese, *wu*). Reinhardt's *Abstract Paintings, Black* seemed to be moving towards the spiritual state of Zen Buddhist *mu* (in his notebooks Reinhardt spoke of the Zen concept of *wu wei*, or non-action).[14]

In Princeton Art Museum at the university in New Jersey, there's a wonderful display of an Ad Reinhardt painting in the midst some Oriental art. One of Reinhardt's *Abstract Paintings, Black* has been hung in between two Asian statues.

In Sixties painting, the object-in-itself was all. Sixties painting aimed to be non-symbolic, non-relational, and non-objective. In this it shared its aims with mysticism. 'It is the mysticism of non-objective art rather than its forms that shocks', wrote Peter Fingesten (28). For Sixties painters, the emotional content of the painting, as well as the traditional elements, had to go. Frank Stella said '[y]ou want to get rid of things that get you into trouble'.[15] The old techniques – of easel painting, the process of doing preliminary studies, drawing from life, using traditional iconography – was dropped. However, this pursuit of form-lessness can be seen as religious in itself; it partakes of a 'cosmic religiosity'.[16]

Ad Reinhardt's project was 'religious' –

Reinhardt's esoteric, erudite and eclectic writings refer frequently to Zen, Taoism, Buddhism, the dark night of the soul of Christianity, Rosicrucian occultism, Mother Night, the dark-on-dark of mystics such as Meister Eckhart (who spoke of the 'divine dark'), *The Cloud of Unknowing*, St John of the Cross, and so on. Reinhardt's square black paintings can be seen as equivalents for this kind of religious darkness, which was defined by Reinhardt in countless notes and essays with the terms of Buddhism – 'not this, not that'. Reinhardt spoke about the use of black in the *Bible*, Geoffrey Chaucer, John Milton and William Shakespeare (in *Macbeth, Othello* and *Love's Labour's Lost*); in the black castle and the black knight; the realm of hell and Pluto; the Kaaba, the black cube at Mecca; the black rock in the dome of the rock in Jerusalem; and blackness in the *Tao Te Ching* ('the Tao is dim and dark', says Lao-tzu, while Reinhardt wrote that the 'Tao is through and through mysterious and dark').[17] Reinhardt acknowledged the maternal, 'dark-earth-mother' of night and blackness, and related it to Goddesses such as Diana of Ephesus (1991, 97). He spoke of darkness as regressive, prime matter, 'primordial darkness', the void, a place of rebirth, the subterranean zone, the 'alchemist's lair', lightlessness, 'negative presence', 'melting away', dematerialization, non-being, the 'black monk', 'prince of darkness', 'black-humour, Black-Protestant, black-blasphemy, black-mass, black arts', emptiness, 'Dark-flame, dark-fire, coal, charred wood', and night as 'mother of all things, veil of stars' (1991, 96-98). But it wasn't these myriad connotations and symbolisms associated with black that Reinhardt wanted to explore, but rather 'the idea of black as intellectuality and conventionality'. 'It's the negativeness of black, or darkness particularly, in painting, which interests me', he wrote (1991, 87).

Ad Reinhardt wanted to '[p]ush painting beyond its thinkable, seeable, feelable limits' (1991, 104). 'I'm just making the last paintings anyone can make', he added.[18] Reinhardt was not messing about, he was really serious about making a series of five-foot square black paintings. An ancestor of Reinhardt's black paintings was the occultist Robert Fludd's five-by-five inch magic square (a black square of religious abstraction made hundreds of years before Reinhardt's canvases).[19] For Reinhardt, black was 'negation' (1991, 87), 'pure non-being' (91). The emphasis on blackness links Reinhardt's paintings to the connotations of the color black: night, chaos, formlessness, creation, madness and mysticism. Black night is also the time of the feminine or maternal realm, but Reinhardt's *Abstract Paintings, Black* depict a cold, lonely and egoless night which aims to eradicate all traces of humanity. Reinhardt appropriated the language of Buddhism, with its perennial emphasis on negation and nothingness, as in the *Heart Sutra* of Buddhism which speaks of 'no body, no mind; no shape, no color, no sound, no smell, no taste, no touch, no concept; no visible world'.[20]

☆

Staring into an Ad Reinhardt painting is a curious experience. The black, for a start, is not black, but tinged with red, blue and green. A cruciform structure can be vaguely discerned. The surface is matt yet reflective, inviting absorption but also repelling it. One might evoke the sheen of death in Reinhardt's paintings, but it might also be the no-non-blackness of timelessness (and therefore death*less*ness). The light Reinhardt's paintings breathe out is steady, dim, gleaming, a 'total light', to use Sidney Tillim's term.[21] The surface of the *Abstract Paintings, Black* is smooth, blemishless, yet also hand-painted. No use of masking tape or spray guns here. The cruciform shape is only faintly visible, but definitely there. Each painting, too, is not exactly the same as the others. The paintings are of varying quality, some of them have become quite scruffy with the passing of time. 'The matt black surface starts to sing: we recognise the vibrations given off by the inexplicably living surfaces of all authentic works of art', remarked David Sylvester (1996, 69).

For some critics, Ad Reinhardt's spacing of blackness went further than almost any other painter. For critics such as Priscilla Colt[22] and Nicholas and Elena Calas,[23] Reinhardt's black paintings had taken purity to extremes ('pushing of the visible toward the brink of the invisible', as Colt put it). Wassily Kandinsky was not so convinced about black: 'the silence of black is the silence of death', he asserted.[24] For Lawrence Alloway, 'Reinhardt's choice of black was an æsthetic and philosophic choice, an aid in investing 'abstract art with a momentous subject'.[25] Reinhardt wanted to paint everything out in the history of art, to negate it all by painting over it all.[26]

Ad Reinhardt's search for the Ultimate Black Abstract Painting marks the end of one kind of 20th century painterly abstraction. Into the black spacelessness of Reinhardt's five-foot canvases all the abstractions of Cubism, Surrealism, Suprematicism, Expressionism and Pure Painting fall, to be eaten up alive. There are other ways past Reinhardt's end-point of Post-Painterly Abstraction: Brice Marden, Gerhard Richter, Thérèse Oulton, Jasper Johns and Frank Stella have demonstrated that abstract painting can be developed (Marden, for example, went on to paint his *Annunciation Series* of monochrome abstract paintings in the 1970s which took the Virgin Mary's story as its starting-point).

Ad Reinhardt's black paintings mark the end of a particularly masculinist form of abstraction, an absolute reductionism. He never reached his goal.[27] Reinhardt's paintings mark the end of a strain of religious painterly abstraction that began in Byzantine icons and developed into the Renaissance images of Leonardo da Vinci, Michelangelo Buonarroti, Matthias Grüne-wald and Rogier van der Weyden. Brilliant and necessary though Reinhardt's *reductio ad absurdum* was, it was not the final word in Minimal, Colorfield, Sixties or contemporary painting, nor was it the final pronouncement in religious painting.

QUOTES BY AD REINHARDT

Art is Art. Everything else is everything else.

•

Art is too serious to be taken seriously.

•

Only a bad artist thinks he has a good idea. A good artist does not need anything.

•

Intellectually and aesthetically the important thing was that there was absolutely no relation between the abstractionists and the surrealists.

•

I finally made a program out of boredom. After all these years I think now that for a long time I've paraphrased Schopenhauer.

•

Abstract art centered pretty much around art-as-art or that art either had involve with aesthetic essence or not.

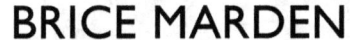
BRICE MARDEN

BRICE MARDEN

Like artists such as Frank Stella, Carl Andre and Donald Judd, Brice Marden (b. 1938) has always made abstract art. There was no period of early figurative work, as with the Abstract Expressionists, Mark Rothko, Jackson Pollock, Willem de Kooning and Robert Motherwell. They all drew and painted figurative art, much of it influenced by the Surrealists, before they turned to abstraction in the 1940s and 1950s. Frank Stella and Marden, though, were abstract artists from the beginning (although there are one or two early figurative works by Marden).

Brice Marden's art draws on Abstract Expressionism, however: he did not reject it as much as did Donald Judd and other Minimal artists. Marden speaks of the relation between himself and the two movements with which he is often associated, Abstract Expressionism and Minimalism:

> Rothko was talking about painting, about death and I was much more interested in that than in Judd's Minimalist æsthetic. Emotions? I wanted to keep that open. Subject matter was no longer valid but I felt my work was much more of a continuation of Abstract Expressionism than a rejection of it. (1992a, 55)

Although Barnett Newman's form of painting seems much more in tune with 1960s Minimalism than Mark Rothko's 'tragic' and 'transcendent' art, Brice Marden came to admire Rothko. In Rothko's mural series (especially in the 'Rothko Chapel' at Houston), Rothko had refined his sense of color and form radically, aligning it with the Christian Passion. Marden visited the Rothko Chapel in 1972, and the solemn, massive panels of color made a deep impression upon him (1992a, 24). Later in the Seventies, Marden created his own series of religious abstract panels, the *Annunciation Series*. Interestingly, while Rothko moved through different phases from pseudo-figuration (in his post-Surrealist period), through the intense subjective expressionism of the radiantly colorful 1950s 'clouds' or 'things', to the radicalization of the dark, sombre, maroon murals series (the Seagram, Harvard and Houston paintings), Marden went the opposite way: beginning very austere and monotone, all in grays, in the 1960s, Marden opened up (like Frank Stella), relaxing into colorful reds, yellows and blues in his multi-canvas paintings of the 1970s, and branching out (literally – he used twigs to draw) into the 'calligraphic' drawings/ paintings of the 1980s and 1990s.

For a time, in the late 1960s, Brice Marden and Mark Rothko were both making ascetic gray-on-gray abstract rectangular paintings. Rothko's dual-tone vertical gray rectangles were associated (by critics) with a cosmic, tragic exhaustion – the works presaged Rothko's suicide in February, 1970. Marden's Minimalist gray horizontal rectangles, meanwhile, were associated with personal depression, alienation from his wife, and the *ennui* of a young artist searching for his voice.

Brice Marden's surfaces take time to open up and reveal themselves. The first perceptions of emptiness and denial of physicality give way to a formal (spiritual) richness and palpable physical presence. The dense planar geometry loses its initial reductive impenetrability, and depth is soon asserted. Denial becomes affirmation, and self-erasure becomes self (and world) glorification. Marden's canvases suggest layering, with colors underneath leaving ghostly traces on the surfaces. Not all art critics saw the underlying colors and gauzes of paint: Scott Burton wrote of Marden's Bykert Gallery show of 1966 that Marden's colors were 'closed', like skin: 'you can't look into them, only at them.'[1]

At the Jewish Museum, where he worked, Brice Marden admired Jasper Johns' work, in retrospective, in particular Johns' gray paintings, such as *Gray Numbers*. Gray became one of Marden's (and Minimalism's) key colors of the mid-1960s. Robert Rauschenberg's influence on Marden is harder to spot than Johns' quiet intensity: Rauschenberg is an extraordinarily dynamic artist, whose work displays an energetic exploration of painterly possibilities. Rauschenberg had, for example, painted all-white paintings years before 1960s Minimalism, Colorfield and Post-Painterly Abstraction (in 1951). Interestingly, one of Marden's jobs when he worked for Rauschenberg was to

repaint the white paintings as they yellowed with age.[2]

Brice Marden's sense of color and abstraction draws largely on the Old Masters, the Spanish Golden Age masters, and Northern European painting. Robert Rosenblum, in his influential book *Modern Painting and the Northern Romantic Tradition,* saw Northern European painters as being the precursors of modern abstraction, and the masters of modern abstract art – Piet Mondrian, Wassily Kandinsky, Kasimir Malevich, Paul Klee – are distinctly Northern European figures. Marden sees himself as a Northern painter (M. Poirer, 52), and his paintings, especially the ones of the late 1960s and early 1970s, have the austerity and mystery of Northern European painters such as Caspar David Friedrich, Emil Nolde and Kasimir Malevich. The spiritual discourse of the modern abstract artists (the affinities with Rudolf Steiner, theosophy, occultism, Rosicrucianism, Qabbalism, and so on), is a key element in the art of Malevich, Kandinsky, Mondrian and Klee. This European taste for the sublime and mystical was later developed by the Abstract Expressionists (the *Qabbalah* in the work of Barnett Newman, Judæo-Christianity in Mark Rothko, Zen Buddhism in Ad Reinhardt, Robert Motherwell and Franz Kline), and in Brice Marden there is Classical mythology, sacred architecture, the Christian Annunciation, the symbolism of numbers (numerology), alchemy, and so on. While fellow 1960s Minimalists and Colorfield artists rejected such spiritual hankerings (Frank Stella, Donald Judd, Dan Flavin, Robert Morris, Robert Mangold, Richard Serra and Kenneth Noland), Marden embraced them. Other Sixties artists, in their own way, also acknowledged a religious dimension to their work: Carl Andre, David Novros, Richard Long, Eva Hesse, Ad Reinhardt, Robert Smithson and Morris Louis.

For a long time, Brice Marden's colors were extremely subdued. Though Marden is grouped with Kenneth Noland, Ellsworth Kelly, Jules Olitski and others, Marden's 1960s colors were nowhere near as brilliant and saturated as theirs. Compare a canvas by Olitski, Noland or Kelly with one by Marden and one sees bright greens, radiant yellows and pulsating scarlets in the former, while Marden's canvases sink deep into gray, light brown, beige, and more gray. For Minimal sculptors, gray, white and black were suitably 'neutral' colors which did not scream expressively, as reds and purples had done in Mark Rothko's or Willem de Kooning's paintings. It was years, really – until the mid-Seventies – before Marden used colors as glowing as the Post-Painterly Abstractionists.

Brice Marden's paintings, like those of Morris Louis, Robert Mangold, Agnes Martin and Robert Ryman, were not concerned with creating 'illusionistic space', with the space of traditional Western post-Renaissance art, but with a new flatness. On the other side of the flat painting camp, there were artists whose aim was to destroy the rigid flatness of painting. One painter who threw anything onto the picture plane was Robert Rauschenberg (see his many 'combine' paintings, those mixed media extravaganzas). Claes Oldenburg's soft telephones and toilets far outdo Rauschenberg for pure eccentricity. Oldenburg like Andy Warhol in questioned the holy notion of 'Art' with a capital 'A'. The picture plane, which had been so scrupulously flat throughout the Renaissance (ignoring the embossed and punched gold), suddenly burst open in contemporary art. As Clement Greenberg put it: '[p]ictorial space has lost its "inside" and become all "outside"'.[3] Of course, some contemporary artists asserted the flatness of the picture plane even more fervently: Morris Louis with his stained, furled canvas, Frank Stella with his black stripes done with housepaint direct onto cotton duck, Mark Rothko with his cloud-like shapes, Agnes Martin with her finely pencilled squares, and Sol LeWitt with his spacious wall-drawings. Lucio Fontana, though, destroyed the flatness of the canvas in a phallic, penetrative fashion: he slashed the canvas. Fontana explained his seemingly violent, nay, pornographic act thus:

> I want to open up space, create a new dimension for art, tie in at the cosmos as it endlessly expands beyond the confining place of the picture. With my innovation of the hole pierced through the canvas in repetitive perforations, I have not attempted

to decorate a surface, but, on the contrary, I have tried to break its dimensional limitations. Beyond the perforations a newly gained freedom of interpretation awaits us, but also, and just as inevitably, the end of art.[4]

Brice Marden employed many of the æsthetics of Minimalism in his paintings: seriality, repetition, symmetry, flatness, abstraction, functionalism and monochromism. In terms of color, Marden's paintings of the 1960s and 1970s were sombre, restrained, impenetrable, physical, tactile, sonorous. When he uses one color, Marden generally fills the whole painting with it; it's an evenly-spread field of color. When he takes up two colors, Marden establishes the relationship between them very carefully. In the multi-part paintings, the colors and the panels exist on the same plane, which is smooth and flat.[5] Marden modulates his colors so that they seem to inhabit the same tone zone, even though they can seem to be from different color families. Even though each panel contains different colors, the color value is often the same.[6]

A painting such as *Three Deliberate Greys for Jasper Johns* (1970, Ottawa, and spelt 'grey' not 'gray'), is a work that takes much of its power from the relativity of gray tones. In this homage to (and wry look at) Johns, Brice Marden explores the interaction of the tonal value of the ubiquitous 1960s 'neutral' color. It is a tribute to Marden's talent that he could make the painting work. After all, the project of making a painting using only

gray, without any figurative or representational elements, entirely in abstraction, could have backfired easily. It is the sort of brief, if given to art students, would have them groaning, dissolving into bouts of apathy and dead-ends. Yet Marden's *Three Deliberate Greys for Jasper Johns* is one of his most successful works, the culmination of his exploration of the neutral color.

From the beginning, Brice Marden acknowledged the emotional power of color. Underneath the monochrome grays and beiges there is an emotional subtext. Marden associated his 1960s gray color, for example, with depression. He was depressed at the time he made some of the paintings. A later pen-and-ink set of drawings was entitled *Suicide Notes* (a series of rectangles, some shadowy, some incomplete, some constructed from webs of lines). Marden wanted the viewer to come away from his paintings changed: to go in expecting something, but to get something else. Marden's Post-Painterly Abstract monochrome paintings hide something underneath, which Marden expressed in terms of color:

> Gray was the way I could deal with color at the time. What I liked about it was how you could twist it, how you could make it be gray, and also be red – how you could get two readings out of one thing. (1983)

Clearly the realm Brice Marden was aiming for was quite from different from that of Roy Lichenstein, say, or Judy Pfaff. Of course, it might seem wholly inappropriate to compare Marden's 1960s Minimal project with that of Lichenstein or Pfaff, for he is so different. But then, Marden is different even from those most closely associated with him – Robert Ryman, Agnes Martin, Robert Mangold, Donald Judd and Jules Olitski. Marden is in a world of his own. One can make cultural comparisons, but this is only partially helpful. One only has to compare the subdued gray and pale cobalt panels of Marden with the vivacious, multicolor of Robert Mangold's paintings to see how far Marden was from mainstream Minimalism, Colorfield and Hard Edge painting and most Post-Painterly Abstraction.

In the early 1970s Brice Marden began to loosen up his palette and introduce much deeper, more saturated colors – and tones. Nature was also more apparent, in series of paintings such as the *Grove Group* and the *Sea Paintings*. The *Sea Paintings* introduced much deeper tones, or rather, much stronger contrasts between one tone and the next. Instead of gentle modulations between one panel and another, Marden was happy to make sudden contrasts and leaps. Thus, in *Red, Yellow, Blue* (1974), the red is very dark, while the yellow, as usual in Marden's art, is light. The result was a sharp leap in tone from the left to the middle panel, which the right hand (blue) panel helps to modulate by its tone, which is mid-way between the red and yellow. Paintings such as *To Corfu*, *Le Mien* and *Morada*, from the mid-1970s, featured the narrow

vertical panels which Marden used so effectively in the *Annunciation Series*. Prints contemporary with the time, such as *Untitled* (1973), also featured vertical columns.

New colors in the Brice Marden *œuvre* (part of his 'red yellow blue' period) appeared in *Morada* (1976, Stedelijk Museum, Amsterdam) and *Le Mien* (1976, Zurich): a dark, damson red, which's followed, in both paintings, by a mid-gray or grayish-blue. In *Morada* there are the usual colors of Marden's Seventies Greek period: olive greens, light grays, and a dark gray. Into this mélange of familiar light/ mid/ dark grays, the damson hue is really surprising. It is, literally, a 'splash' of color – living color, the color of life (blood, anger, passion, fecundity). Imagine this damson-red entering the austere Greek paintings, such as *Lethykos, Moon I* and any of the *Grove Group Paintings*. In *Le Mien* the damson color takes up one of the wide panels on the left, and is echoed by the mid-red in the right-hand narrow panel. Against these sonorous hues, Marden places his olive grove greens and grays. The painting is symmetrical, in terms of color (though not with the perfect symmetry of *Lethykos (for Tonto)*): warm green is set against deep crimson; lighter red is set against light gray.

In the paintings of the late 1960s and early 1970s, Brice Marden's palette warmed up, with mid-earth-browns in *For Pearl*, lemon yellows in *Rodeo* and buttercup yellows in *Range, First Figure*

(*Homage to Courbet*) and *Starter,* and one of Marden's most radiant colors, the orangey-red outer panels of *Pumpkin Plumb*. The outer panels in *For Pearl* (1970, Lannan Foundation, Los Angeles), contain and moderate the warmest color, the earthy brown, with two more restrained hues (a gray-blue on the left, and a sand tint on the right). *Rodeo* (1971, Lannan Foundation) is one of the first of Marden's horizontal format dual color paintings: an expanse of lemon yellow in the upper half; dark slate gray in the lower half. *Untitled* (1971-72, Walker Art Center, Minneapolis) is unusual for Marden at this period: three warm colors, rather than, as is more usual, one warm and two cooler colors. The central band of light orange is modulated and contained by the outer panels of light carmine. The colors in *For Pearl* and *Untitled* are rare in Marden's art of this time.

In *First Figure (Homage to Courbet),* the usual three Brice Marden panels are set on top of each other, unusually, creating a tower of three near-square panels. The colors, crowned with a mustard yellow in the upper panel, are those of Seventies works such as *Summer Table, Range* and *Starter* (yellow plus a light and dark neutral color). *Pumpkin Plumb* (1970/73, collection: Helen Harrington Marden), contains a vivid contrast between the subdued gray of the 1960s monochrome paintings (in the central panel) and the bright orange, a hue which looked towards the primary colors of the *Red, Yellow,*

Blue series of the following year (1974). *Summer Table* (1972-73, Whitney Museum, New York) uses the color-configuration of *Range, First Figure (Homage to Courbet)* and *Starter*: a warm yellow panel in amongst two cooler panels. *Summer Table* is clearly a part of the (Greek) landscape works of the first half of the 1970s (the *Grove Group* and *Sea Paintings*). The warm color is at the centre, but the flanking two blues (one pale, one dark) cannot restrain it. The yellow of *Summer Table* is dominant, overwhelming the outer panels. The structure of the three rectangular panels in a horizontal format of *Summer Table* recalls *Point, Range* and the *Moon Series.* The sullen, recalcitrant grays and blues of the 1960s monochromes are left behind decisively with paintings such as *Summer Table, Pumpkin Plumb* and the *Red, Yellow, Blue Series*. With his new, colorful palette, Brice Marden's art gained a new intensity, no longer tied to an introspective, 'depressed' mood.

Miranda (1972, New York) is three panels of closely-valued color in a horizontal format making a 72 by 72 inch square. The allusions to landscape in the upper olive-gray-green, middle mid-blue and lower sand-earth colors are unmistakable. *Blue Painting* (1972, private collection) is also a part of the group of landscape-based works of the early 1970s. *Blue Painting,* like the *Moon, Hera,* and *Red, Yellow, Blue* paintings, is a vertical three-panel configuration. The colors are those of the *Grove Group* and *Sea Paintings* (light and mid-toned blues). In *Blue Painting* Marden explores the sense of narrative and progression (moving from light through mid to dark blue), which became increasingly important (culminating in the *Annunciation Series*).

Two paintings based on Brice Marden's experience in Morocco also employed earthy colors, like *Starter* and *Summer Table*. Both *Moroccan Painting* (1978, New York) and *Helen's Moroccan Painting* (1979, collection: Helen Harrington Marden) set a mid-green against an earth red-brown. In the former work the panels are side by side vertically, in the latter they are set one above the other (this vertical format was another reworking of a format used in the early Seventies). In both the effect is of an exploration of landscape. In this case, a response to the particular landscape of Morocco, with its abundant greenery that grows out of what appears to be nothing but dust and partial desert. Such deep green plants amongst such seemingly arid, barren soil is an astonishment to the traveller used to the lush green of temperate Northern Europe and North America. Brice Marden's Moroccan panels explore the wonder of the North African landscape, where the dry, apparently lifeless browns of *Hydra* and the early *Untitled* paintings gives way to a luscious, fertile green.

These hues broaden considerably the narrow range of colors Brice Marden had employed in works such as *For Otis,*

T.K.B., Wax I, Nebraska and *Decorative Painting.* In those 1960s monochromes, Marden seemed to be working in the rarefied and extreme realm of abstraction occupied by the likes of Ad Reinhardt and late Mark Rothko; with the post-1969 multi-panel paintings, and the new, luminous palette, Marden joined the ranks of Post-Painterly Abstract artists such as Morris Louis, Frank Stella, Kenneth Noland, Richard Diebenkorn and Ellsworth Kelly. Even so, paintings such as *Rodeo, For Pearl, D'après la Marquise de la Solana, Point, Starter* and *Miranda* were still more severe and restrained than anything in the art of Louis, Kelly, Murray or Diebenkorn. In amongst the more colorful works of the 1970s (such as *Starter* and the *Red, Yellow, Blue* series), there were still ascetic grays and near-blues, such as in *Gober* (1971, Spiegel Family Collection). This is a narrow vertical dual-color panel whose two muted grays look straight back to the *Untitleds* of the early 1960s. The first *Hydra* (1972, New York), too, is extremely closed-in and muted, quite unlike the later hymns to the Greek landscape (such as *Thira* and the *Grove Group*). *Shunt* (1972, New York) is also restrained, in *Hydra*-like beiges and grays.

In amongst the many colorful paintings of the first half of the Seventies, then (such as *Pumpkin Plumb, Blue Painting, Starter,* and *For Hera*), Brice Marden was still producing quiet panels in earth, gray, olive and brown hues (*Hydra, Shunt,*

Gober, Three Deliberate Greys for Jasper Johns and so on). Even with a subject such as the one-off rock star Patti Smith, Marden produced a piece in subdued light and dark grays (*Star (For Patti Smith)*, 1972/74, private collection).

Brice Marden's *Grove Group* paintings are in the landscape or horizontal format, like other paintings that referred to nature (*Seasons, Summer Table, Winter Painting, Moon I, Thira* and *Gulf*). The thematic dimensions of the *Grove Group* is that they are about, well, olive groves; or, more specifically, they take as their departure point Marden's experience of sitting in olive groves. The olive dominates so much of Greece. Indeed, Lawrence Durrell speaks of the Mediterranean as that area marked out by the olive tree. The shiny, silvery underside of the leaves, and the dark tops of the leaves, the extraordinary twisted trunks and branches, the sound of leaves in the wind, the shelter they offer from the noonday sun, all these aspects and more of olive trees would interest a poetic painter such as Brice Marden. He is a painter who comes across more and more as someone who has spent a long and careful time observing nature. His paintings are born out of lengthy immersions in the natural world. He wrote in his notebooks of the importance of considering nature, and of feeling a part of nature, even though this absorption in nature can be problematic.[7] Nature is the teacher, the inspiration, the starting-point for many of Marden's works.

The *Grove Group* employ 'natural' colors, the blues, greens and grays one finds in the natural world. The *Grove Group* paintings are large – the five paintings are 72 x 108 inches. The series begins with a single-color panel, one of Brice Marden's largest expanses of a single hue (*Grove Group I*, 1973, MOMA, New York). The sheer scale and breadth of *Grove Group I* invites comparisons with Barnett Newman's work, but how subdued Marden's painting is compared to the sonorous ultramarines of Newman's works (*Cathedra*, 1951, for example). The expanse of blue is consuming, especially as, in *Grove Group II,* the soft cobalt on the left is only partially held back by the darker, mid-ultramarine. *Grove Group III* (1973-80, private collection) is in the familiar 1970s Marden horizontal tripartite format (there are two three-panel *Grove Group* paintings, two dual-plane pieces, and one single panel, *Grove Group I*).

Grove Group III, which was reworked in 1980, does not contain blue, like *Grove Group I* or *Grove Group V*. Instead, Brice Marden concentrates, as in other Greek/ Hydra paintings, such as *Lethykos*, on his beloved grays. A pale greeny-gray begins the three-panel work, with a very light gray in the centre. Harnessing these pale grays is a dark gray in the right-hand panel, bringing the painting down to Earth. *Grove Group V* (1976, Chicago) is a much warmer painting than some of the other *Grove Groups*: a panel (horizontal this time) of a pale sky blue is at the centre of this painting. A simplistic analogy may be the sky (or sea) glimpsed between the green of the olive leaves. In *Grove Group V* Marden reprises the mid-green of *Grove Group I,* which sandwiches the sky blue panel.

In the *Grove Group* paintings the paint reaches right to every edge. There is no strip of canvas kept bare, as in the mid-1960s monochromes. Like subsequent multi-panel paintings of the Seventies, the *Grove Group* paintings are self-contained, they offer a unified sense of space, with none of the relics of gesture that occurred in the single panel canvases of the Sixties with their strip of splashed or runny paint (Marden's paintings, a critic writes, follow the rule that 'a painting contains within itself its *raison d'être*').8

Of all Brice Marden's paintings, the *Grove Group* are among his most tranquil and self-absorbed. They have a mute passivity, which one discerns elsewhere – in the *Back Series* or in *Lethykos (For Tonto)* – but the *Grove Group* works are not aligned with the emotions of depression and anxiety, which were so much a part of the 1960s monochrome paintings.

The sheer number of Brice Marden's paintings that deal with Greece, or the sea, attest to the significance the Mediterranean country had (and has) for Marden. Hydra, where he has a house, appears in many works (in the early 1970s multi-panel oil and wax paintings, in the 1979 *Hydra Group*, 1987's *Hydra* (Art Institute

of Chicago) and again in the *Hydra (Summer 1990) Series* of 'calligraphic' paintings). The *Sea Paintings* were about the sea, as one might expect. Like *To Corfu, Towards Brindisi,* the three *Hydra* paintings and *Adriatic,* the *Sea Paintings* were part of Marden's response to the way the sky and sea dominate the landscape. Marden had begun to paint vertical format works divided into light and dark halves with *Gober* (1971, New York) and *Urdan* (1970-1). The upper-lower format of the *Sea Paintings,* as with the *Hydra Paintings* of 1972, derives from Marden's response to the experience of staring at the sea on the voyages he made between Greece's beautiful islands.

Lawrence Durrell eulogized Greece many times, in his novels and poetry. This is a stanza from 'On Ithaca Standing':

> Tread softly, for here you stand
> On miracle ground, boy.
> A breath would cloud this water of glass,
> Honey, bush, berry and swallow.
> This rock, then, is more pastoral, than
> Arcadia is, Illyria was. (CP, 111)

And from 'Limits: Mykonos Windmills':

> The pure form, then, must be the blue
>   silence
> And the archaic shape of whiteness posed
> On blueness utterly bemused, a sort of
>   coyness
> Which garners the wind of the four quarters.
> (*The Mediterranean Shore,* 144)

In Greece, one cannot help but be impressed by the sheer hardness and purity of the horizon line, where sky meets water: it is this pure line that bisects not only the *Sea Paintings*, but also many prints of the same period. The obviousness of the *Sea Paintings* does not detract from their power. There is an upper panel in one color and tone, which is clearly related to the sky, but poetically, and a lower half which is the sea. Sometimes the upper half is lighter, as the sky often is over the sea, as in the London *Sea Painting*. This is not a rule, however: it is the *relationship* between the two panels that interests the artist. In the second Saatchi *Sea Painting*, for example, the tones and hues are very close. Hardly anything differentiates them, except that one lies above the other. As he sailed over the Adriatic and other parts of the Mediterranean, Marden would have seen many lighting changes, many different hues of blue. Sometimes the sea and sky are very close, color-wise, so that one cannot differentiate between the two, and sometimes the horizon is very misty: this is what the second *Sea Painting* depicts.

The prints related to the *Sea Paintings*, *Adriatics*, are also about the different weights and densities of the sea and sky: sometimes close, sometimes far apart. The first three of the *Adriatics* prints echo the format of the *Sea Paintings* – an upper and lower half relates to ocean and air. In these prints, the contrast between the top and bottom rectangle is very strong, even though Marden modulated the contrast with foul-biting, wiping the plates and drawing on the prints. A lithograph of 1969, *Gulf* was a horizontal format image

divided into two halves. The upper half is very dark, the lower half is mid-gray. *Gulf* relates directly, Marden said, to the view out of Robert Rauschenberg's window at his house in the Gulf of Mexico, at Captiva Island. The bottom edge of both rectangular blocks of color is left roughly hewn, in keeping with Marden's practice in the 1960s canvases.

Number One (1983-84, Whitney Museum, New York) is another of the large, multi-panel *Thira*-type paintings Brice Marden was working on during 1983-84 (such as the *Elements Series*, *Green (Earth)*, and others). With its twelve panels (as with *Green (Earth)*), *Number One* is nearly as complicated, structurally, as the 18-panel *Thira*. *Number One* is among the darkest of the *Thira* era paintings, with over half (seven) of the panels very dark tonally (in blacks and ultramarines). The reds, too, are severe, especially those in the right-hand *tau* shape. Two central panels, though, stave off the darkness that threatens to consume *Number One*: the mid-red and yellow of the central uprights of the *tau* crosses in the centre are left-hand groups of panels. Although these paintings are 'aggressive', as Marden accepted, he did not let them become wholly consumed by darkness. Actually, the *Thira* paintings are amongst his brightest works. Only one painting appears relentlessly 'negative' or 'depressed', in the old, 1960s Marden sense, and that is *Green (Earth)*. But even this painting is actually (partly) about the fecund powers of the Earth, its dark soil and green plants.

The post and lintel multi-panel format of *Thira, Numbers One* and *Two,* the *Elements Series, Coda, Green (Earth)* and other paintings proved to be loose enough for any number of serial variations. Brice Marden could vary the hues and tones *ad infinitum*, it seemed. The severe shapes of the rectangular panels was a rigorous framework to hold down the explorations of color and tone.

Elements II (1981-82, Stedelijk Museum) is just one *tau* cross shape, composed of four panels. The colors relate to Brice Marden's alchemical concept of the four elements (fire, air, earth, water): blue, earth-brown, dark green and mustard yellow. Though alchemically-allusive, these hues in *Elements II* are kept firmly earthbound, closely tied to colors found in the natural world. The shape of the *tau*-cross is emphasized by Marden placing the two warmer colors (ochre and yellow) on either side of the viridian panel which forms the upright of the cross. *Elements I* has three vertical panels (red, blue, yellow) capped by a horizontal green (earth) panel.

The colors in *Elements IV* (1983-84, New York) are the vivid, near-primary colors of the *Red, Yellow, Blue Series*: the red, yellow and blue appear twice, but modulated each time. On the left is a mid-red, which is repeated but lightened a little in the fourth panel from the left. In amongst the bright primary colors in

Elements IV there are the colors of the *Thira*-type paintings: dark blues and olive greens. The presence of these darker, earthier colors moves *Elements IV* on from the more joyful exchanges in the *Red, Yellow, Blue Series.*

☆

Brice Marden's influence continues to be seen in contemporary painters, and his works have remained some of the most enduring and valuable productions of the Minimal and 1970s period. Marden's art, however, transcends its origins in Minimalism, and takes its place among the richest artworks of the contemporary era.

QUOTES BY BRICE MARDEN

Working on these paintings, there's always an idea which is an ideal. It's always impossible... But I think every time, maybe, I just get closer to some impossible thing...

•

A painting, you know, it's all dirty material. But it's about transformation. Taking that earth, that heavy earthen kind of thing, turning it into air and light.

•

Painters are amongst the priests – worker priests of the cult of man – searching to understand but never know.

RICHARD DIEBENKORN

RICHARD DIEBENKORN

Like many painters of the second half of the 20th century, Richard Diebenkorn (1922-93) started out in figurative art and moved into abstraction. Artists who helped influence Diebenkorn included Edward Hopper, Paul Cézanne, Henri Matisse, Pablo Picasso and Pierre Bonnard, as well as Willem de Kooning, Robert Motherwell, Arnold Gottlieb, Clyfford Still and Mark Rothko.

Richard Diebenkorn's most celebrated work was the *Ocean Park* series of paintings, named after an area in Santa Monica. In 1966 Diebenkorn moved from the East coast to L.A. and used Sam Francis's studio in Ocean Park.

Prior to the *Ocean Park* series, Richard Diebenkorn had painted hundreds of figurative works: Hopperesque landscapes of Middle America; Bonnard-like female nudes; and not a few pictures of open windows or doorways, recalling a favourite motif of Henri Matisse. The seeds of the great *Ocean Park* series can be seen in Diebenkorn's early and mid-period works, however. There is not such a sudden leap between figuration and abstraction. Many of Diebenkorn's landscapes contain large rectangular areas of flat color – blues, yellows, white – the palette later used in many of the *Ocean Park* paintings. One can see, in the canvases of the mid to late Sixties such as *Recollections of a Visit to Leningrad* (1965, San Francisco), *Window* (1967, Stanford University Museum of Art), *Cityscape* (1963, California), and

Interior With Doorway (1962, Pennsylvania Academy of the Fine Arts), the elements that became the æsthetic basis of the *Ocean Park* series: the areas of flat color, the light tones, the use of horizontals and verticals, the foundation in an appreciation of landscape.

The first *Ocean Park* paintings, such as *Ocean Park No. 16* (1968, Milwaukee Art Museum), *Ocean Park No. 21* (1969, New York) and *Ocean Park No. 39* (1971, New York), predominantly consisted of areas of monochrome organized on a vertical grid, with sometimes a band of diagonal lines of color in the middle section of the composition (as in *Ocean Park No. 9* [1968, Los Angeles], *Ocean Park No. 40* [1971, private collection] and *Ocean Park No. 27* [1970, Brooklyn Museum]).

The *Ocean Park* paintings are large abstract canvases which relate to the Californian coastline: the clear Pacific light, the white of gables, the sloping hills descending into the sea. Diebenkorn's abstract canvases took as their departure point the view of the sea, roads, fences, pier and sky that Diebenkorn could see framed in his large transom windows.

The *Ocean Park* paintings (such as *Ocean Park No. 60* (1973, Buffalo), *Ocean Park No. 30* (Metropolitan Museum) and *Ocean Park No. 78* (1975, Honolulu)), are large, spacious works, serene, clear. They are both gestural in the Abstract Expressionist manner and filled with substantial areas of Minimalist monochrome.

Ocean Park No. 60 was one of the

bluest in the series of Richard Dieben-korn's paintings, as if this painting was devoted almost entirely to the ocean. Large areas of *Ocean Park No. 60* were painted in the same cerulean blue hue, with all the fiddly bits occurring around the edge. Similar blue-dominated paintings included *Ocean Park No. 79* (1975, Phila-delphia), *Ocean Park No. 115* (1979, Museum of Modern Art), *Ocean Park No. 125* (1980, Whitney Museum), *Ocean Park No. 128* (1984, New York) and *Ocean Park No. 129* (1984, private collection). As with so many of the *Ocean Park* paintings, *Ocean Park No. 60*'s comp-osition set the lines and panels of differ-ent colors along the top and right-hand edge of the canvas. There were red and black lines suggesting architectural structures in *Ocean Park No. 60* and others, such as *Ocean Park No. 83* (1975, Washington) and *Ocean Park No. 87* (1975, Virginia), with cream and yellow pigment put into the rectangles the lines made. Only in those rectilinear spaces did Diebenkorn allow a departure from the generally consistent monochrome pass-ages of the main part of the painting.

In many *Ocean Park* paintings a size-able proportion of the canvas is taken up by one block of color. Some of the *Ocean Park* paintings are in pale hues, which sometimes look pastel (pale blue, green, yellow, cream) – for example, *Ocean Park No. 114* (1979, California). Some are primarily cream and yellow, such as *Ocean Park No. 48* (1971, California),

Ocean Park No. 91 (1976, California), *Ocean Park No. 95* (1976, San Francisco), *Ocean Park No. 96* (1977, Guggenheim Museum), *Ocean Park No. 100* (1977, California), *Ocean Park No. 118* (1980, Miami), *Ocean Park No. 123* (1980, California) and *Ocean Park No. 131* (1985, California); some were predomin-antly deep blue, such as *Ocean Park No. 92* (1976, private collection) and *Ocean Park No. 137* (1985, Los Angeles); some were mostly dark green (*Ocean Park No. 111*, 1978, Hirshhorn Museum, Wash-ington); while others used large areas of mid-green and mid-blue, such as *Ocean Park No. 45* (1971, Art Institute of Chicago), *Ocean Park No. 105* (1978, private collection), *Ocean Park No. 66* (1973, Albright-Knox Art Gallery) and *Ocean Park No. 140* (1985, Los Angeles).

Unusually, canvases such as *Ocean Park No. 70* (1974, Des Moines Art Center, Iowa), were mainly red and pink. Paintings such as *Ocean Park No. 63* (1973, private collection), *Ocean Park No. 49* (1972, Los Angeles County Museum of Art), *Ocean Park No. 43* (1971, San Francisco) and *Ocean Park No. 64* (1973, Carnegie Museum of Art, Pittsburgh), consisted of large areas of flat white. A canvas such as *Ocean Park No. 107* (1978, Oakland Museum) layered green, yellow, gray, pink, dark blue and red above a large pastel blue rectangle. They are often light, airy paintings, with few dark tones. The *Ocean Park* series exhibit echoes of the Minimal grid: the paintings are sometimes divided into rectilinear blocks of color by black lines, which are sometimes painted over. But the square pattern of the grid is still visible.

The force and impact of the *Ocean Park* series derives partly from the sheer number of canvases, from the Conceptual and Serial art notion of doing one thing then another. 'Do it again', repeat and repeat: how many impressive contemporary works of art have we seen that comprise essentially of nothing more than one element replicated endlessly? You take something than replicate it. A floor tile, repeated... a painted stripe, repeated over a canvas... a metallic box, repeated, up a wall...

On their own, each *Ocean Park* painting is impressive, but when you view the series as a whole, it contains much more power (however, the paintings are scattered all over the planet: *Ocean Park* is not a group of paintings in one place, like Barnett Newman's *Stations of the Cross* in Washington, DC, or Mark Rothko's *Houston Chapel* works).

QUOTES BY RICHARD DIEBENKORN

In a successful painting everything is integral.. all the parts belong to the whole. If you remove an aspect or element you are removing its wholeness.

•

When I am halfway there with a painting, it can occasionally be thrilling.. But it happens very rarely; usually it's agony. I go to great pains to mask the agony. But the struggle is there. It's the invisible enemy.

•

I want painting to be difficult to do. The more obstacles, obstructions, problems.. the better.

•

Abstract literally means to draw from or separate. In this sense every artist is abstract... a realistic or non-objective approach makes no difference. The result is what counts.

•

All paintings start out of a mood, out of a relationship with things or people, out of a complete visual impression.

•

My freedom consists in my moving about within the narrow frame that I have assigned myself for each one of my undertakings.

•

It is not a matter of painting life. It's a matter of giving life to a painting.

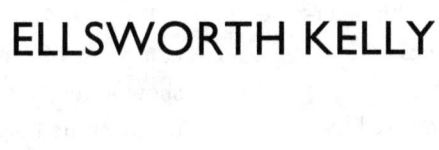

ELLSWORTH KELLY

ELLSWORTH KELLY

Like Kenneth Noland, Richard Diebenkorn and Frank Stella, Ellsworth Kelly's paintings were instantly recognizable as his own. Kelly (born in 1923) moved through a number of different styles, as many young artists do, before arriving at a kind of lyrical Hard Edge painting embodied in works such as *Yellow-Blue* (1963, Des Moines Art Center), *White-Dark Blue* (1962, London), *Blue, Red, Green* (1962-63, Metropolitan Museum, New York) and *Red Blue Green* (1962, La Jolla Museum of Contemporary Art). The latter was made at Coenties Slip, where Kelly shared studios with Jack Youngerman, Agnes Martin, and James Rosenquist.

Ellsworth Kelly's art was marked by brilliant coloration and a harmonious organization of color and shape. Like Brice Marden, Robert Mangold and David Novros, Kelly made multi-panel paintings in which each panel was given a single all-over color. Kelly said he wasn't influenced by the Abstract Expressionists (whom he had seen in 1954), but by Egyptian, Oriental and Byzantine art, by French Romanesque architecture, and Vincent van Gogh, Paul Cézanne, Claude Monet, Paul Klee, Pablo Picasso, Max Beckmann and Henri Matisse.[1] Kelly's *Spectrum* series (such as *Blue Green Yellow Orange Red* [1966, Guggenheim Museum]) were brighter than any of Marden's monochrome paintings.

Ellsworth Kelly expressed a view in his "Notes of 1969" article that was common to many of the Sixties painters: '[t]he form of my painting is the content'. It was not the brushmarks that interested Kelly in his paintings, so much as 'the "presence" of the panels themselves'. It was in 1949 that Kelly started to make objects rather than paintings.

> Instead of making a picture that was an interpretation of a thing seen, or a picture of invented content, I found an object and "presented" it as itself alone.[2]

This encapsulates the fundamental break between traditional art and postwar and contemporary art.

The 1999 Harvard University Art Museum show of early drawings, like the later show at the Tate Gallery in Blighty, demonstrate how immensely creative Kelly's art was, and how he has been overlooked for too long. In *The Early Drawings, 1948-1955*, Kelly's sense of joy in the exploration of painterly abstraction is palpable: especially fine are the mysterious two-color works (such as *Study For a White and Black Painting*, 1955), and the white-on-white studies (*Study For a White Relief*, 1953).

Although Ellsworth Kelly is still not the most well-known contemporary artist – mention his name and I'm sure many people, even dedicated art lovers, won't know who you mean – his art is completely distinctive. In an era (1960s-1970s) when 100s of artists, it seems, were churning out smooth, rectilinear, monochrome works – boxes, canvases, slabs, repeated objects – Kelly's art still stands out as something wholly his own. And that's no mean feat.

Walk into a gallery or museum today, and you can recognize Ellsworth Kelly's art instantly. There's a superb display of Kelly's Serial repetitions on the wall of the Metropolitan Museum of Art in Gotham, for instance (*Spectrum V*, 1969). It's a group of vertical format paintings which run thru the color spectrum, and it's immediately grasped as a Kelly work. And in the atrium of Chicago's Art Institute, there are giant Kelly slabs high on the wall, with his stamp all o (*Chicago Panels*, 1989-99).

You take a form, reduce it and compress it to its most fundamental essence, and somehow it increases the æsthetic impact; then you add those distinctive 1960s primary and secondary colors, and the works bounce off the white walls of galleries and museums.

QUOTES BY ELLSWORTH KELLY

I'm not interested in edges. I'm interested in the mass and color, the black and white. The edges happen because the forms get as quiet as they can be. I want the masses to perform. When I work with forms and colors, I get the edge.

•

I noticed that the large windows between the paintings [in the Musée d'Art Moderne] interested me more than the art exhibited. From then on, painting as I had known it was finished for me.

I usually let them [his drawings] lie around for a long time. I have to get to really like it. And then when I do the painting I have to get to like that too. Sometimes I stay with the sketch, sometimes I follow the original idea exactly if the idea is solved. But most of the time there have to be adjustments during the painting. Through the painting of it I find the color and I work the form and play with it and it adjusts itself.

•

The form of my painting is the content.

•

Instead of making a picture that was an interpretation of a thing seen, or a picture of invented content, I found an object and 'presented' it as itself alone. My first object was "Window, Museum of Modern Art, Paris', done in 1949. After I constructed 'Window' with two canvases and a wood frame I realized that from then on painting as I had known it was finished for me. The new works were to be objects, unsigned, anonymous.

•

I felt that everything is beautiful, but that which man tries intentionally to make beautiful; that the work of an ordinary bricklayer is more valid than the artwork of all but a very few artists.

•

My work is about structure. It has never been a reaction to Abstract Expressionism. I saw the Abstract Expressionists for the first time in 1954. My line of influence has been the 'structure' of the things I liked: French Romanesque architecture, Byzantine, Egyptian and Oriental art, Van Gogh, Cézanne, Monet, Klee, Picasso, Beckmann.

•

In my painting, negative space is never arbitrary. (I believe lithographs to be colored marks printed on a ground – the paper and the measure of the ground and the marks are to be considered of equal importance). In my painting, the painting is the subject rather than the subject the painting.

5

OTHER COLORFIELD, MINIMAL, HARD EDGE, SERIAL AND POST-PAINTERLY ABSTRACT PAINTERS

OTHER COLORFIELD, MINIMAL, HARD EDGE AND POST-PAINTERLY ABSTRACT PAINTERS OF THE 1960S AND AFTER

ELIZABETH MURRAY (1940-2007) was one of many (post) Sixties artists who used multiple panels or 3-D paintings, in the manner of Frank Stella and Robert Mangold. Murray produced marvellous shaped panels, such as her *Simple Meaning* (1982, collection: Jerry & Emily Spiegel, New York) and *Fire Cup* (1982, Paula Cooper Gallery, New York). Murray's *1, 2, 3* (1984, private collection) was a complicated shaped abstract canvas using three layers. *1, 2, 3* was lushly painted in blues, greens, yellows and purples. You will come across Murray's works in many museums and galleries around the world (mostly in the U.S.A., inevitably), and while Murray's isn't as celebrated as many of the other Colorfield and Post-Painterly Abstract artists, her work is always impressive, particularly in the realm of the shaped canvas.

> There's a kind of miracle involved with paint [Murray wrote]. It's just this stuff in a tube... you squeeze out. It's this physical thing, yet you use it as a transforming agent.

ALAN CHARLTON (b. 1948) followed the strictly monochrome route of Ad Reinhardt and Alexander Rodchenko, producing panels of different shades of gray. Victor Burgin and Mel Ramsden had also experimented with the *reductio ad absurdum* of monochrome art. ED

MENEELEY 's shaped canvases recalled Ken Noland's and Ellsworth Kelly's, with stripes bordering the shapes.

One of JAKE BERTHOT's (b. 1939) formal techniques was to put two canvases side by side, inhabited by rectilinear forms, hints at architecture and horizons, and allusions to Romanticism, produced with a return to traditional methods of painting, as in *Walken's Ridge* (1975-76, MOMA, New York). In *Belfast* (1981), Berthot's shadowy rectangular forms and lines recall Richard Diebenkorn's *Ocean Park* series, though the colors (dark blues and blacks, with patches of red and white), are much darker than Diebenkorn's.

SAM GILLIAM (b. 1933) created complexly shaped 'paintings' (such as *Like Today*, 1985, Monique Knowlton Gallery, New York) which, gleefully smash the primacy of the traditional rectangle in painting. Some of Gilliam's distinctive works are canvases hung in loose shapes on the wall, not stretched on a wooden frame, rather like multi-colored versions of the felt works of Robert Morris.

JOHN McCRACKEN (1934-2011) was a Californian sculptor who made Minimal slabs or 'planks' from wood or fibreglass, which were halfway between paintings and sculptures (or neither one nor the other), which he leant against walls (such as *Blue Plank* [1966], *Untitled (Red Plank)* [1966], and *Untitled (Dk Blue)* [1970]).

McCracken saw his unitary slabs as 'meditation devices'. At times McCracken's works looked like Barnett Newman's zips, or Richard Serra's leaning sculptures (*Untitled*, 1967, Saatchi Collection). When they were freestanding (*Untitled* [1966, Los Angeles County Museum]; *Sagittarius* [1988, private collection]), McCracken's sculptures evoked the mysterious, alien obelisk in *2,0001: A Space Odyssey*, perhaps the key Minimal film of the era. But McCracken painted his slabs in bright, Pop Art colors, not the monochromes associated with Minimal art (gray, white and black): the bright *Blue Post and Lintel* (1965), for instance. McCracken was still making his mysterious monochrome sculptures into the 1990s (such as *One* [1997], and *Hill* [1997]).

ROBERT MANGOLD (b. 1937) explores color and architecture in his multi-panelled paintings which often contain a unifying element of drawing (in *Four Color Frame Painting No. 1*, collection: Martin Sklar, New York, for example). Mangold's shaped canvases are usually in bright colors (oranges, reds, blues), usually with one simple geometric idea played out on a large scale (typically on six foot canvases), and often with a black pencil mark drawn on top of the color, marking out some internal geometry (often a square or a circle). Many of Mangold's canvases are simple shapes – a circle, more often a square, but one or two are complex (such as *W Series Central*

Diagonal I (Orange) [1968], and *4 Color Frame Painting No. 3* [1983, both Saatchi Collection]).

JULES OLITSKI (1922-2007) produced formalist abstract paintings that employed Minimal æsthetics (such as the use of large areas of monochrome) with the opulent color of Colorfield painting (as in *Green Goes Around*, 1967, private collection). In *Green Goes Around*, a canvas over seven feet wide is predominantly a field of green, though it has modulations (the green, for example, is darker towards the edges).

In *High A Yellow* (1967, Whitney Museum of American Art), Jules Olitski used a favourite motif of Colorfield painting: a dominant and central warm color with harmonized colors painted around the edge of the painting.

The emphasis on optical effects in Jules Olitski's art, with affinities to Mark Rothko and Morris Louis in particular, are obvious: this is painting as a pure sensory experience, in which colors and abstract forms seem intended to act on the body and the senses immediately. The relations to anything representational are vague and ambiguous. As with Brice Marden's art, Olitski's device of leaving the edges of the paintings worked around with other colors and forms emphasized aspects of the manufacture of the work, and also added some elements of solidity or reference for the central expanses of single colors.

RICHARD TUTTLE (b. 1941) produced shaped canvases for a time, such as *Tan Octagon* (1967, London), made from dyed cloth, and *8th Paper Octagonal* (1970, London). Tuttle's artworks were somewhere between paintings and sculptures, as with so many of the 1960s artists. Tuttle's *Canvas Dark Blue* (1967, private collection, NYC) cut the canvas in an irregular, consciously non-geometric shape, with a roughly rectangular hole in the middle, and pinned the painted result on a wall.

DAVID NOVROS's (b. 1941) paintings include pieces which were complex in terms of physical construction. A work such as Novros's *Untitled* (1967, private collection), consisted of six dacron L-shapes fitted together like a jigsaw, but allowing rectangular spaces in between them. In another *Untitled* of 1967, three L-shaped panels are set on top of each other on the wall, each with a rectangular segment bitten out of them.

Some of JO BAER's (b. 1929) paintings consist of large areas of white, with a narrow band of color around the very edges of the canvas (as in *Sidebare (Lavender White*, 1972), *Untitled* (1963) and *Untitled (Red Wrap-Around*, 1969). This format recalls Morris Louis's stripes, where the major, central section of the painting is either white or bare canvas, color being relegated to the periphery of the spectator's vision.

Canadian JACK BUSH (1909-77) went through the roster of 20th century art styles (Cubism, Expressionism, Abstract Expressionism) before making Colorfield paintings that consisted of his 'sash and fringe' motif: rows of brilliant colors were set beside a neutral-hued vertical ground (as in *Tall Spread*, 1966, National Gallery of Canada). Op Art or optical art of the Sixties had its ancestors in artists such as Josef Albers and Victor Vassarely. Apart from Vassarely, the chief practitioners of 1960s Op Art included Bridget Riley, Larry Poons, Yaacov Agam, Enrico Castellani, Günter Uecker, Jesús Raphael Soto, François Morellet, Piero Dorazio and Richard Anuzkiewiscz.

Linked to Op art and optical art are kinetic art, and light art, where machines or devices move to create optical effects, or neons and lamps are employed, or, as in the art of James Turrell, the sky itself. It's easy to see how expanses of the sky, or the lighting effects of Dan Flavin, the neons of Bruce Nauman and Nam June Paik, have equivalences with Colorfield painting.

Britain's BRIDGET RILEY (b. 1931) produced paintings (such as *Gala*, 1974, private collection and *Shiver*, 1964, private collection), which were as dazzling and vertiginous in reproduction as in the flesh. Look at a reprint of a black-and-white Riley work in a book and it appears like one of those visual puzzles or tricks, designed to depict some aspect of the human eye. Riley's art also attempts an optical play, a sudden and forceful assault on the eye and the way that humans perceive the visual world.

LARRY POONS (b. 1937) developed an Op Art format consisting of a monochrome canvas with small disc-shaped blobs of paint dotted across the surface (the 'jumping beans' were carefully situated in relation to each other). In *Rosewood* (1966, William Rubin Collection), these discs were mainly pink, orange and pale green on a dull yellow ground. In Poons' *Untitled* (1966, Whitney Museum of American Art), blue, green, pink and orange impastoed dots floating disembodied on a pale green ground. As with Jules Olitski, Kenneth Noland, Helen Frankenthaler and Morris Louis, Larry Poons' paintings stressed the sensory thrill of opticality. Like Bridget Riley's or Richard Anuzkiewicz's paintings, Poons' works revelled in creating retinal afterimages. (And Poons' bright dots led directly to the substandard imitations by British pseudo-artist Damien Hirst).

The German painter GOTTHARD GRAUBNER (b. 1930) developed the all-overness of Abstract Expressionism and did away with geometric motifs altogether. Graubner's paintings consist of areas of color which merge like mist, as if Mark Rothko's 'cloud-like' images had been dissolved in fog (as in *Blue-Rose Color-Space*, 1961-62, Kunstmuseum, Düsseldorf). Graubner's art evoked a spaceless meditative zone, which Graubner enhanced at times by placing fabric on top of paintings made with foam rubber on canvas.

One of GÜNTER UECKER's (b. 1930) styles was distinctly Minimalist, austere monochrome canvases (in black, white and gray), which explored the materiality of the painting-as-object: some of Uecker's paintings were reliefs using nails (*Painting Nailed Over* [1957, collection: the artist] and *Informal Structure* [1957, Staatliche Museen zu Berlin]), others mixed oil and silver leaf, as in *Silver Spiral* (1957, collection: the artist), some recalled the textured white panels of Robert Ryman (*Vertical Structure White*, 1958, collection: the artist), and some were classic Minimal pieces (half of a painting in white, the other half in black), recalling Ellsworth Kelly and Brice Marden (*Black-White*, 1956-57, collection: the artist).

RALPH HUMPHREY (1932-90) was one of the earlier Minimal painters, whose monochrome canvases (such as *Atlanta* [1958] and *Olympia* [1959]) were precursors of Brice Marden and Robert Mangold (who admired Humphrey). Like Jo Baer, Robert Ryman and Agnes Martin, Humphrey explored the formal possibilities of all-over white in pieces such as *Rio* (1965) and *Camden* (1965). The edges of the painting become the zone of interest, the central area being all white.

BLINKY PALERMO (1943-77) was also influenced by Minimal painting, as well as Conceptual art and performance art, as in his *Textile Picture 18* (1968, Stuttgart) and *Softspeaker* (1965, Frankfurt). Palmero's 1960s paintings were typically made using colored fabrics (as in *Fabric Painting, Pink-Orange-Black,* 1968). Some of Palermo's paintings (*Fabric Painting,* 1969, private collection) were archetypal Minimal works, echoing Brice Marden and Ellsworth Kelly with bands of mono-chrome (though in painted fabric). Later, Palermo produced installations of wall drawings (Hamburg, 1975).

LUDWIG SANDER produced mono-chrome post-Mondrian explorations of grids (such as *Chincoteague II* [1961, New York]). WILLIAM ANASTASI turned in monochrome Minimal paintings as part of his *œuvre* (as in *North Wall, Dwan Main Gallery* [1967]).

DAVID HOCKNEY (b. 1937), though associated with Pop Art, used Minimal means at times. In his most famous painting, *The Splash* (1966), he employed large areas of unbroken single colors, reminiscent of Robert Mangold or Ellsworth Kelly (Tom Wesselmann was another Pop artist with a similar painting technique of flat, opaque color).

PAINTERS AFTER COLOR-FIELD, MINIMAL, HARD EDGE AND POST-PAINTERLY ABSTRACTION

Other painters who have affinities with Colorfield art and Post-Painterly Abstraction include: GERHARD RICHTER (b. 1932), who is renowned as an influent-ial figurative and abstract painter, a painter of representations such as the softly smeared *Annunciations After Titian* (1973), a series of meta-paintings, paint-ings about paintings, which explored Renaissance art in terms of postmod-ernism.

The art of Gerhard Richter is not wholly (or nearly wholly) abstract. Eighties paint-ings by Richter such as *Untitled (531-4)* and *Group of Trees (628-1),* are near-abstract pieces, consisting of thick brush-strokes, in the Willem de Kooning or Howard Hodgkin manner. The more abstract painting, *Untitled*, still retains notions of representation: it has a 'back-ground' space to the foreground shapes which is a light blue, something like the smooth, clear skies of Yves Tanguy.

Photography is one of Gerhard Richter's recurring concerns. Many of his paintings have been based on photos, but Richter's use of photography is much more complic-ated than that (though those paintings from photographs are beautiful enough on their own). Richter's photographic paintings combine plenty of theoretical and philosophical explorations with sensual, visual magic. They work on many levels, and seem designed to delight people who still think postmodernism is important. (That is, Richter's art is tailor-made for art history students or for art critics for whom terms like 'postmodernism' and 'Baudrillardian' and 'hyper-reality' still hold some weight).

Aligned to photography is Gerhard Richter's exploration of monochromism, so that many of his paintings begin with a black-and-white photograph, reproducing its black-and-white æsthetic make-up (though not in the same way as Andy Warhol). Richter has also gone far into Minimalism's beloved area of gray art, of exploring multiple shades of gray.

Later pieces by Gerhard Richter developed his striking technique of smearing paint wet-in-wet, which, combined with employing vivid hues, lend his works an appealing sensuality and impact. Richter builds on the Colorfield art of the 1960s and 1970s (particularly the Washington school) – by Gene Davis, Morris Louis and Kenneth Noland – and takes it even further in areas of pure optical pleasure. Richter's smeared abstractions are works which refer to nothing but themselves, and they create the means and ways by which they are to be consumed. The æsthetic and painterly force of these paintings is undeniable.

Gerhard Richter is also an artist, I think, who demonstrates for all to see that painting is not dead, but vibrantly alive. The *energy* coming off the walls in Richter's art is so strong. You can't ignore it. This man knows what he's doing, and he

does it so well – indeed, he does it better, more skilfully and more flamboyantly than almost any other of his contemporaries. (Recent displays of Richter's work in Gotham, L.A. and London have demonstrated the vibrancy of his art).

If you are losing your faith in contemporary painting, go straight to Gerhard Richter: he will restore it, he will make you realize why you loved painting in the first place. In that respect, he is supremely a 'painter's painter', someone who both technically brilliant and thematically inspiring.

SEAN SCULLY's (b. 1945) painterly surfaces recall Jasper Johns' oil and wax treatments, as do those of Howard Hodgkin. Scully's use of the grid, or vertical stripe motifs, also directly recalls painters such as Barnett Newman, Frank Stella, Kenneth Noland and Agnes Martin. Scully's formal innovations with a small separate square canvas pushed into a larger set of panels bolted together also recall Johns' multi-part paintings and Stella's shaped canvases.

Sean Scully painted thickly in horizontal and vertical stripes. His subject was the way the stripe was painted. 'The stripe is neutral and boring and that makes the stripe receptive to interpretation', Scully said. The variations in the way the stripes were painted were intended to make different sorts of paintings: some

> may have a kind of intimacy, another a sort of wildness, or a brutality, an ugliness, a

lyricism, a brightness, a darkness, a claustrophobic feeling, a powerfully aggressive feeling.[1]

☆

There are many painters who traverse the boundaries between abstraction and figuration, who make blurred shapes and patterns on canvas which hint at representation, while remaining inexplicable and 'abstract': Gerhard Richter, Andreas Schulze, Helmut Middendorf, Helmut Federle, Julian Schnabel, Anselm Keifer, Thérèse Oulton, Albert Oehlen, Mimmo Paladino and Herbert Brandl. The painters, sometimes called Neo-Expressionists or *Neue Wilde,* make powerful gestures which are also deliberately vague, ambivalent and non-didactic. Their paintings are very strident, in the 'expressionist' style, with much fierce, energetic application of paint. But the shapes, patterns, forms and tones suggest figuration (figures, bits of architecture, shadows), while also simply being brushstrokes.

PER KIRKEBY's *Winter VI* is a tall canvas with tones ranging from white to black, yet the forms, which hint at architectonics, remain abstract. HERBERT BRANDL's (b. 1959) *Untitled* is an Expressionist mass of dark reds and blacks, a swirl of paint which suggests a storm in the manner of J.M.W. Turner's paintings of the Alps. This is a simplistic, Romantic reading of a painting which is nothing to do with a Turnerian storm, even though, at a physical level, in terms of the physical look of paint on canvas,

there is a similarity between Turner's and Brandl's technique.

The 'Neo-Geo' artists, the East Village artists of the early 1980s, influenced by Jean Baudrillard and his concept of *simulcra* and surfaces (Peter Halley, Ashley Bickerton, Meyer Vaisman, Jeff Koons and Haim Steinbach), produced postmodern, hybrid, ironic, Neo-Conceptual art, which sometimes developed and parodied Colorfield, Minimal and Post-Painterly Abstraction. PETER HALLEY's paintings, for example – *Asynchronous Terminal* (1989) and *Nirvana* (1992) – drew on Joseph Alber's squares, Sixties Day-Glo colors, computer diagrams, comics, and the large scale of the New York School. 'My work will use everything that it can to communicate', admitted Jeff Koons. 'It will use any trick; it'll do anything – absolutely anything – to communicate, and to win the viewer over'.[2]

PHILLIP TAAFE (b. 1955) parodied Barnett Newman's zip in his *Abraham and Isaac* (1986, a Newmanesque title), turning the revered stripe into a decorative twisted cord (a motif that also evoked Henri Matisse, who used Hermès silk scarves).

ROSS BLECKNER (b. 1949) made Hans Hofmann-like Neo-Op paintings, all energy and light (*Cage* [1986], *Fallen Object* [1987], and *The Oceans* [1984]). Bleckner's is an art of dim phosphorescences glowing out of dark monochromy (*God Won't Come* [1983] and *Delaware* [1983, both private collection]), or vague, antiquated motifs (leaves, snow-flakes, monograms), as in *Fallen Summer* (1988, private collection).

JENNIFER BARTLETT (b. 1941) has explored the dynamics of perception and space using multiple panels and rainbow-curved can-vases (in, for example, her *Horizon*, 1979, enamel, silkscreen and baked enamel on steel plates, oil on canvas, 20 plates, 1 canvas, 48 x 250 in, collection: Martin Sklar, New York).

HELMUT MIDDENDORF's (b. 1953) *Aeroplane Dream* has a more descriptive title than the ubiquitous *Untitled*, the most popular title in contemporary art. The dark black plane, though, is barely visible in the deep blue of the sky. The painting is more about the application of paint in luscious colors than about an aeroplane, although the dream-like quality is affirmed in the use of dark blues.

HELMUT FEDERLE's (b. 1944) *Three Shapes, Two Crossed* reworks Ad Reinhardt's reductive Minimal painting, with its dark blue crosses on dark green. The religious connotations are close to Brice Marden's paintings, and the cross motif recalls Marden's *Thira*. JOHN ARMLEDER's *Untitled* is very Mardenesque: a horizontal painting of two colors: flat yellow/ ochre and beige,

and nothing else. But it has a round wooden table in front of it, which radically alters the abstract painting hanging behind it.

There are a host of Post-Painterly Abstract artists who make the sensuality of surface primary in their works: Jean Dubuffet and Antonio Tàpies love to crowd their surfaces with mixtures of materials such as oil and sand on canvas, in ANTONIO TÀPIES' (1923-2012) *Great Painting* (1958, Guggenheim Museum, New York), mixed media in *Brun et Ochre* (1959, private collection). Tàpies's art has some of the most gloriously OTT textures and surfaces in contemporary art, as if Tàpies wanted to cut up slices of the world itself and glue them onto his canvases (and in the process, scoring deep lines in them, sometimes in grids, and allowing cracks and fissures to occur everywhere).

In JEAN DUBUFFET's (1901-85) art, such as *Run Grass, Jump Pebbles* (1956, private collection, Paris) and *Texturology* (1958, private collection), the example of Jackson Pollock is employed, flattening everything onto a single picture plane, spreading all of the elements over the plane evenly, and mixing in a variety of materials, includ-ing sand, glass, plaster, glue, tar, stones and asphalt.

MILTON RESNICK's (1917-2004) *Elephant* (1979, New York) was a field of impastoed gray, on a large, 209-inch wide canvas, recalling Brice Marden's gray Sixties panels. Britons Peter Joseph and Bob Law made Postminimalist paintings; **BOB LAW** had an exhibition of all-black canvases at the Whitechapel in 1977. **TERRY SHAVE** (b. 1952) produced mixed media paintings, such as *Walkabout I* (1992), *Reflections* (1993) and *Stalker 4* (1992-93), which explored notions of space, materiality and the sublime, using techniques such as painting onto nylon flock.

ANSELM KEIFER (b. 1945) sticks all manner of materials onto his oil paintings, including bits of straw, to radically alter the painting's surface (such as *Margarethe*, 1981, oil and straw on canvas, 9'2" x 12'6", Saatchi Collection, London; and *Nurnberg-Festspiel-Weise*, 1981, oil, straw, mixed media on canvas, collection: Eli & Edythe L. Broad, Los Angeles).

There are any number of contemporary painters for whom touch and surface are crucial: such as Julian Schnabel, Thérése Oulton, Gillian Ayres and Jennifer Bartlett. But Anselm Keifer is amongst the most impressive: coming across a Keifer canvas in a museum is a reminder of just how dynamic and playful his art can be. Of course, there are deep thematic and philosophical aspects to it, but merely at the level of paint and objects and sculpture, Keifer's art is striking.

Anselm Keifer's heroes were Joseph Beuys, Andy Warhol, Jackson Pollock, Vincent van Gogh, and plenty of German Romanticism: Caspar David Friedrich, Richard Wagner, Friedrich Nietzsche, and poets such as Friedrich Hölderlin and Johann Wolfgang von Goethe.

But many of Anselm Keifer's subjects are of big political and ideological concerns, many to do with Germany and its troubled past in the modern era. Keifer's art has made powerful, impossible-to-ignore references to Nazism, to World War Two, and the Wagnerian, Christian and Bavarian aspects of the modern German psyche (Keifer was born in the Black Forest).

With contemporary German artists such as Anselm Keifer, Sigmar Polke and Gerhard Richter, the purely sensual, optical and pleasurable elements of Colorfield painting are given a powerful political twist, reversing the self-absorbed dive into Matissean hedonism of American art of the 1960s.

ILLUSTRATIONS

Including some influences on Colorfield art and artists

Mark Rothko in Washington, DC

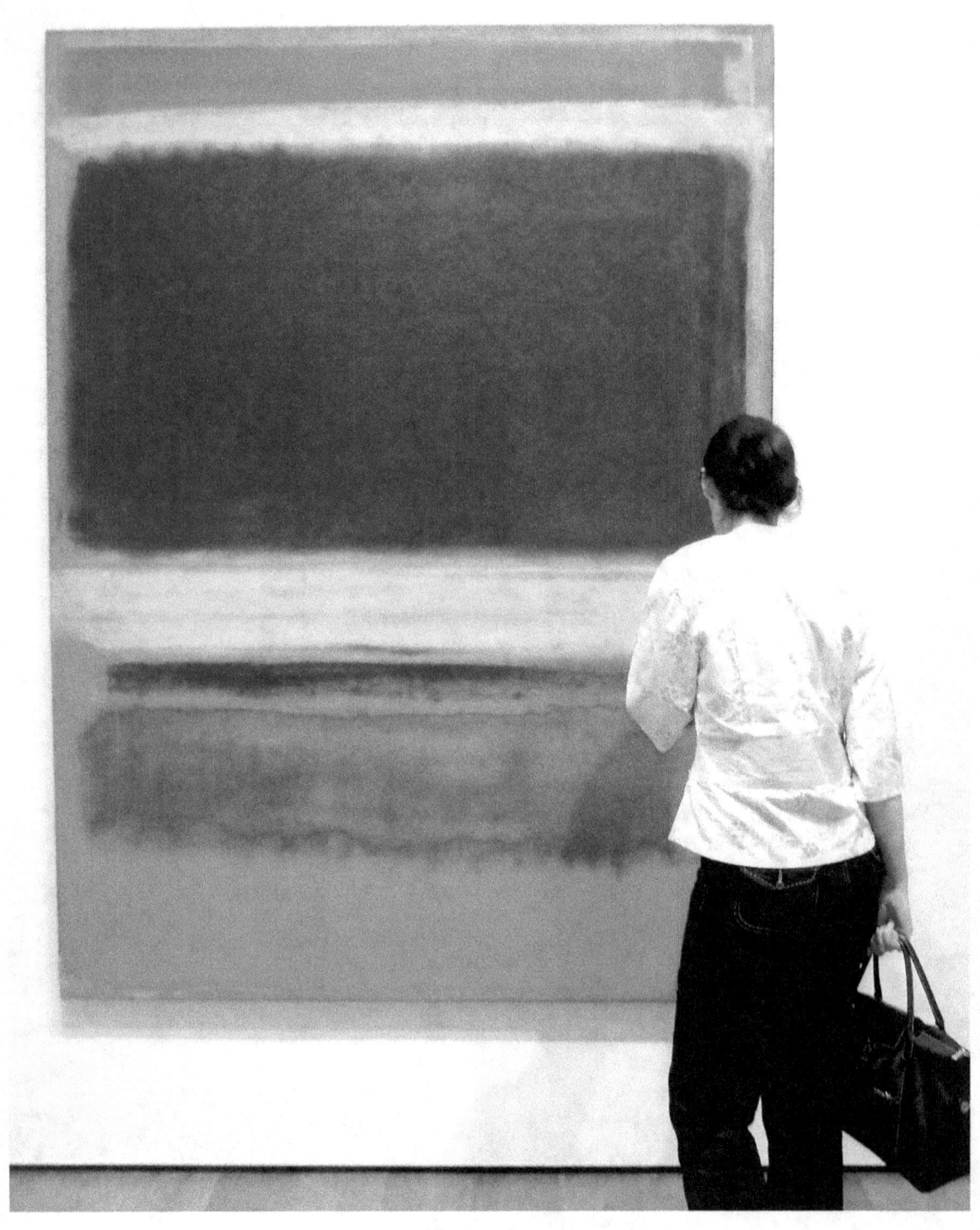

Mark Rothko at MOMA, New York City

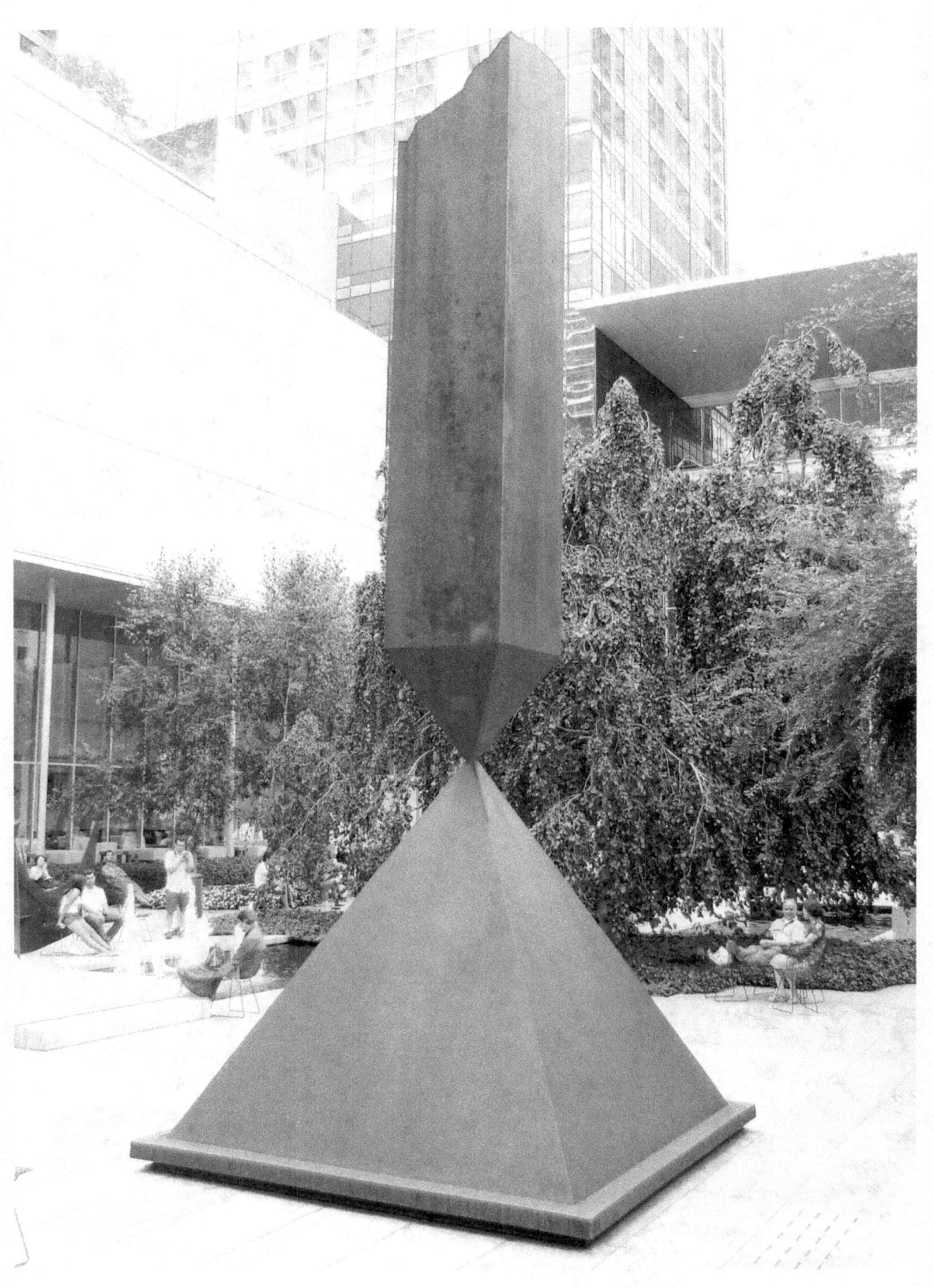

Barnett Newman, Broken Obelisk, MOMA, New York

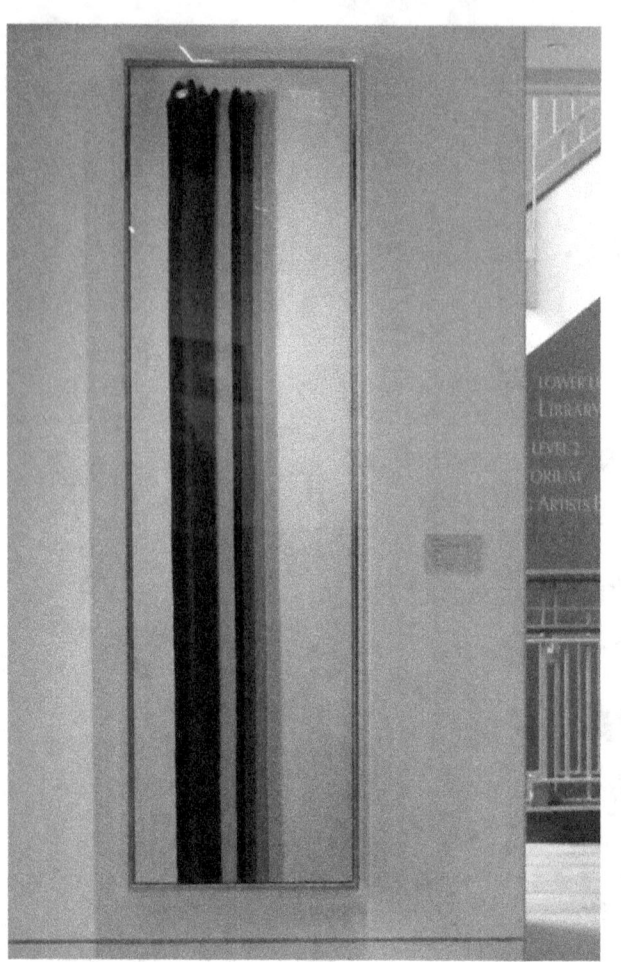

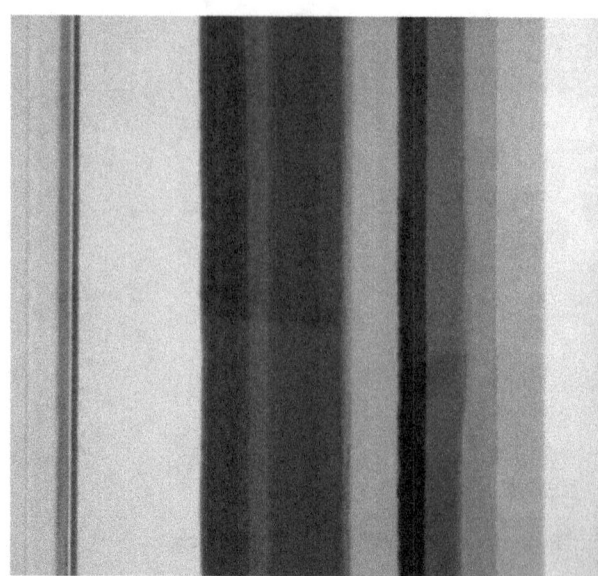

Morris Louis

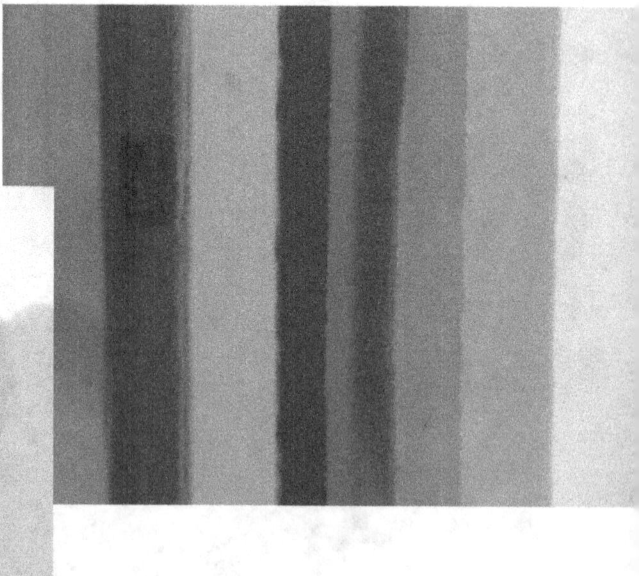

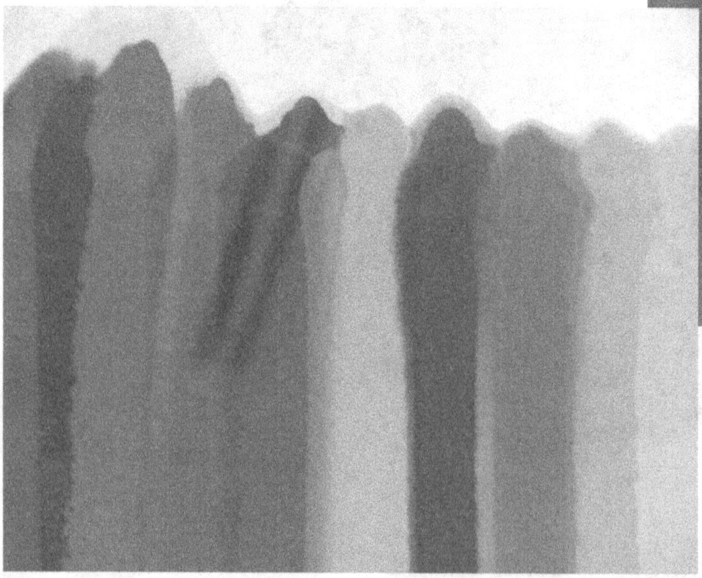

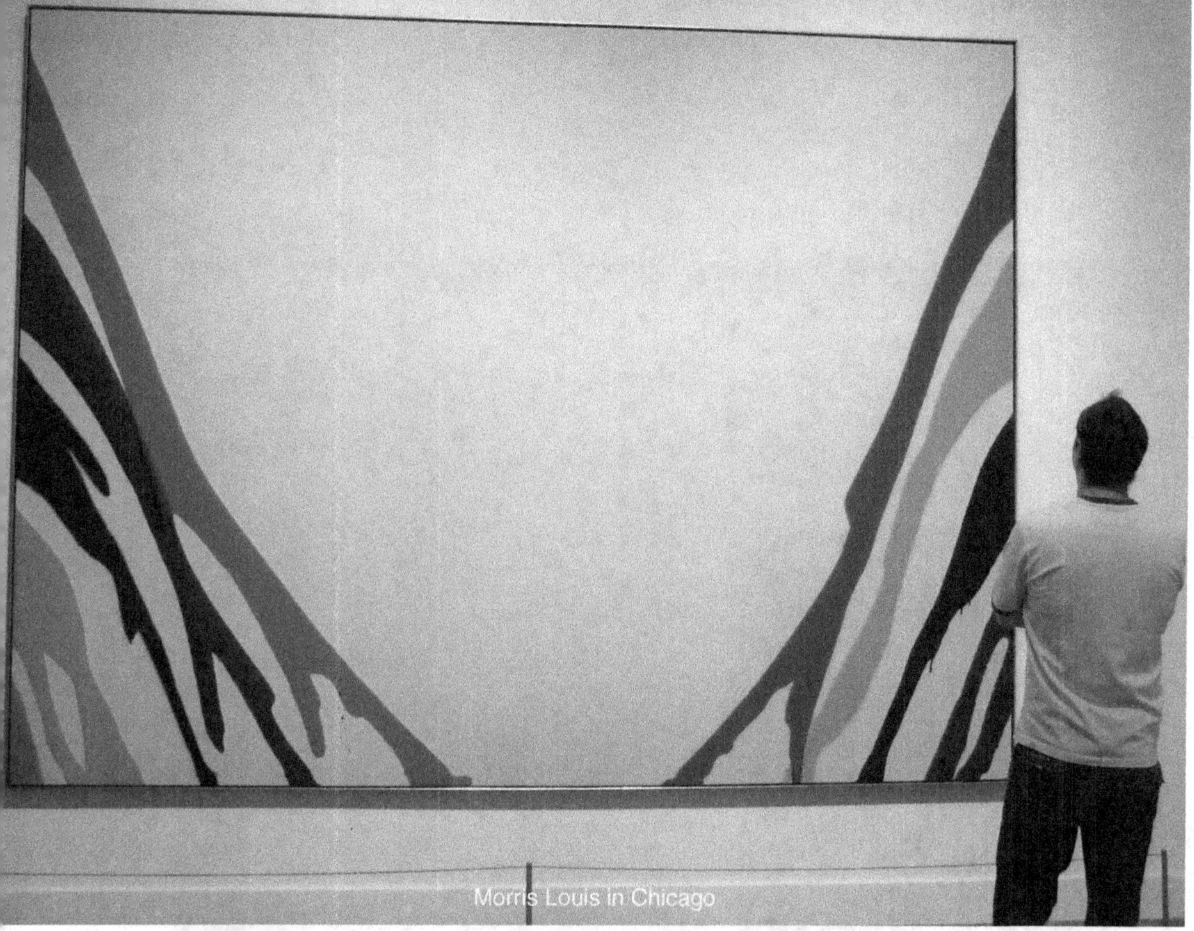

Morris Louis in Chicago

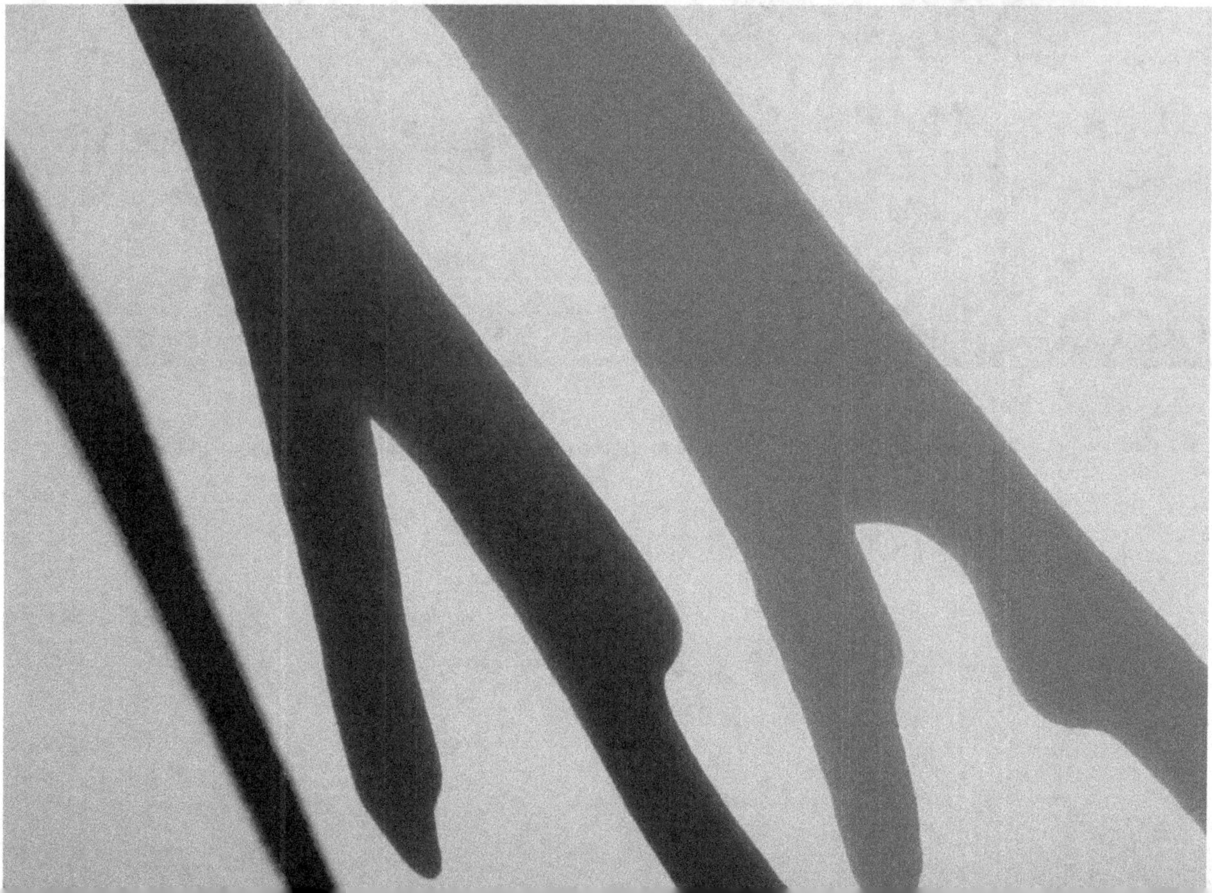

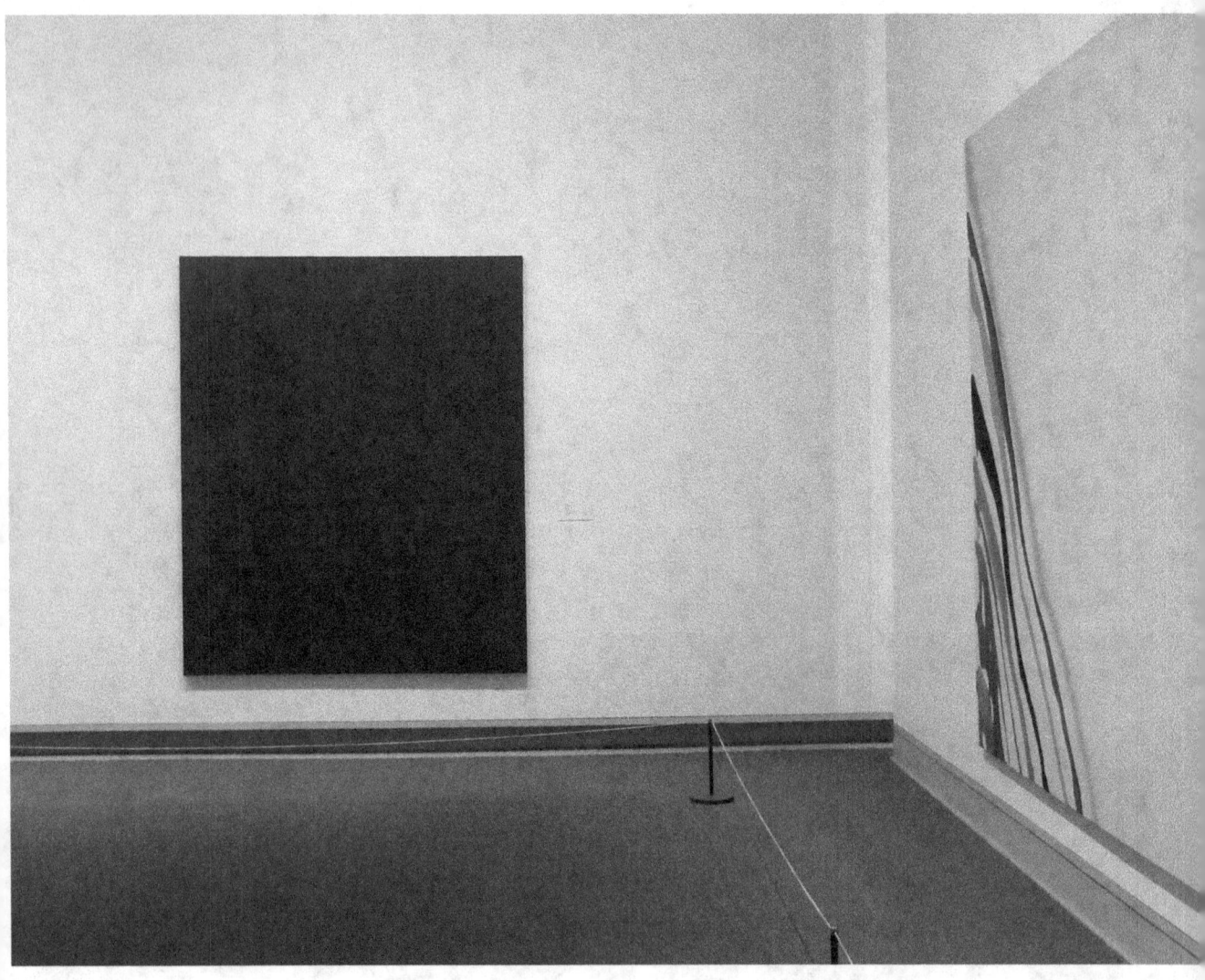

Ad Reinhardt in Gotham, at the Metropolitan Museum of Art, with Morris Louis on the right.

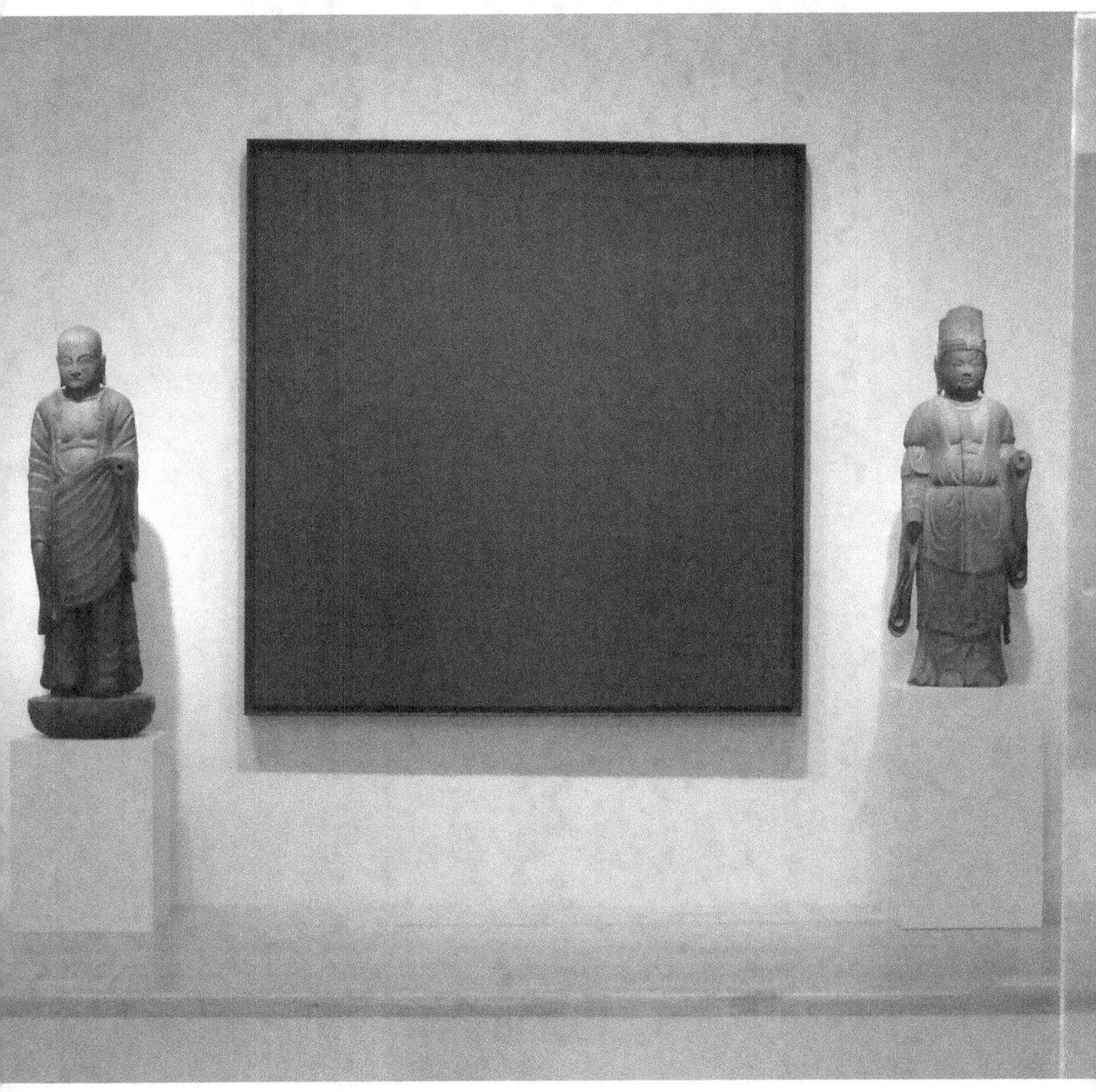

An inventive display of Ad Reinhardt's work in Princeton Art Museum, New Jersey, putting modern New York abstract art in amongst ancient Asian art

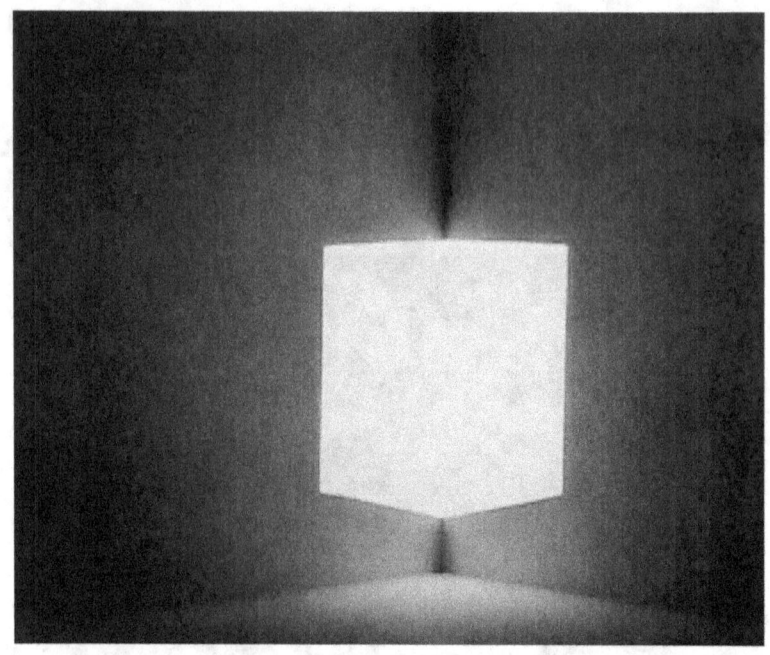

James Turrell

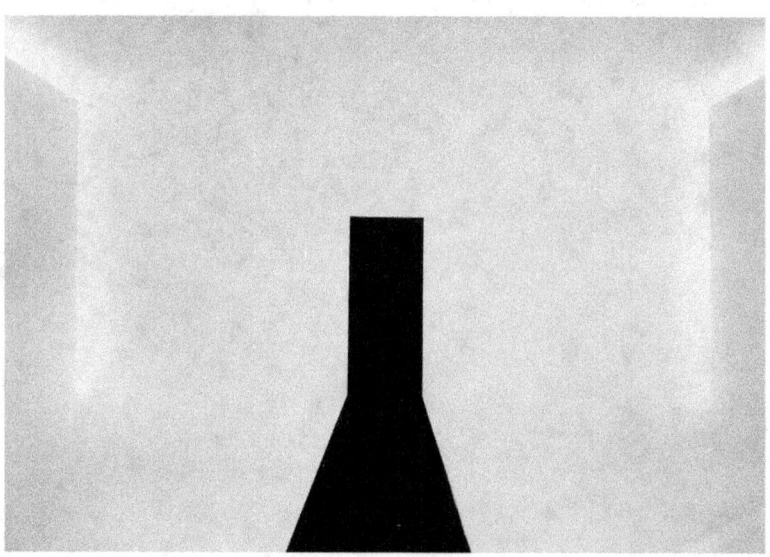

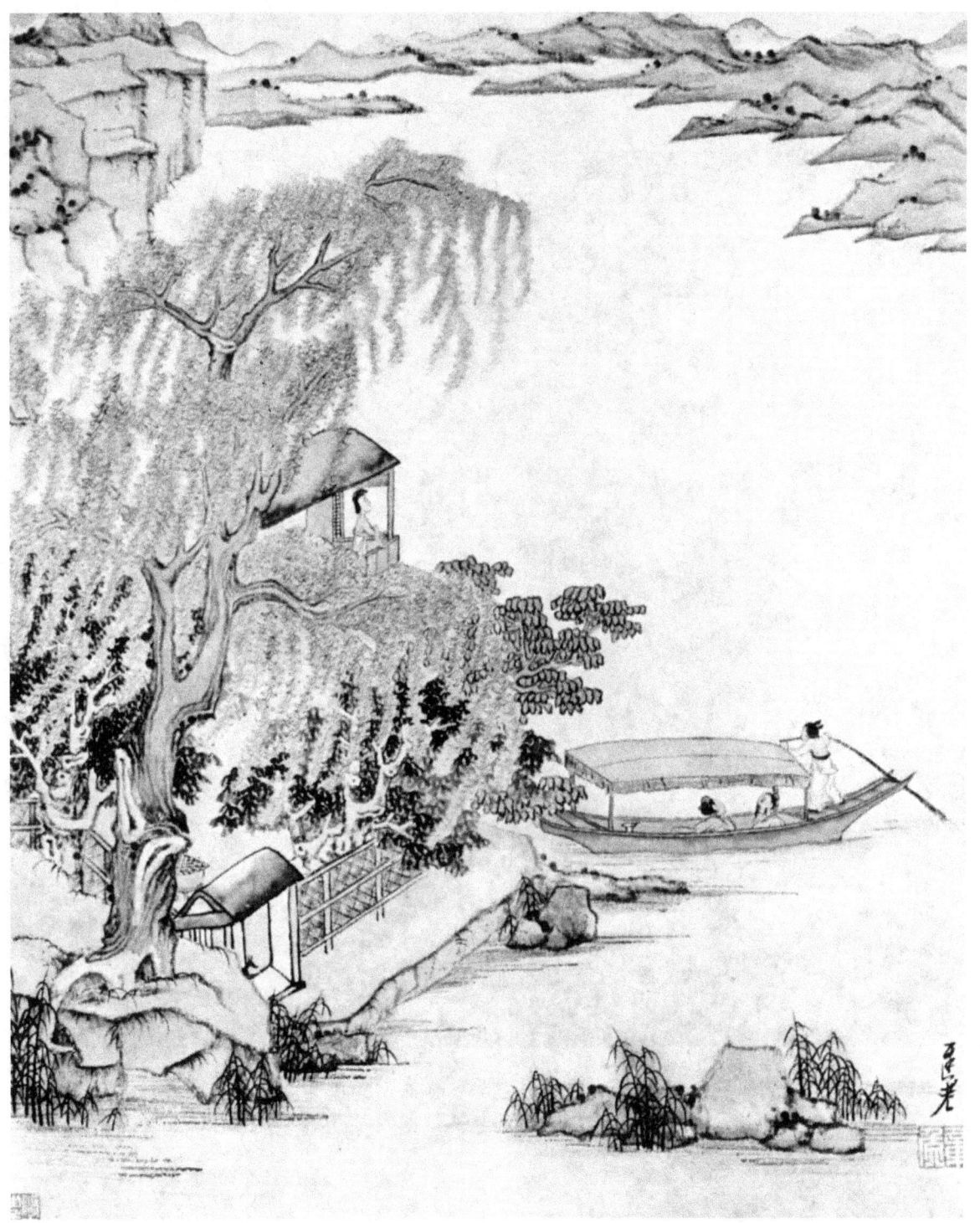

Chinese Landscape, Ming Dynasty, 1630-1650

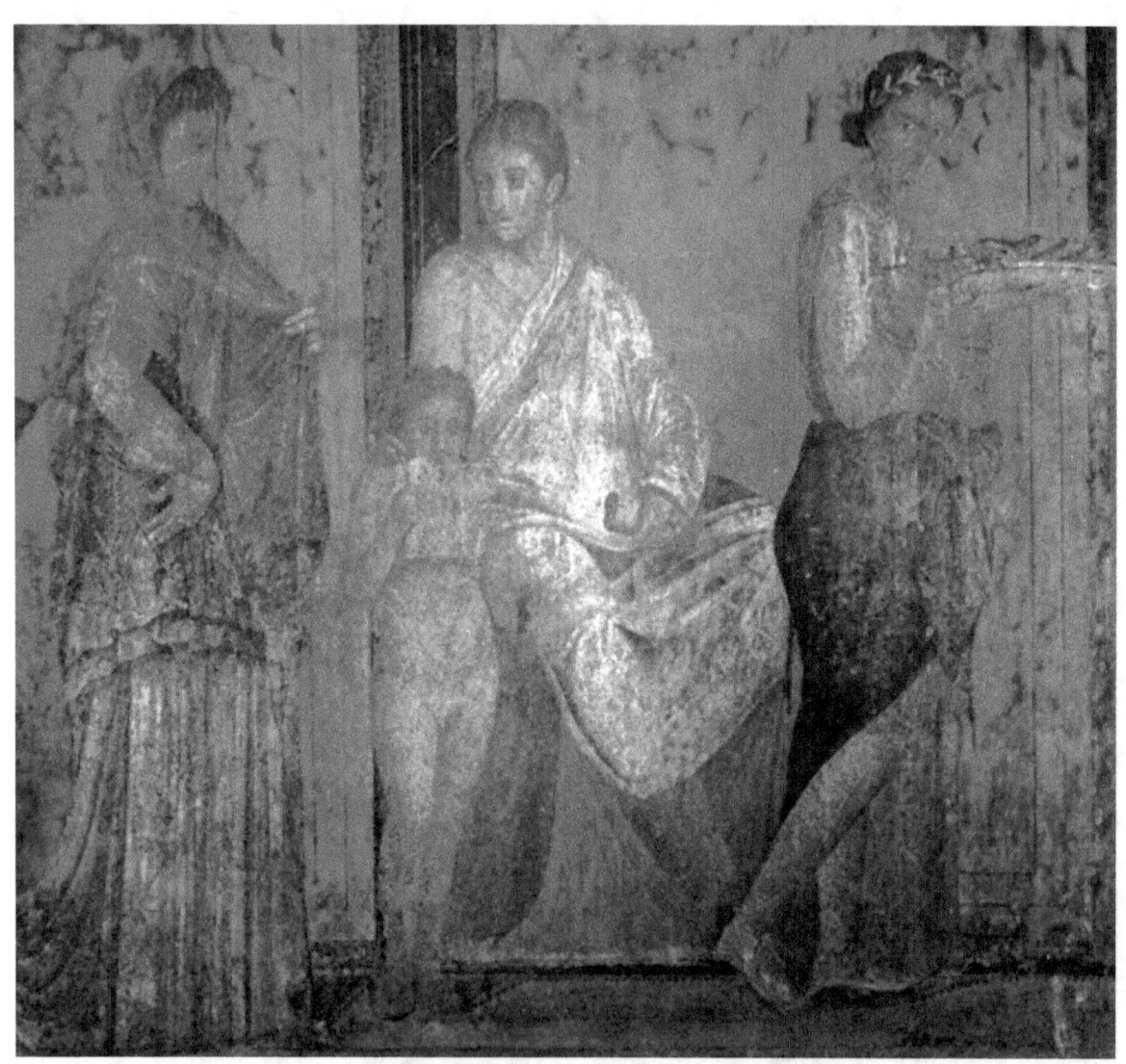

Villa of the Mysteries in Pompeii, c. 50 B.C.

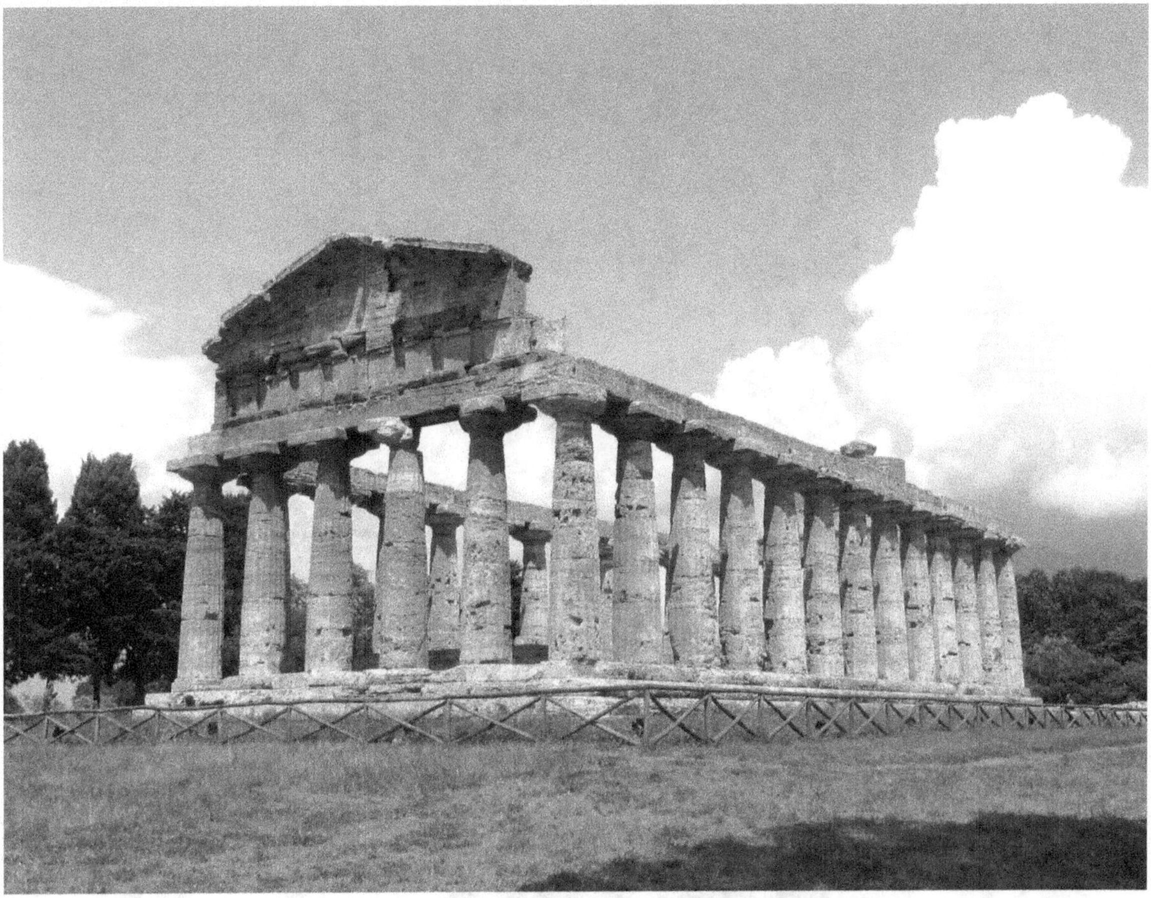

Temples at Paestum

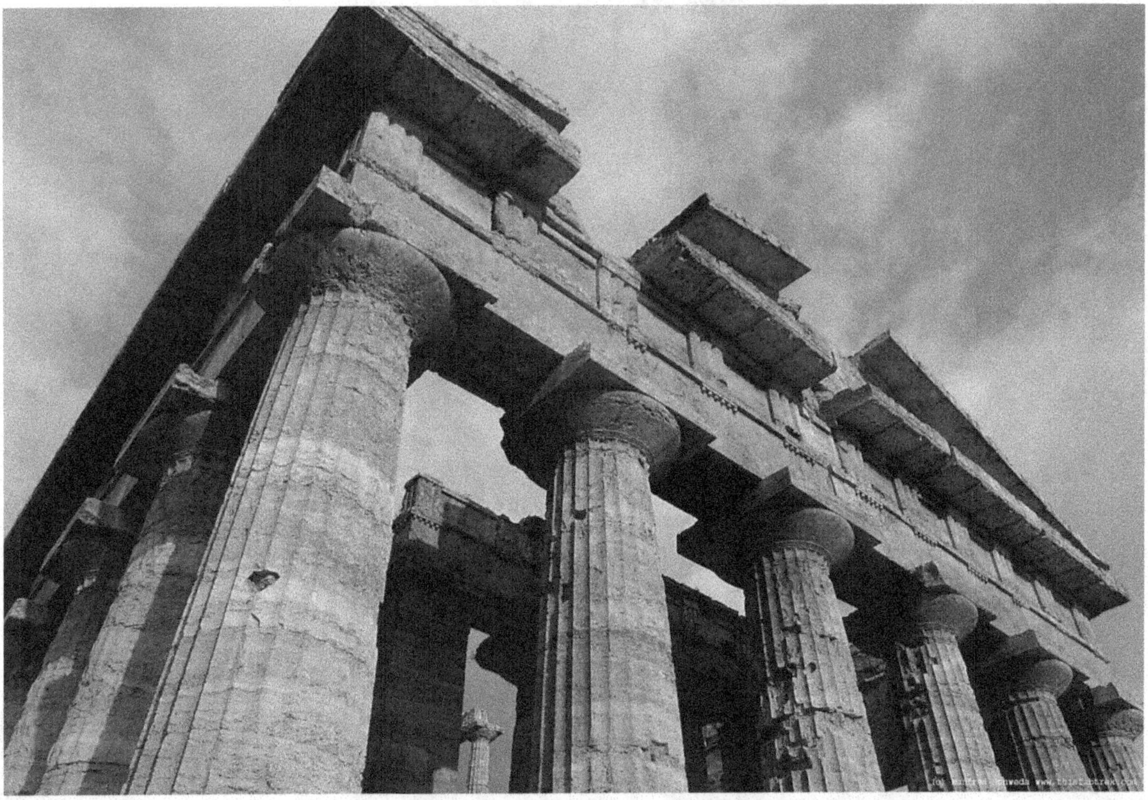

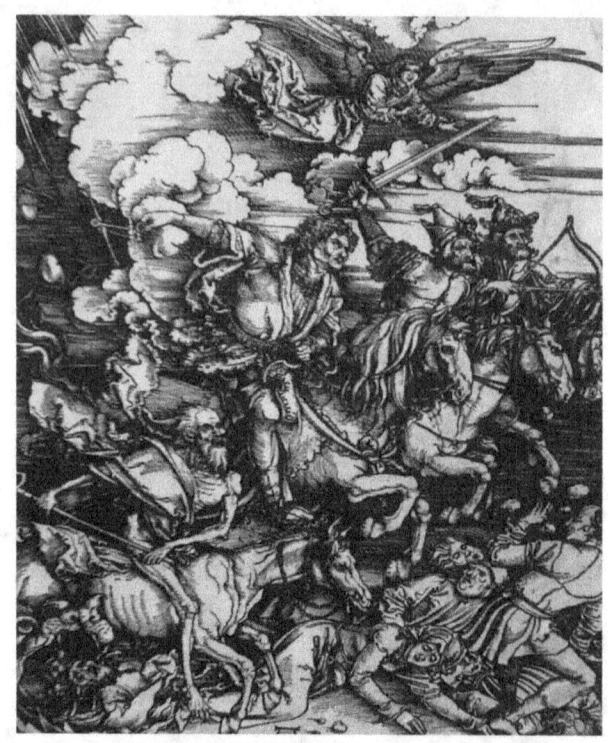

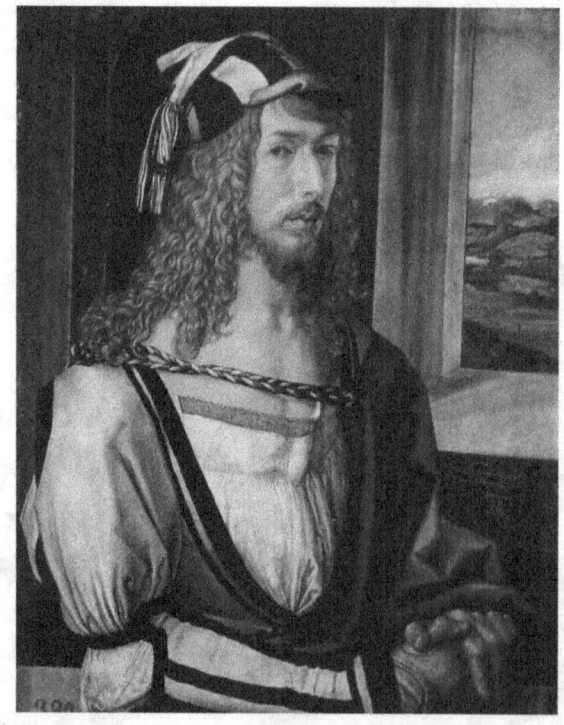

Albrecht Dürer

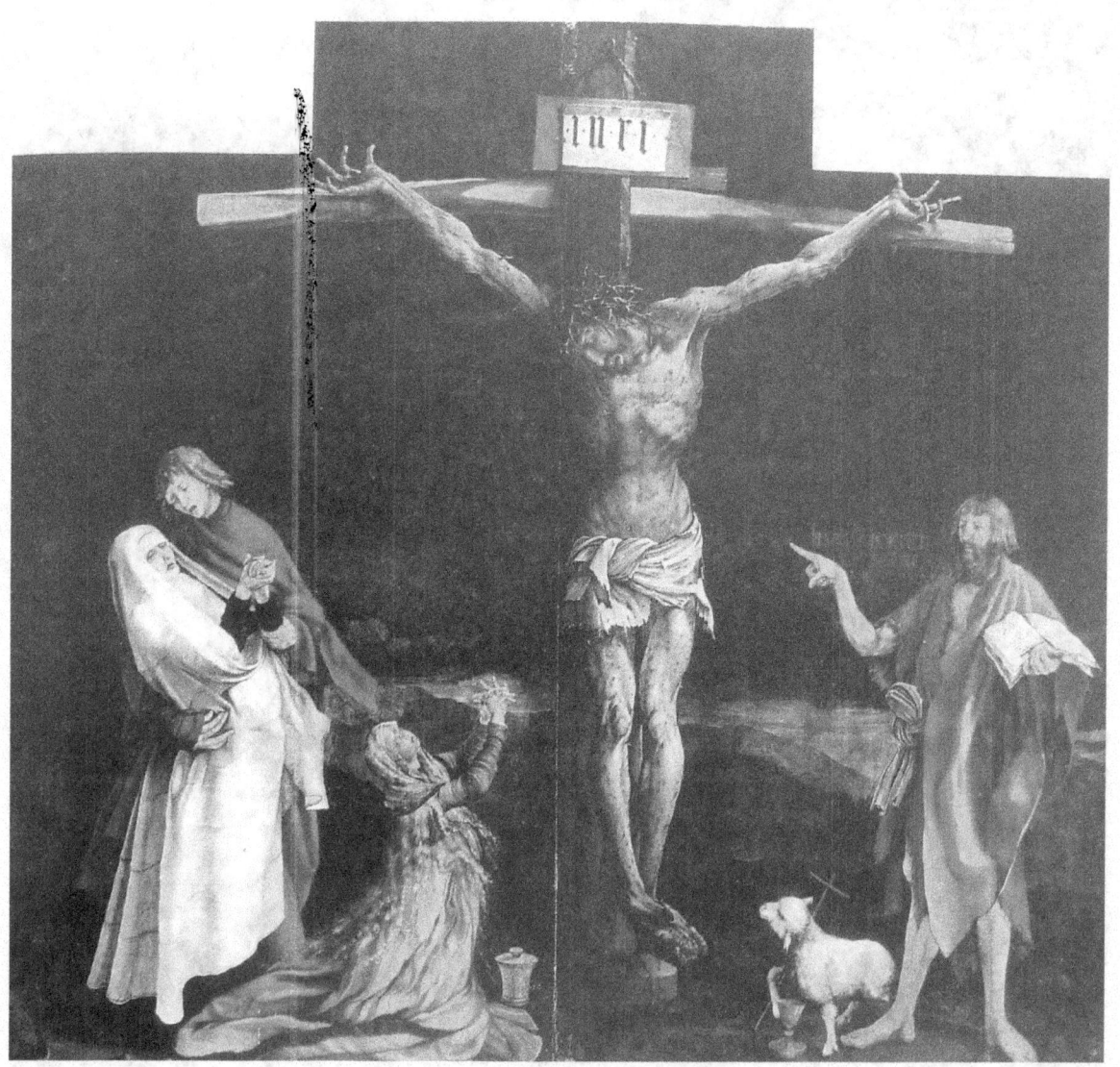

Matthias Grünewald, Crucifixion, Isenheim Altarpiece

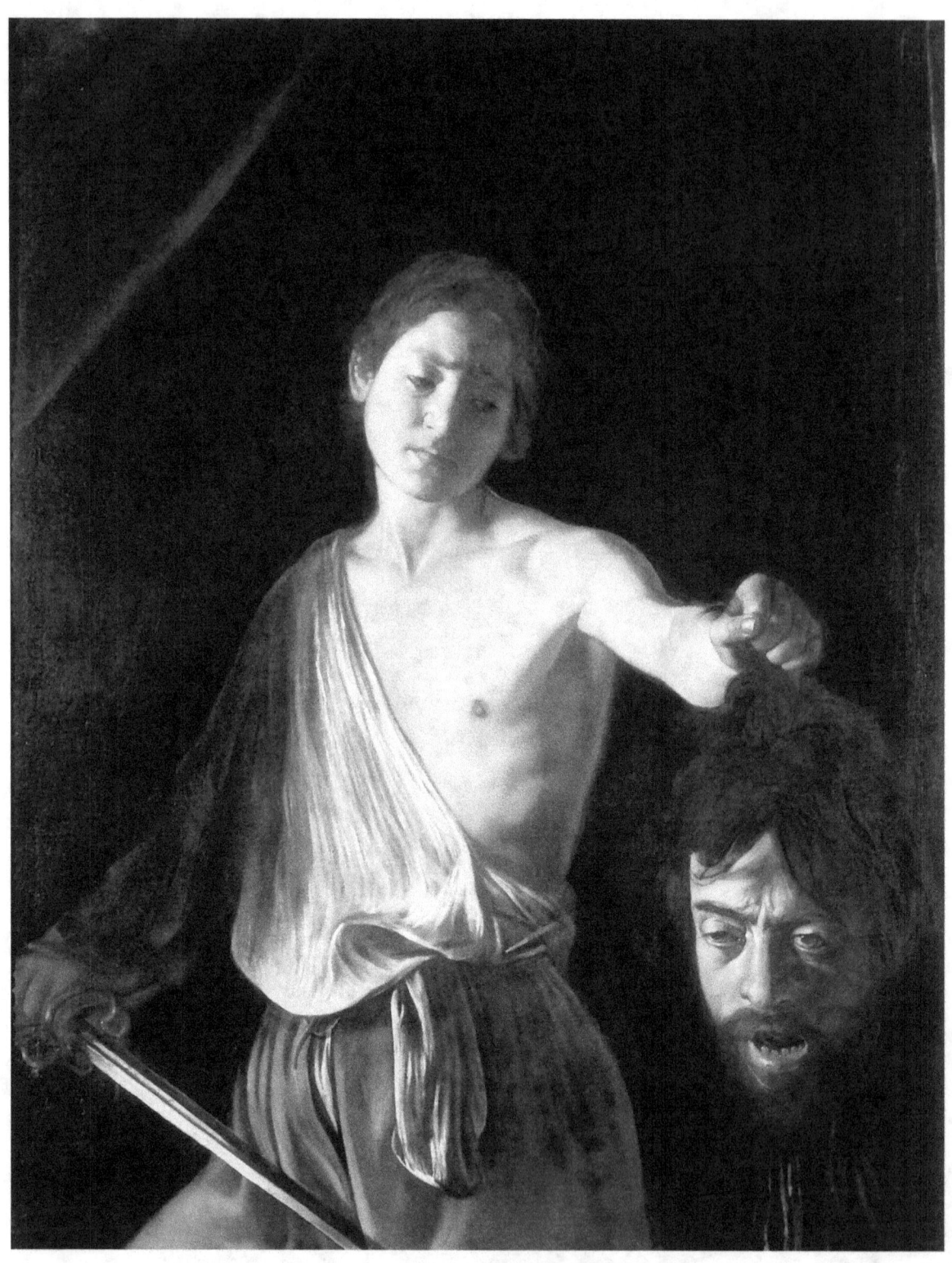

Michelangelo Merisi da Caravaggio, David With the Head of Goliath,
1605-06, Galleria Borghese, Rome

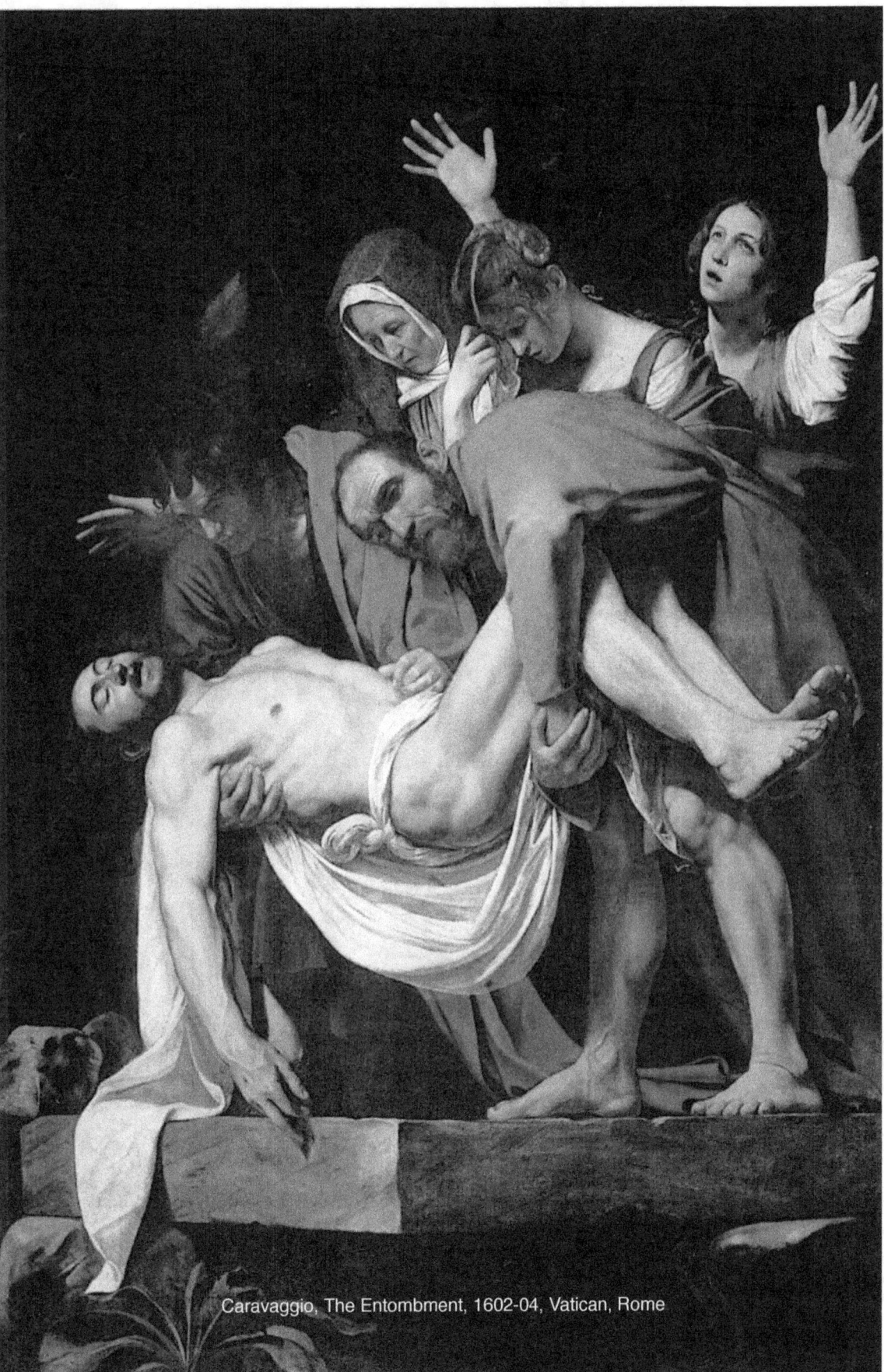

Caravaggio, The Entombment, 1602-04, Vatican, Rome

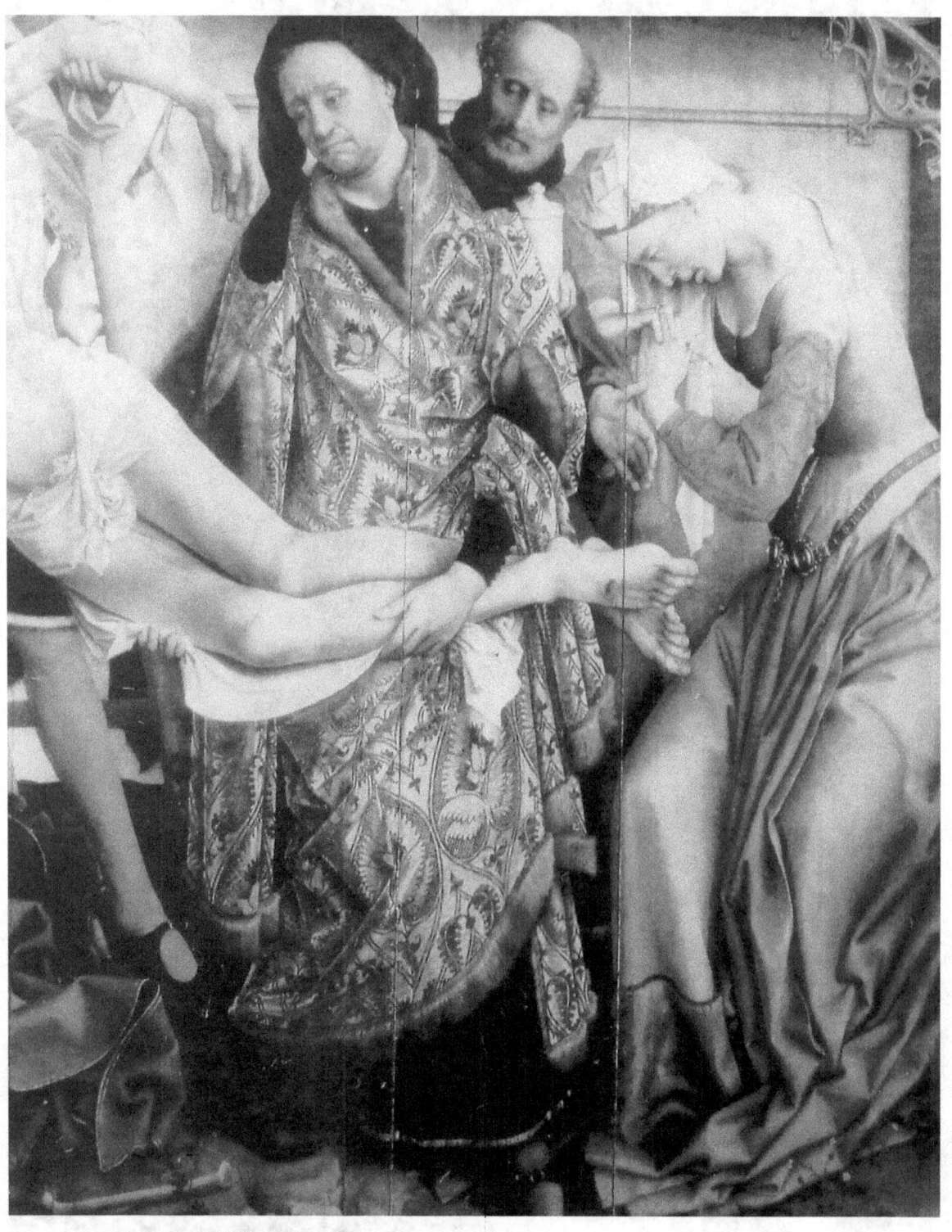

Rogier van der Weyden, Descent From the Cross, detail, Madrid

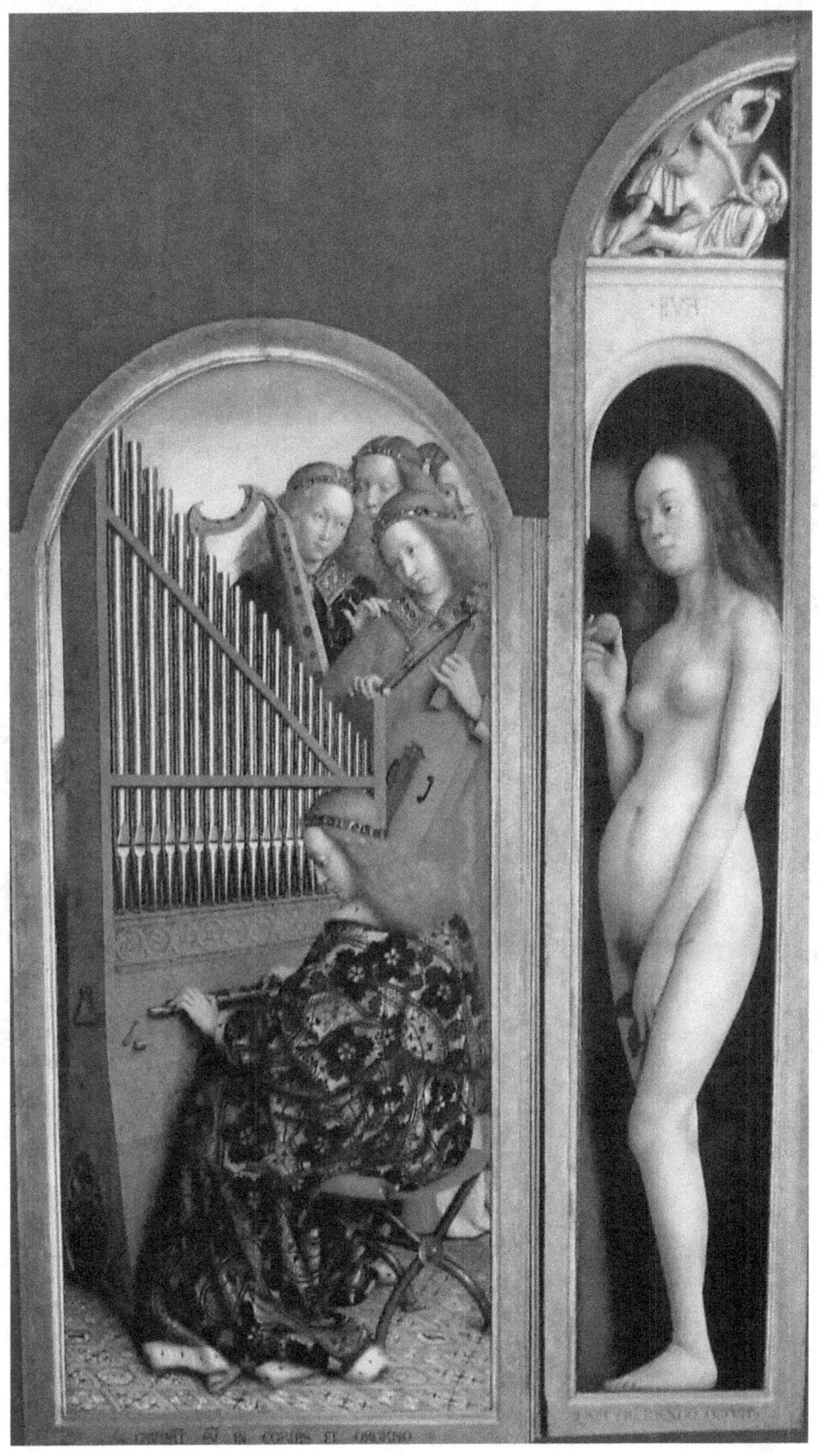

Jan van Eyck, The Ghent Altarpiece, wing

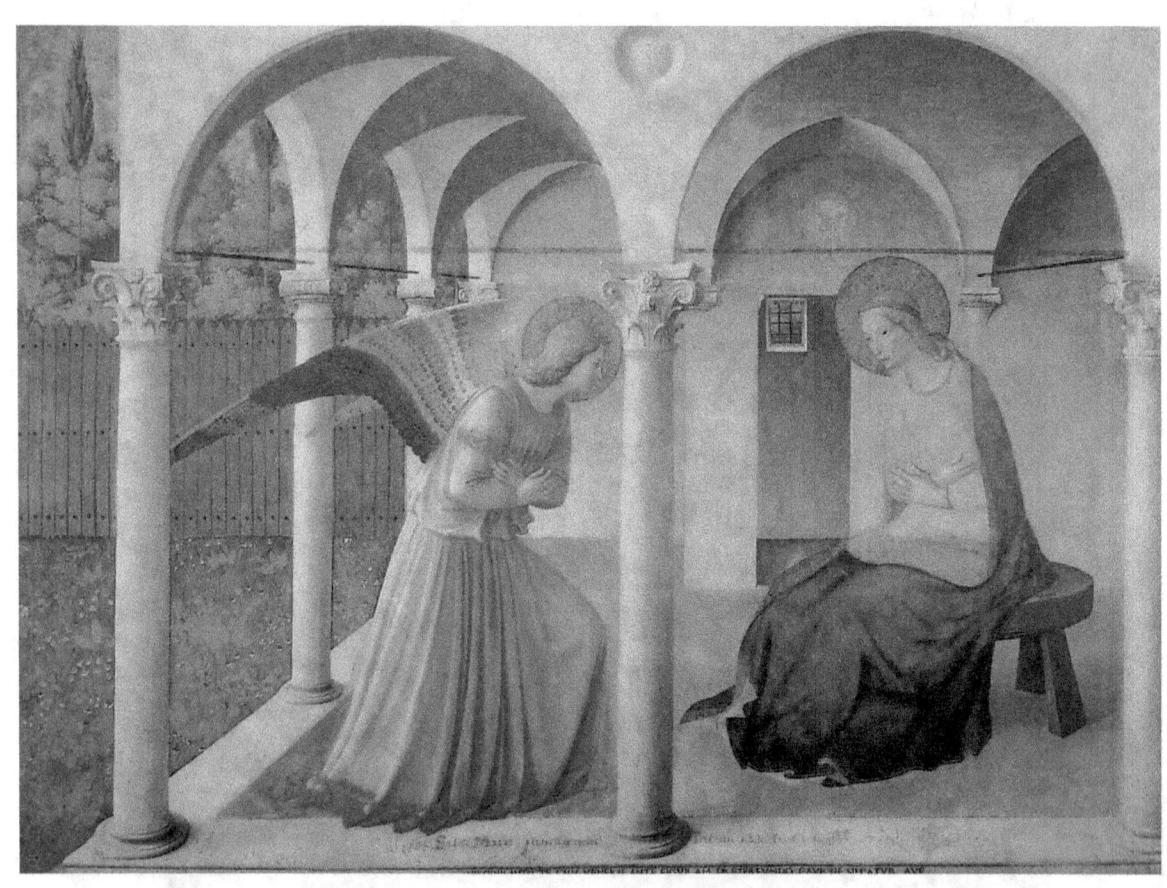

Fra Angelico, The Annunciation, San Marco, Florence

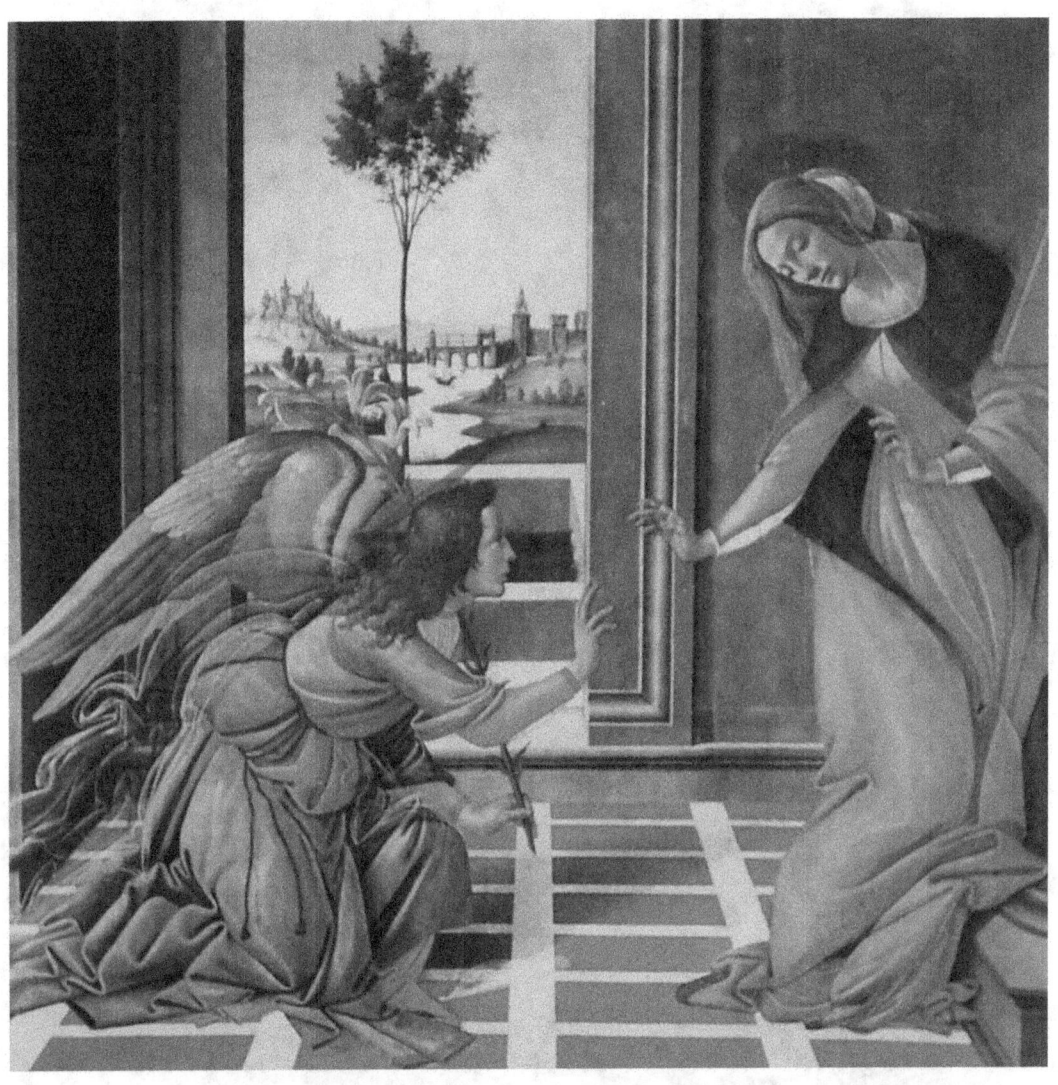

Sandro Botticelli, The Annunciation, Uffizi Gallery, Florence

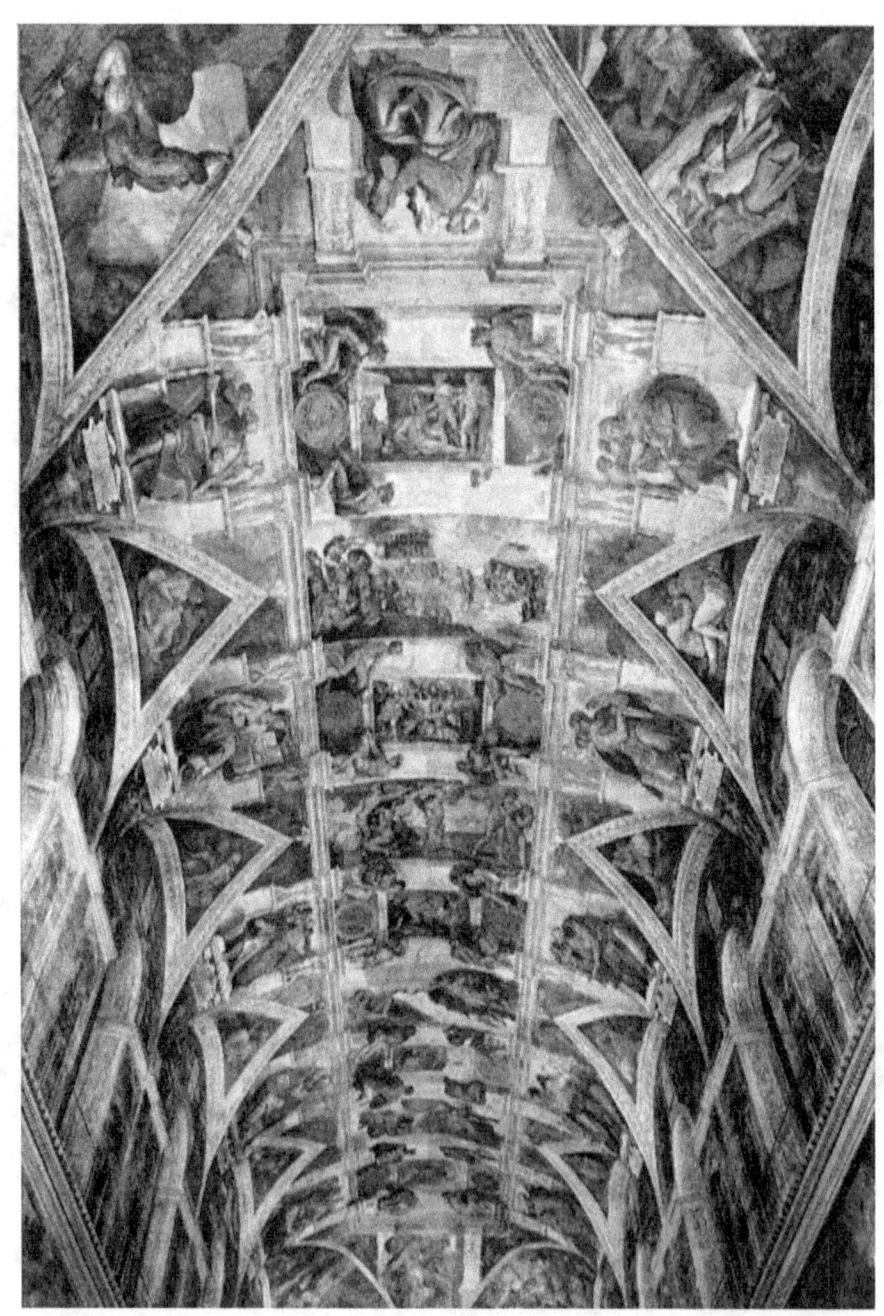

Michelangelo Buonaroti, Sistine Chapel Ceiling, Rome

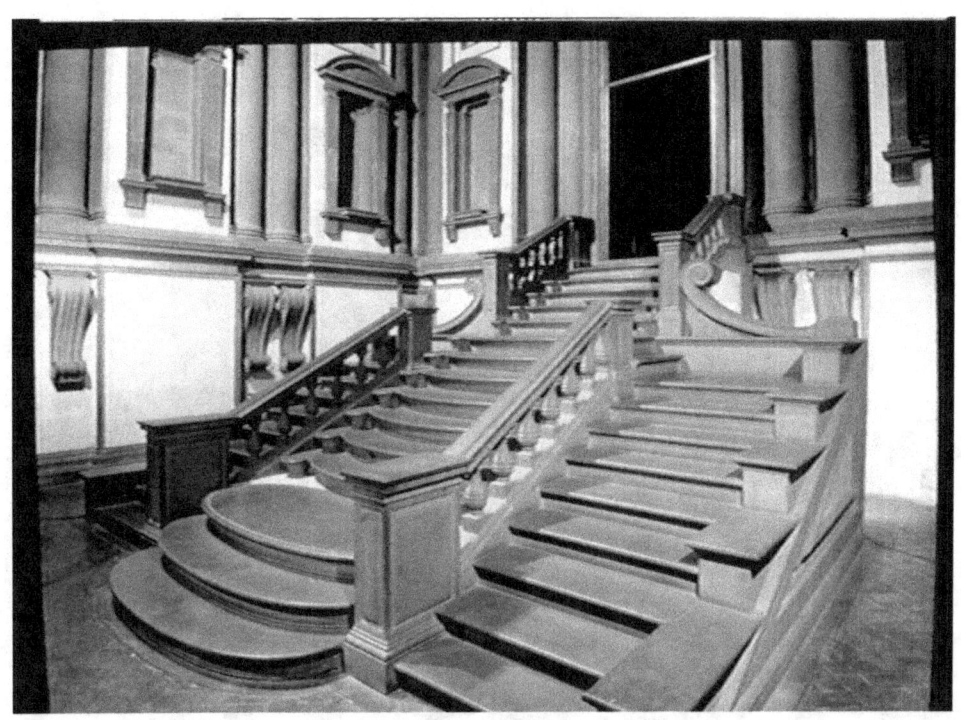

Michelangelo's Medici Library in Firenze. 1524-26
Michelangelo, Mark Rothko said:
'makes the viewers feel that they are trapped in a room where all the
doors and windows are bricked up, so that all they can do is butt their
heads forever against the wall.

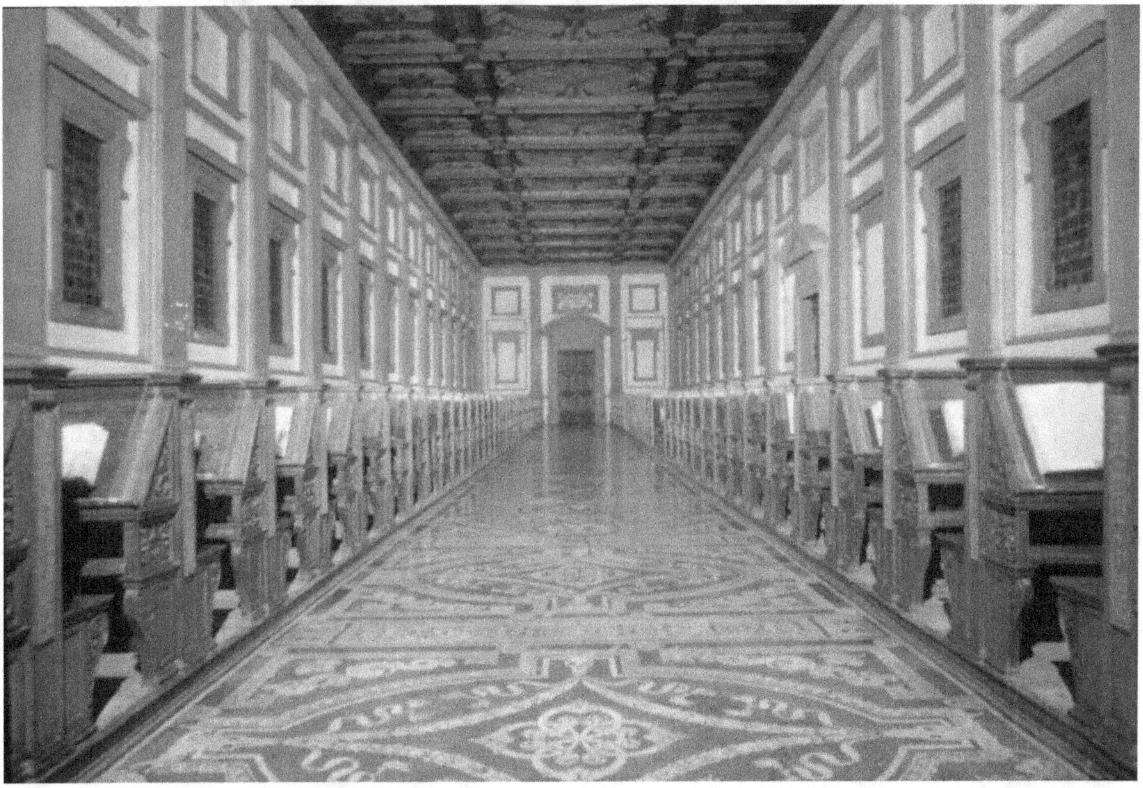

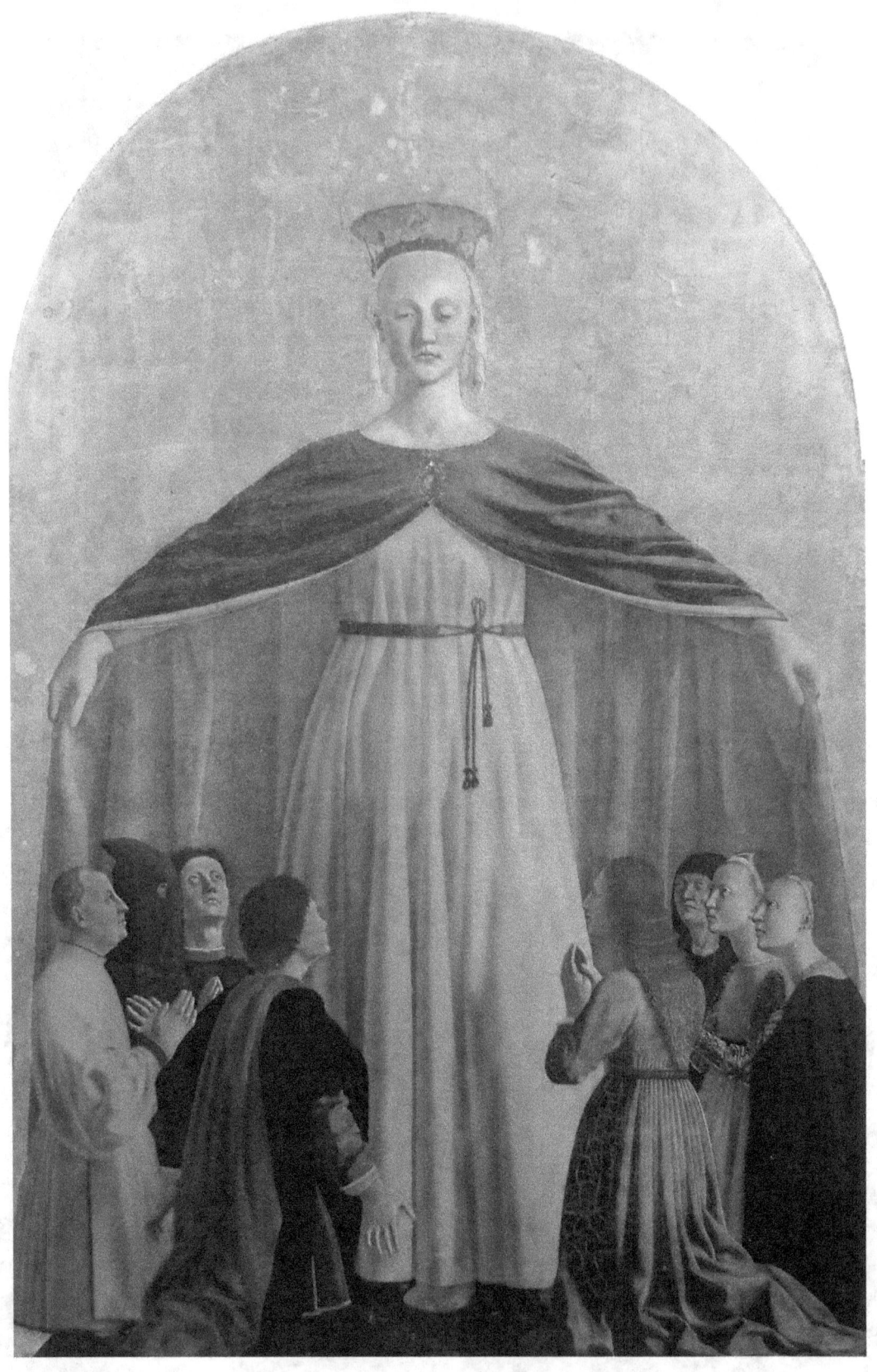

Piero, Madonna della Misericordia, Sanepulchro

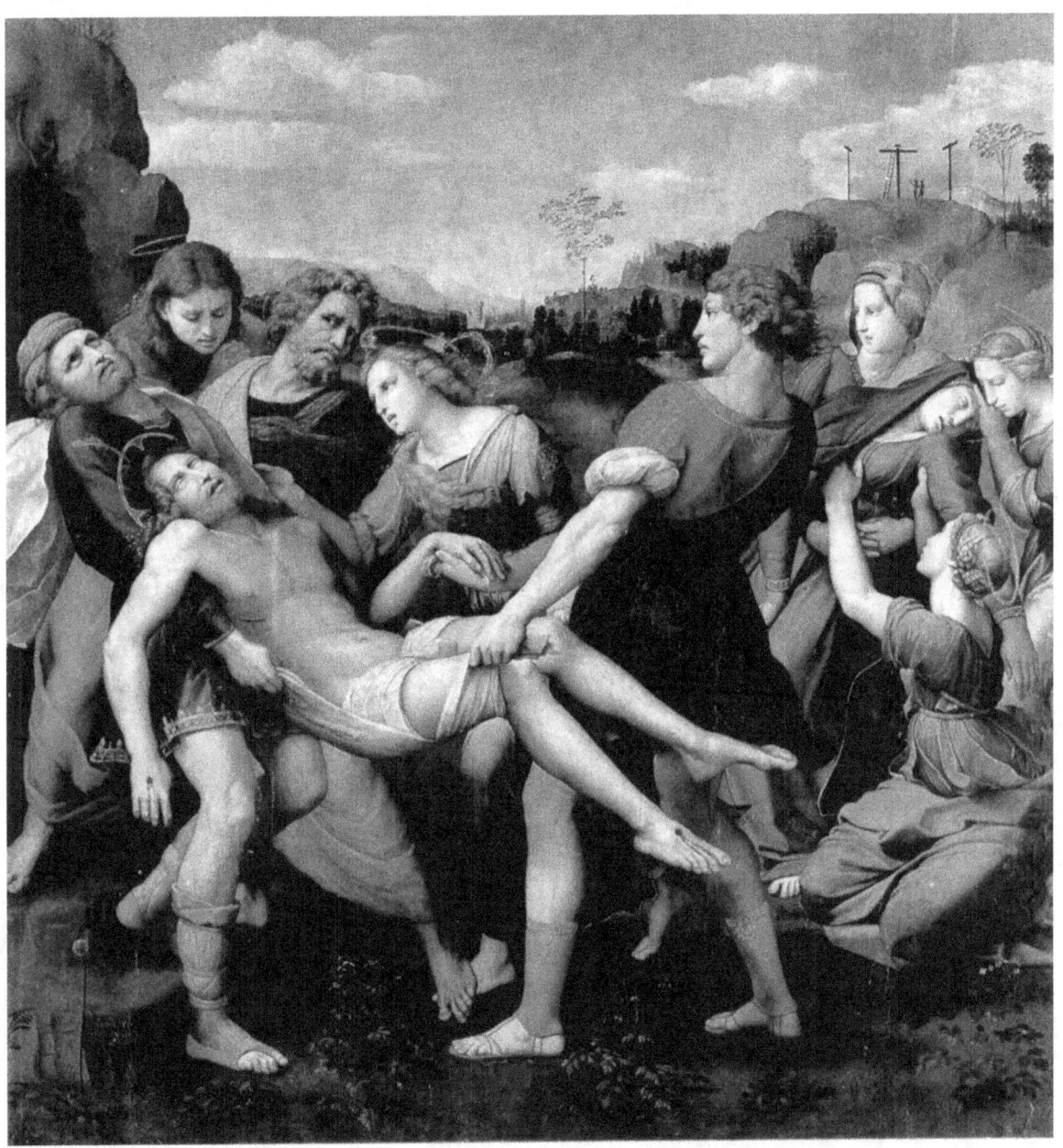

Raphael, The Descent From the Cross, Galleria Borghese, Rome

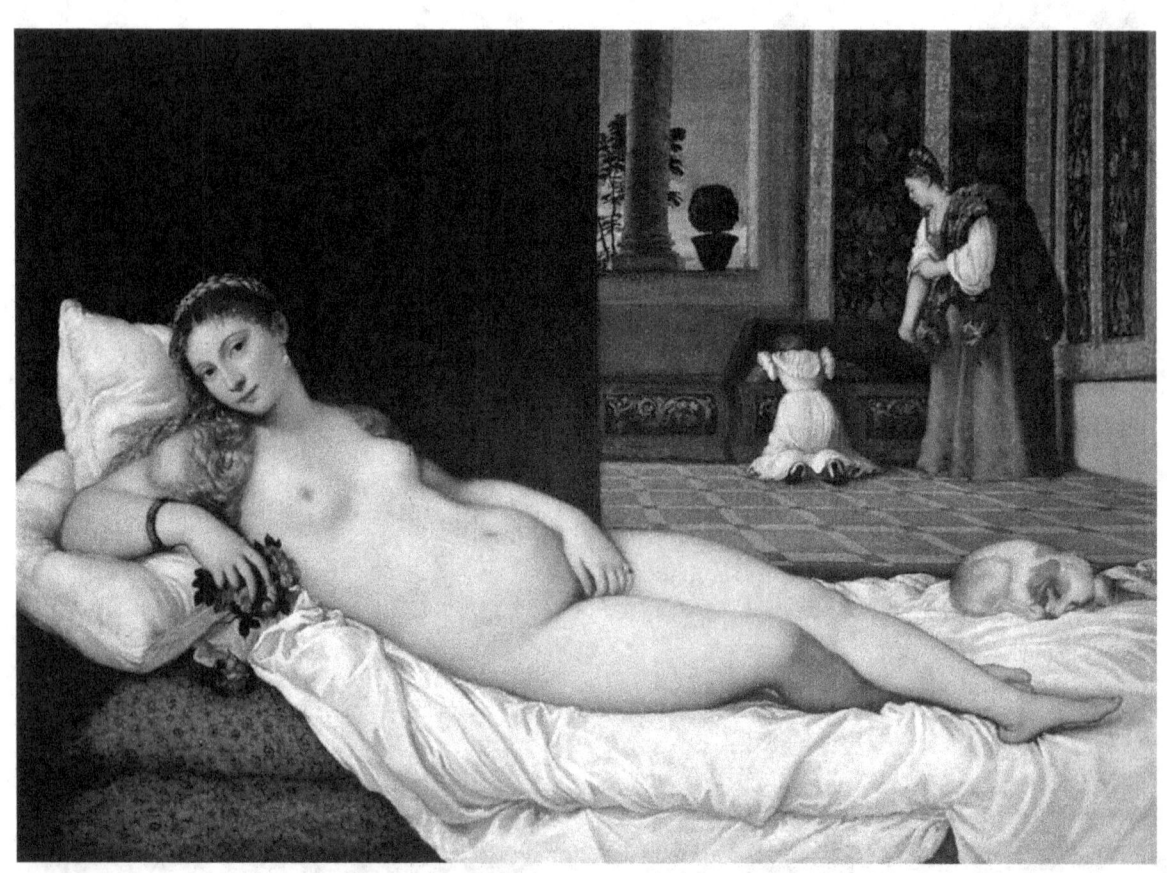

Titian, The Venus of Urbino, 1538, Uffizi, Florence

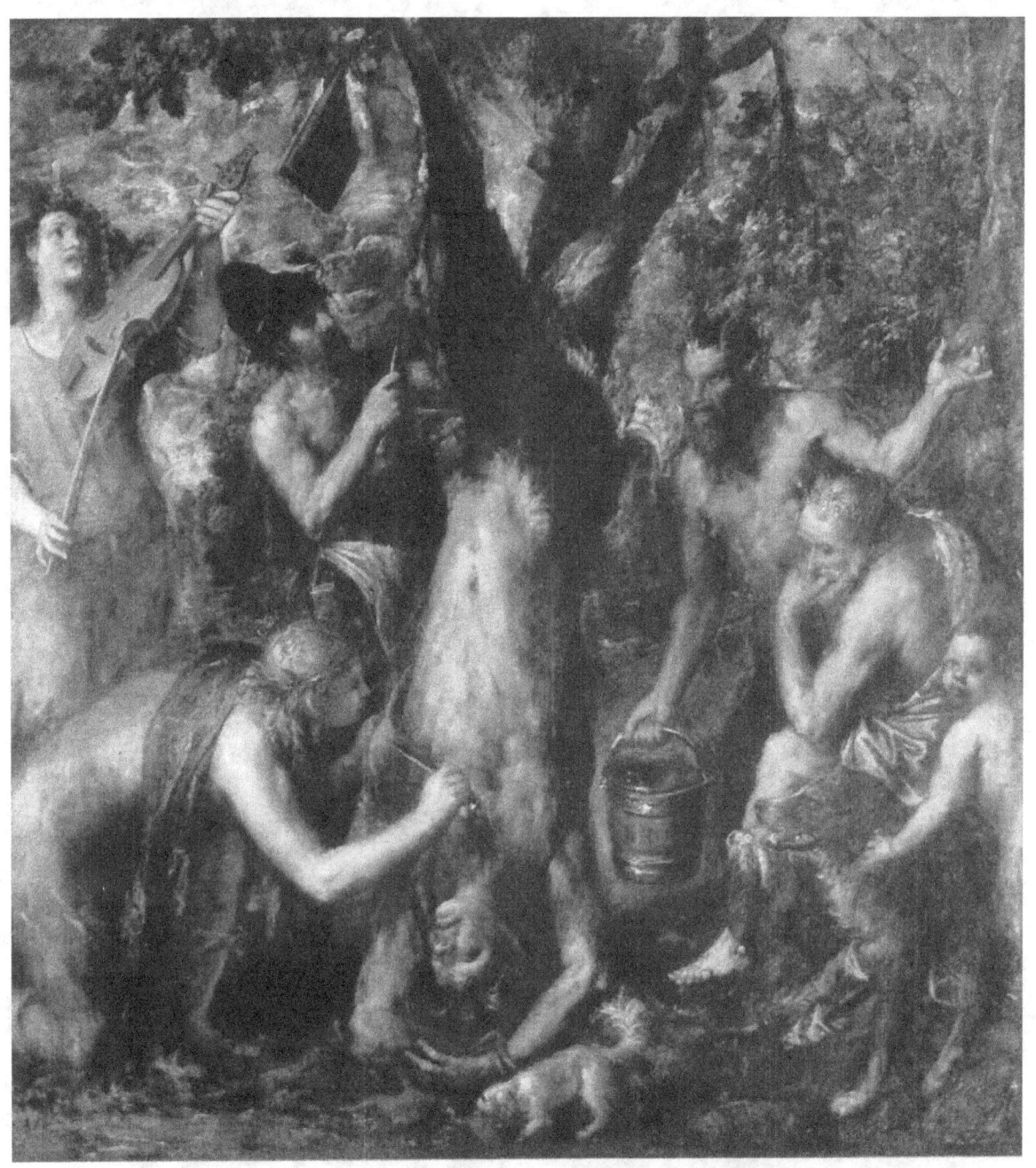

Titian, The Flaying of Marsyas, c. 1570-76, Kromeriz,

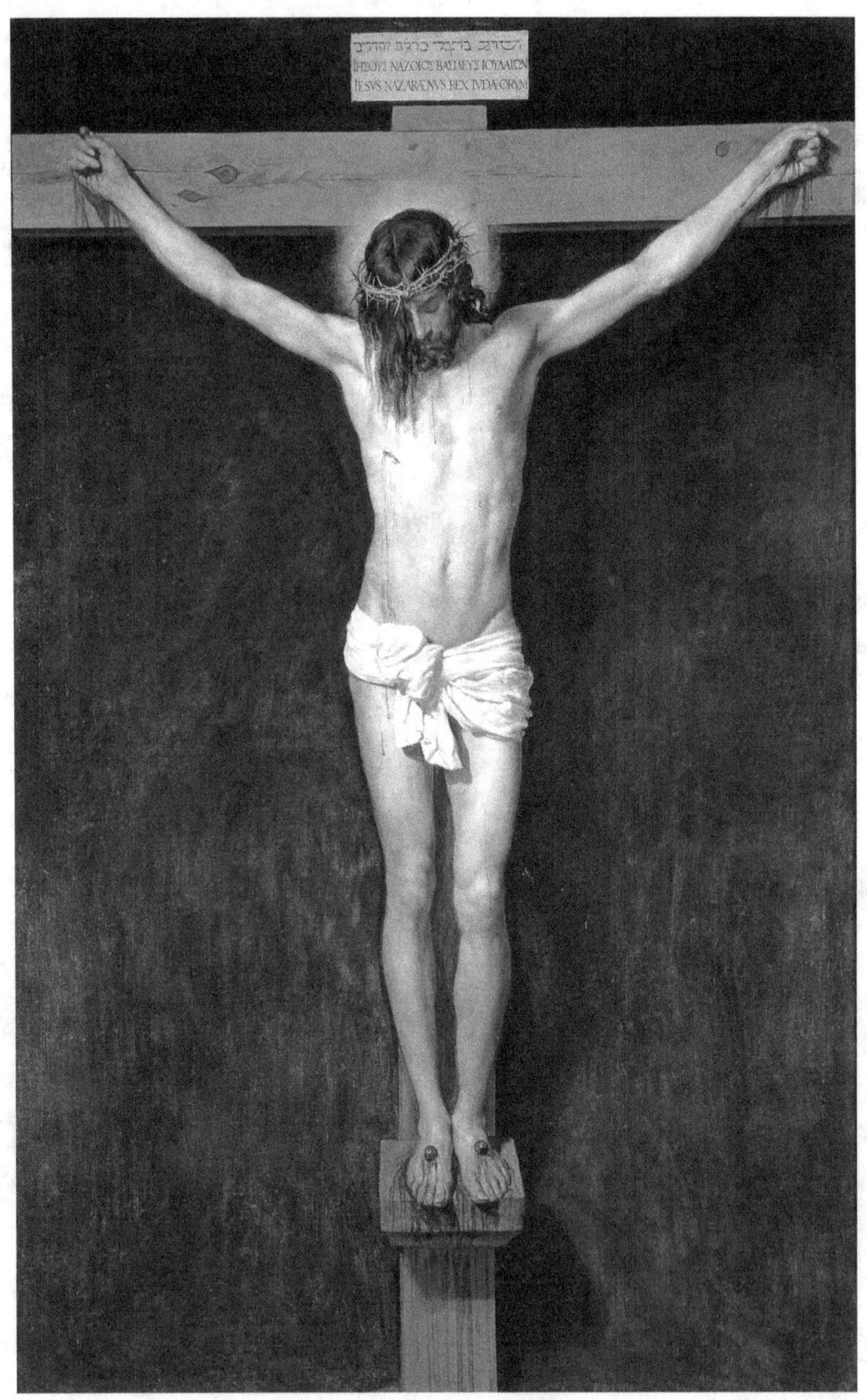

Diego Velásquez, Christ Crucified, 1632, Prado, Madrid

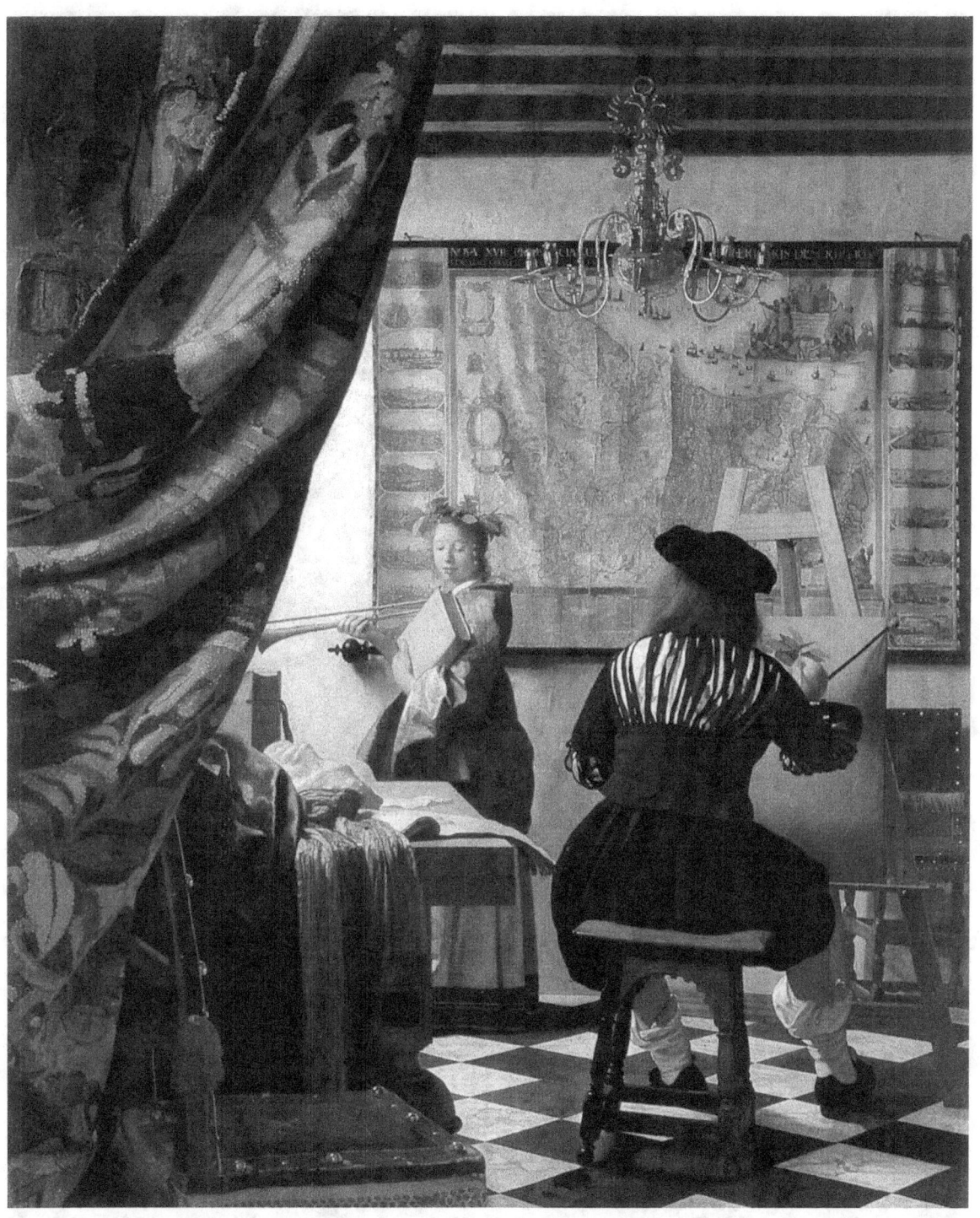

Jan Vermeer, The Allegory of Painting, 1666-67,Kunsthistoriches Museum, Vienna

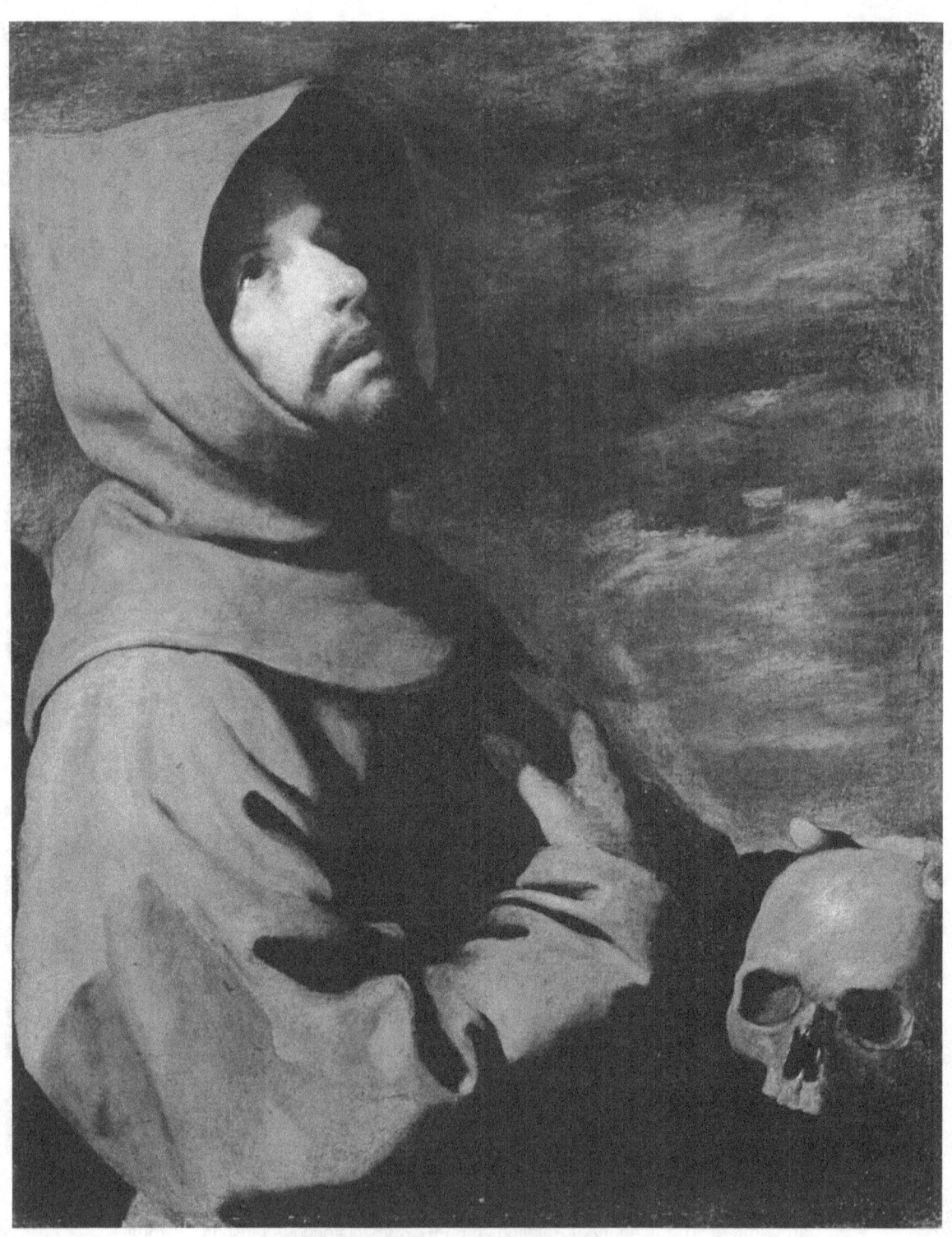

Francisco de Zurbarán, St Francis, Munich

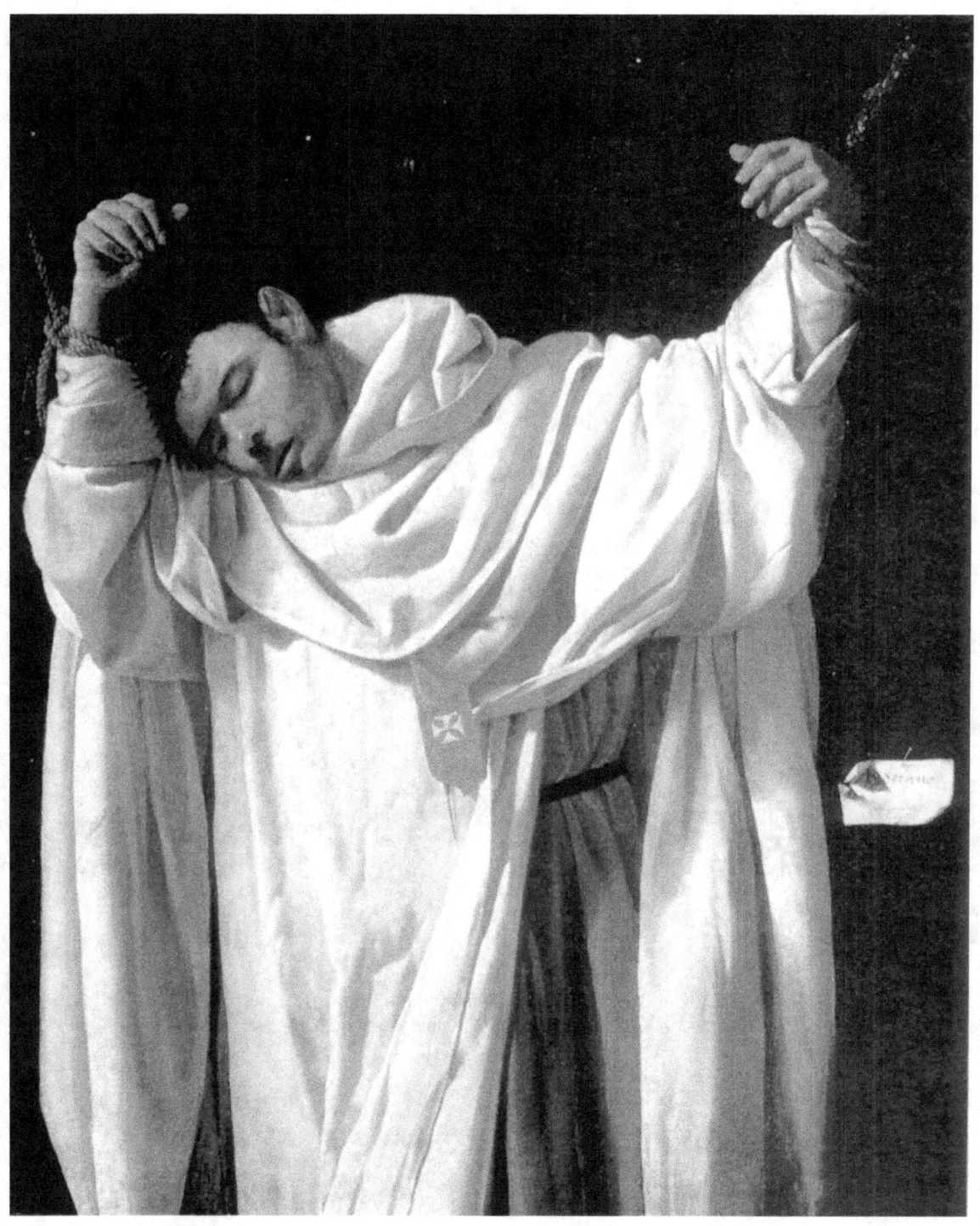

Francisco de Zurbarán, St Serapion, 1628, Hartford, Connecticut

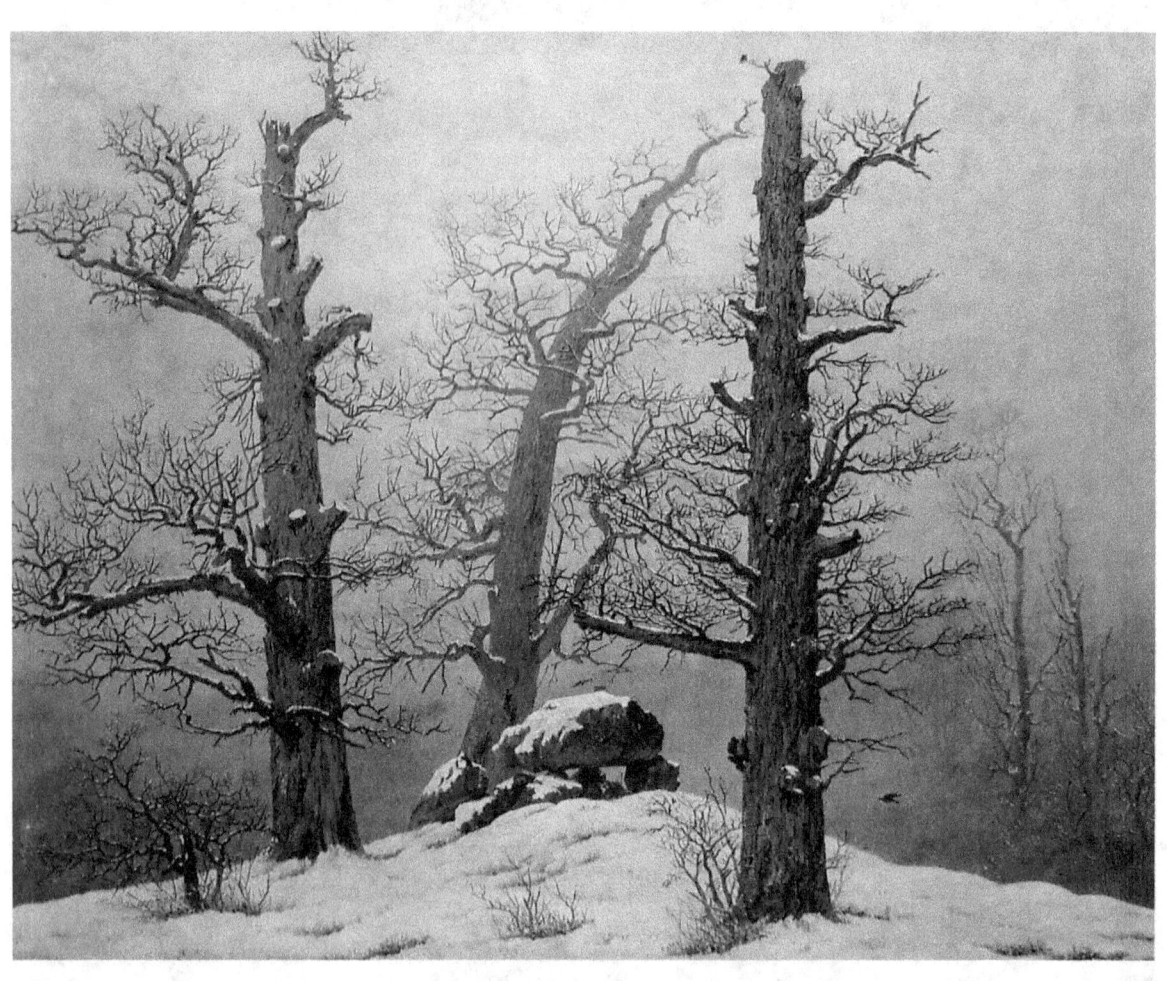

Caspar David Friedrich, Dolmen In the Snow, 1807,
Staatliche Kunstsammlungen, Gemäldesgalerie, Dresden

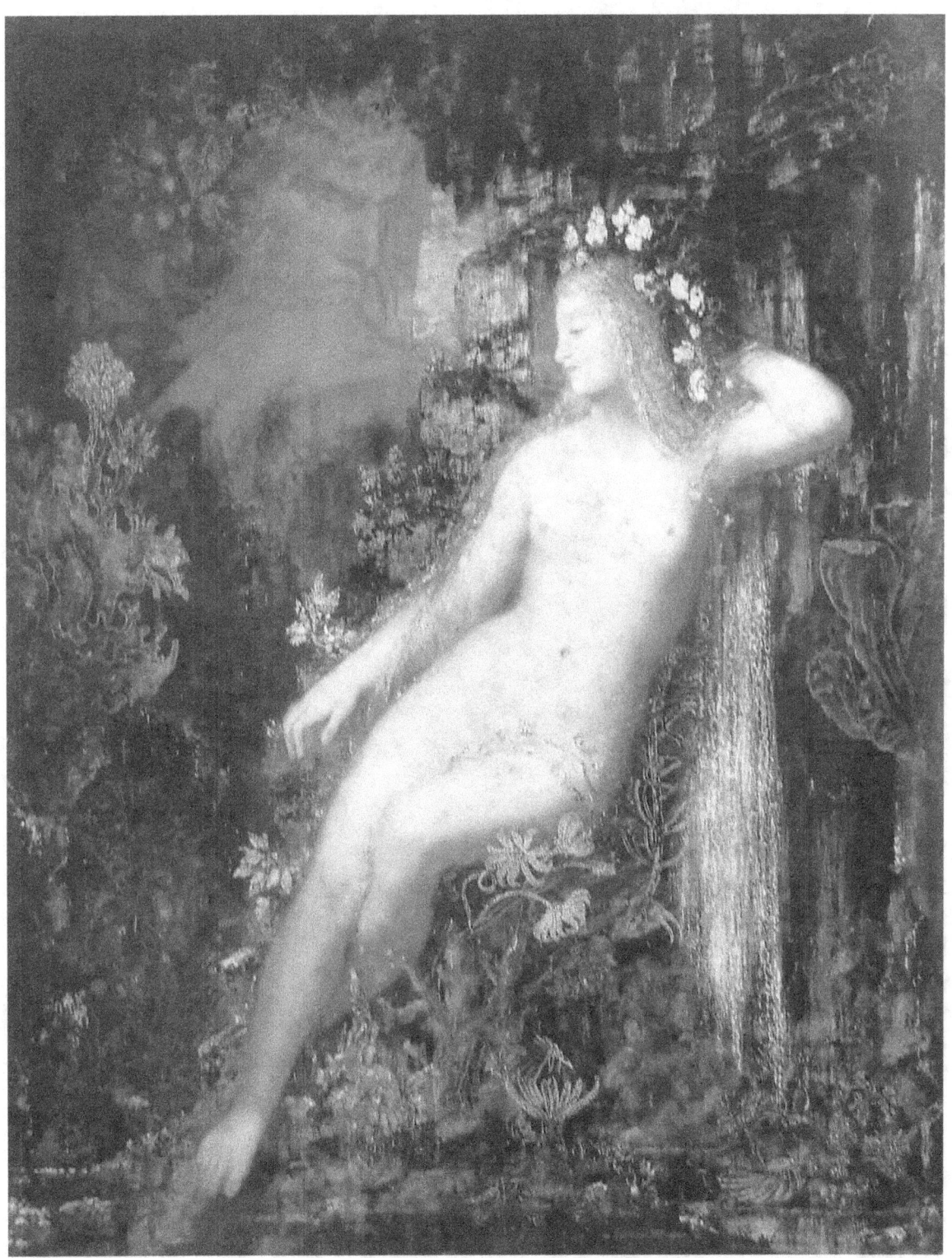

Gustave Moreau, Galatea, 1880

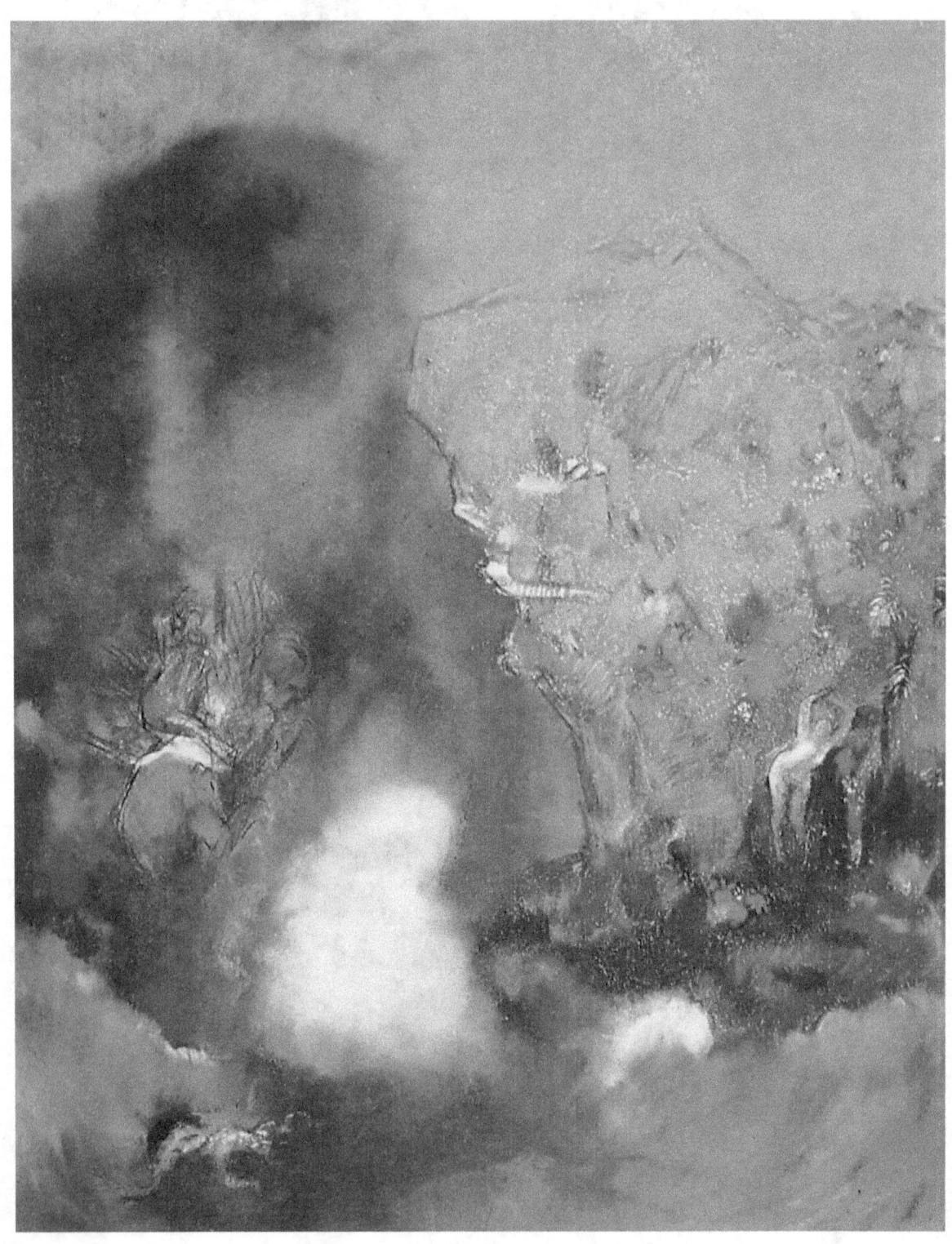

Odilon Redon, Roger and Angelica, c. 1910,
Museum of Modern Art, New York

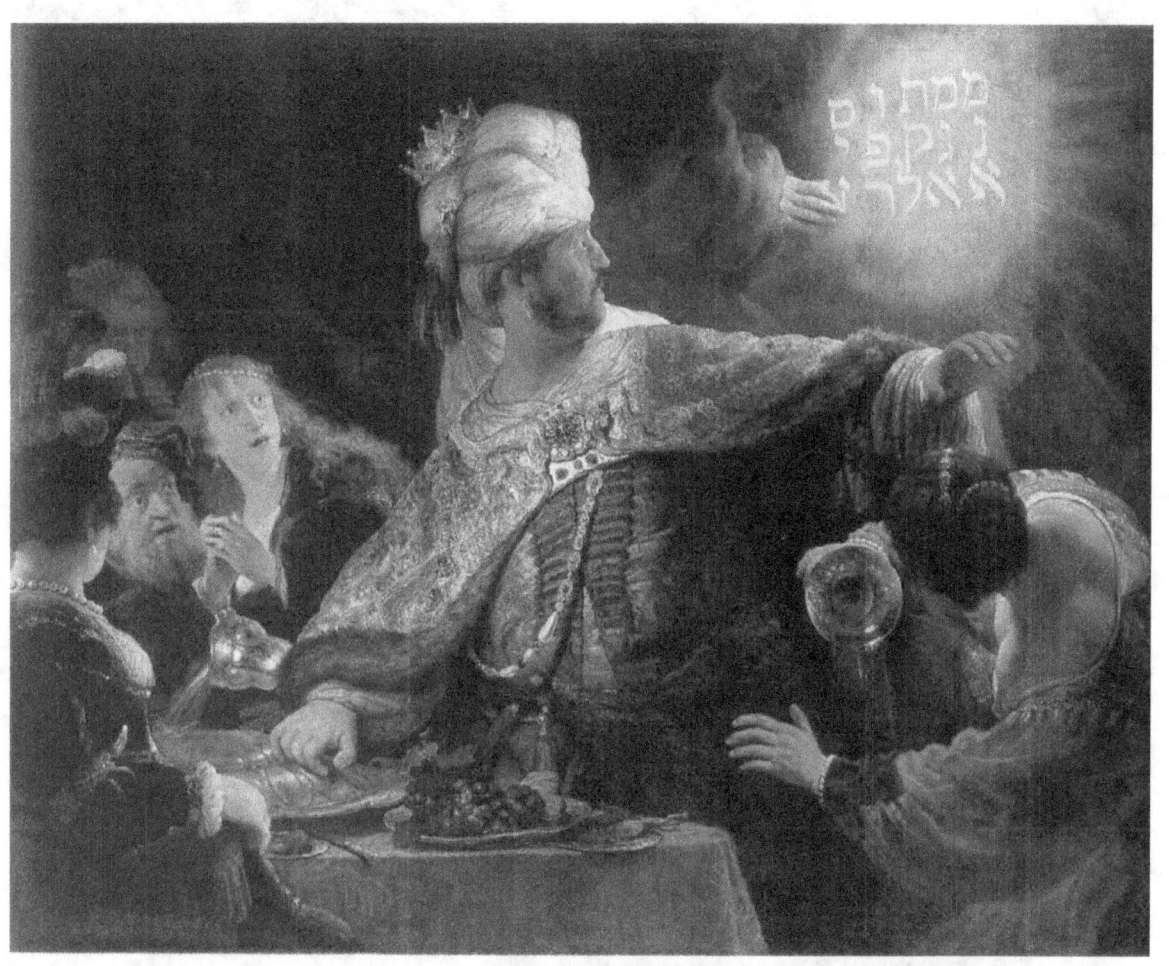

Rembrandt van Rijn, Belshazzar's Feast, 1635, National Gallery, London

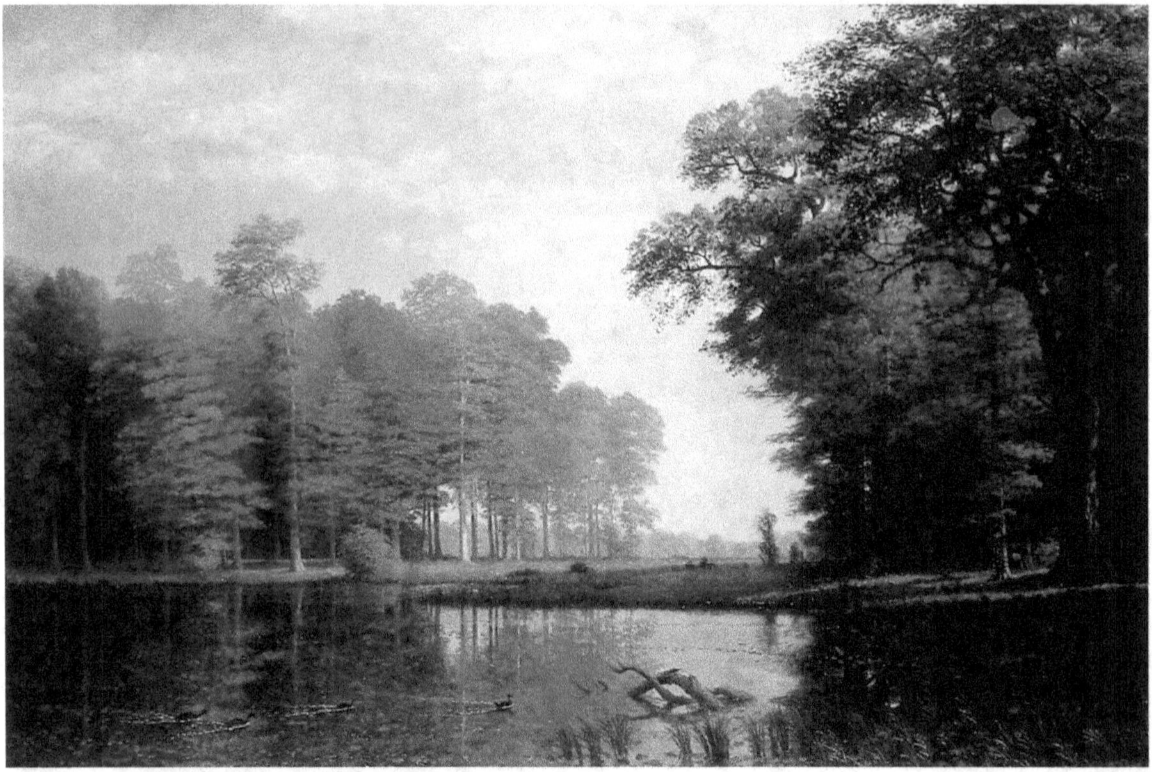

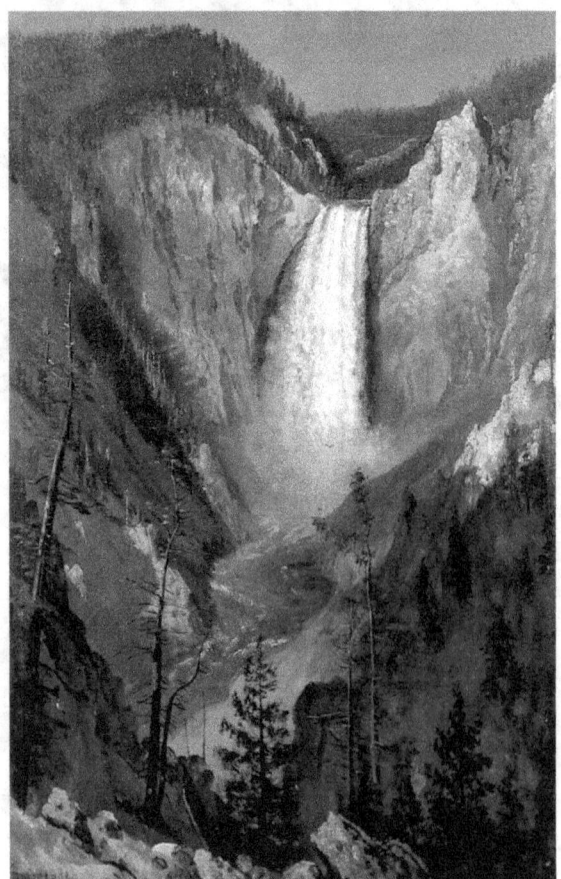

Albert Bierstadt,
Autumn Woods (above), and
Lower Yellowstone Falls (left).

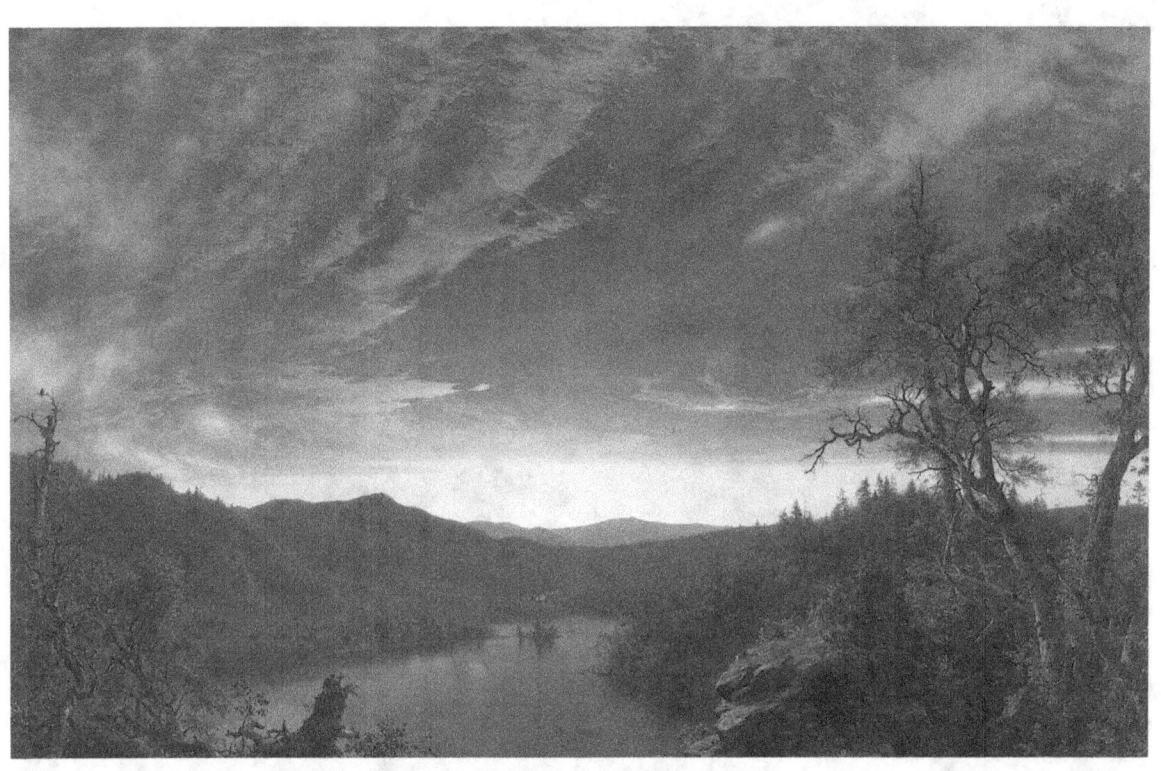

Frederic Edwin Church, Twilight In the Wildnerness, 1860,
Cleveland Museum of Art

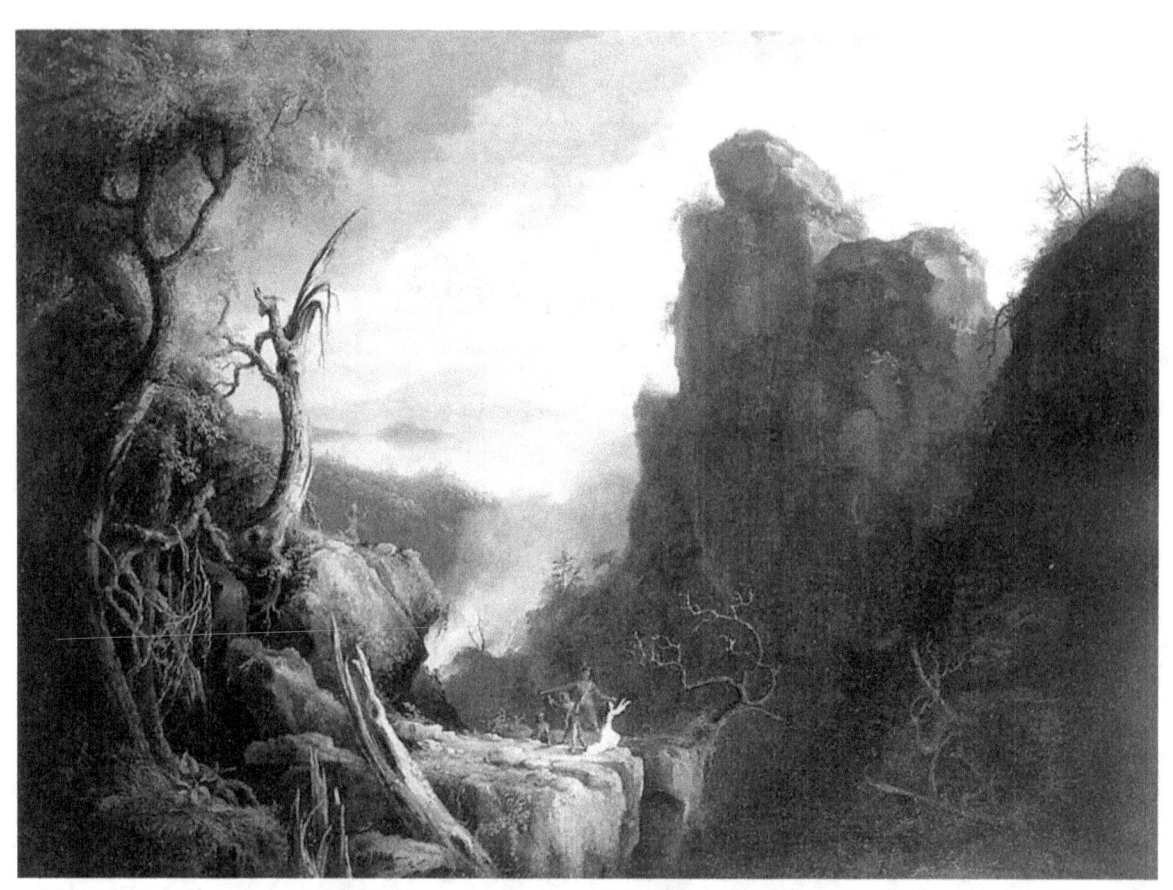

Thomas Cole, Indian Sacrifice, 1826

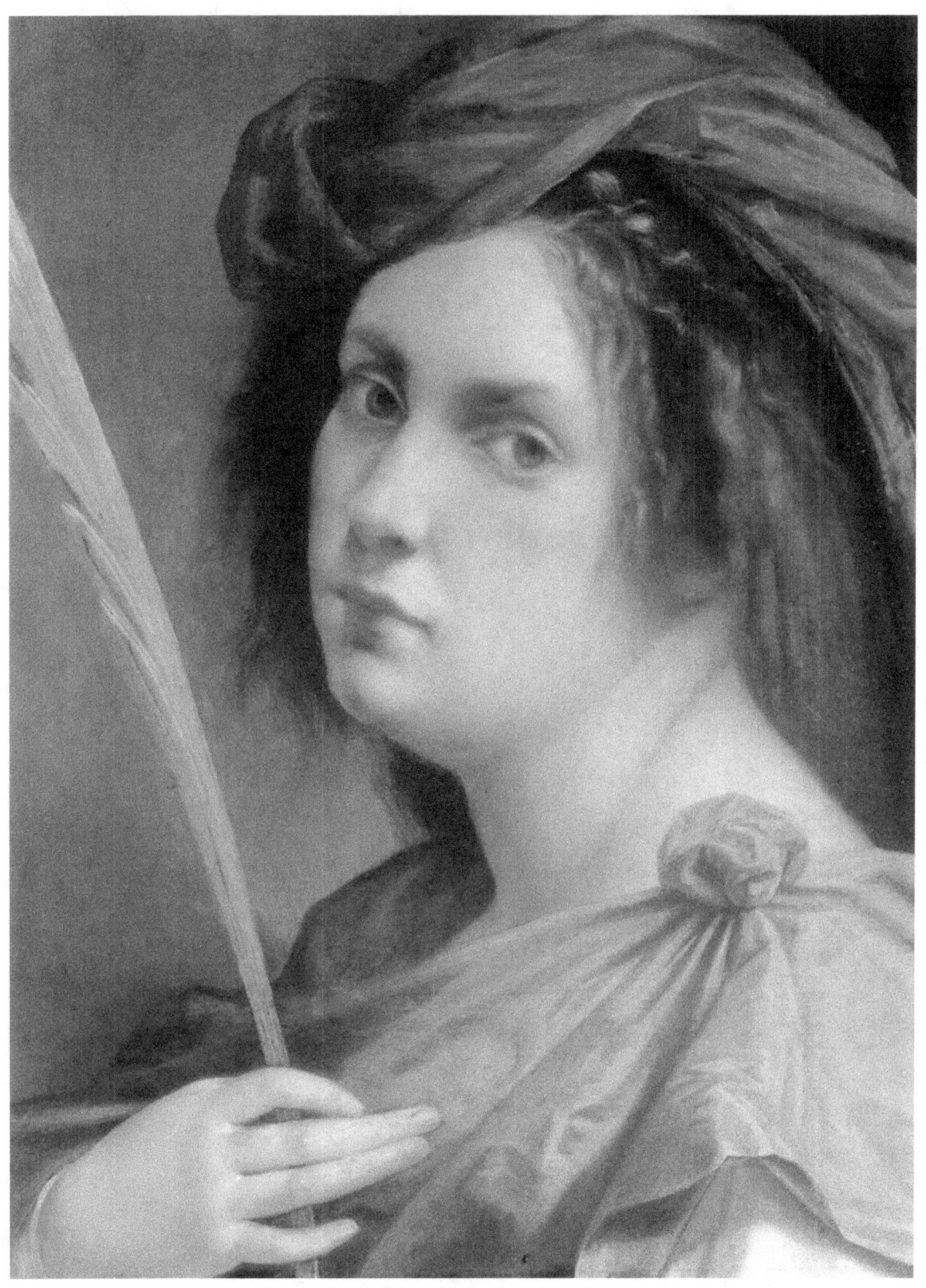

Artemisia Gentileshi, Self-Portrait as a Martyr, 1615

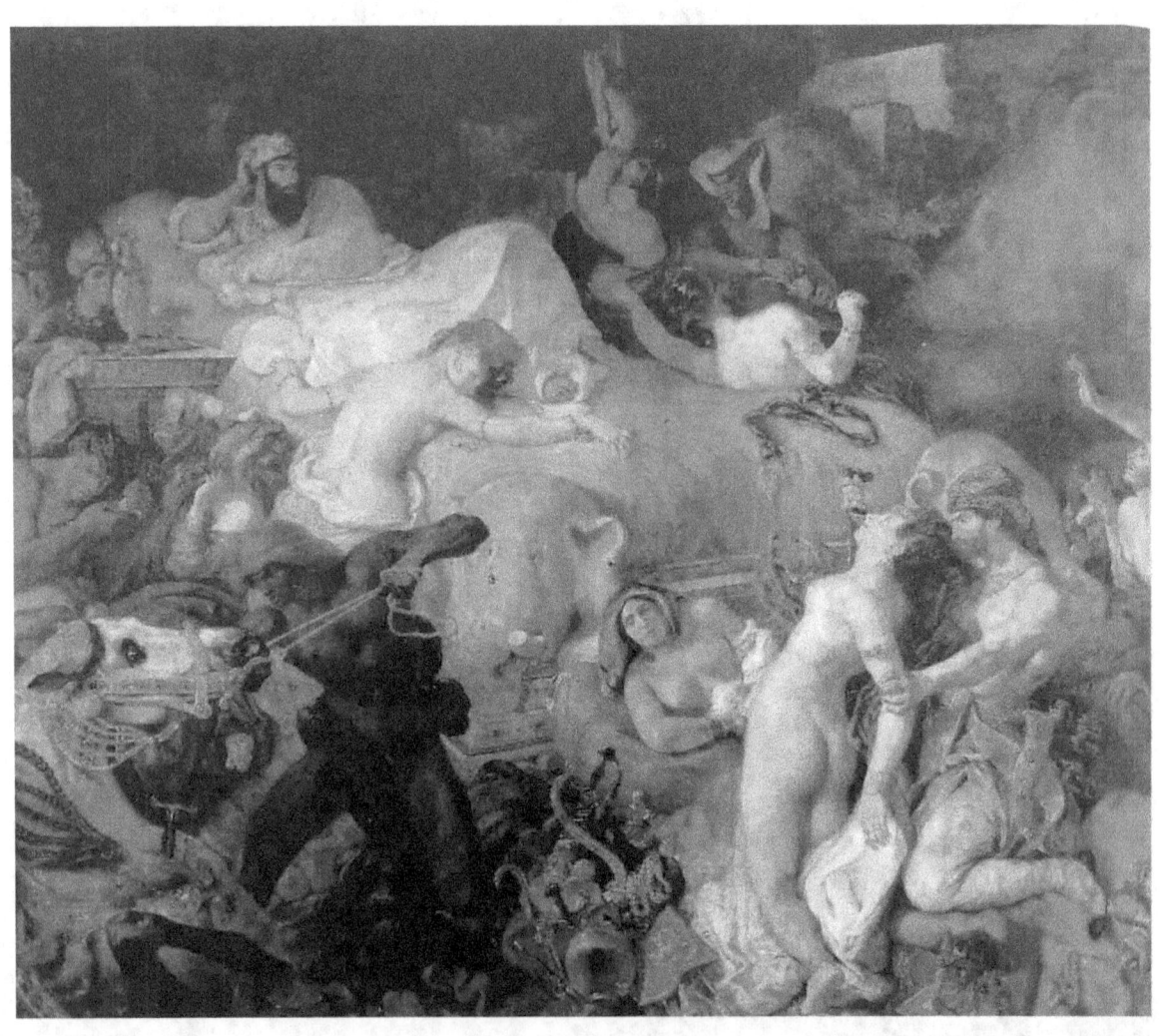

Eugene Delacroix, The Death of Sardanapalus, 1827

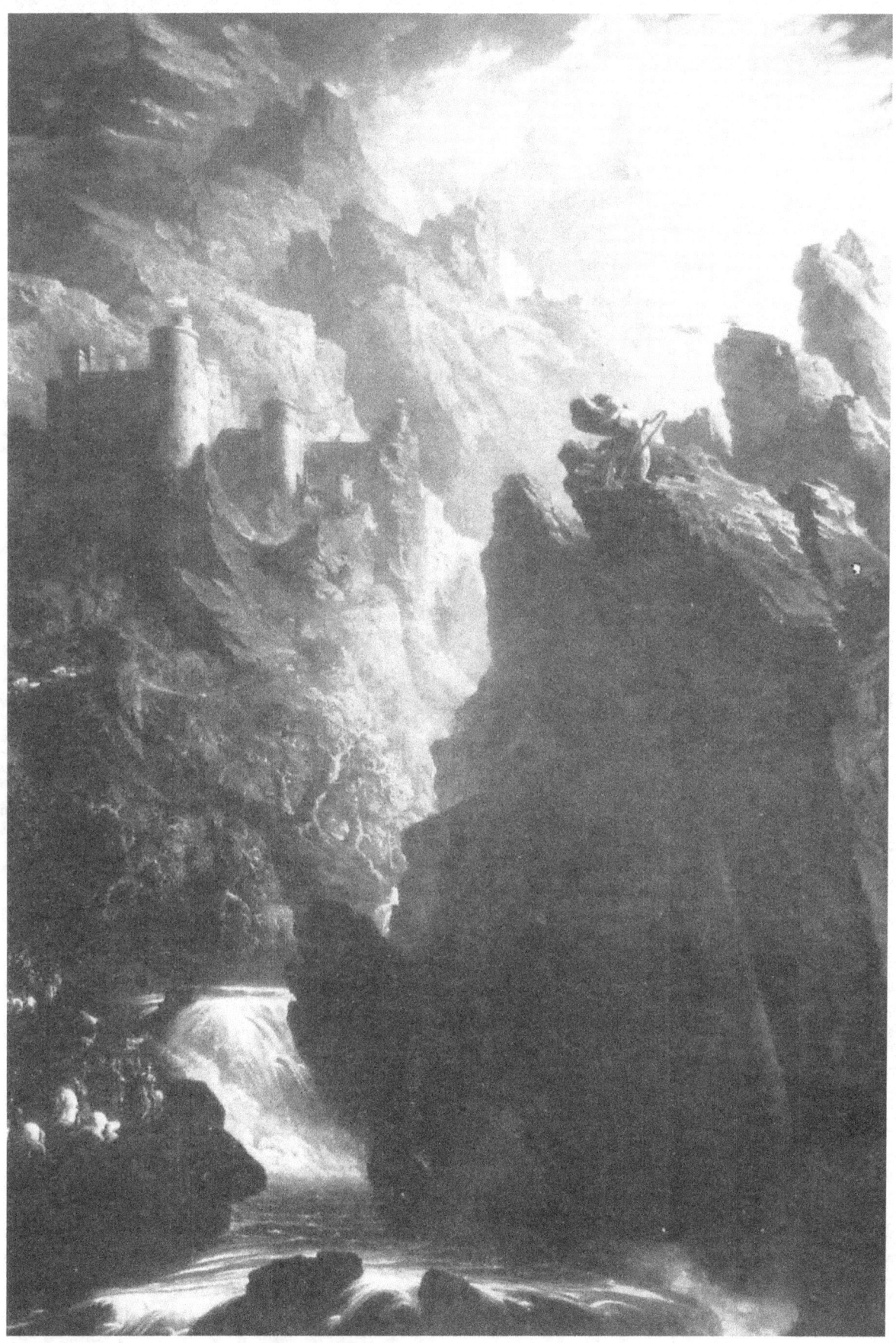

John Martin, The Bard, 1817

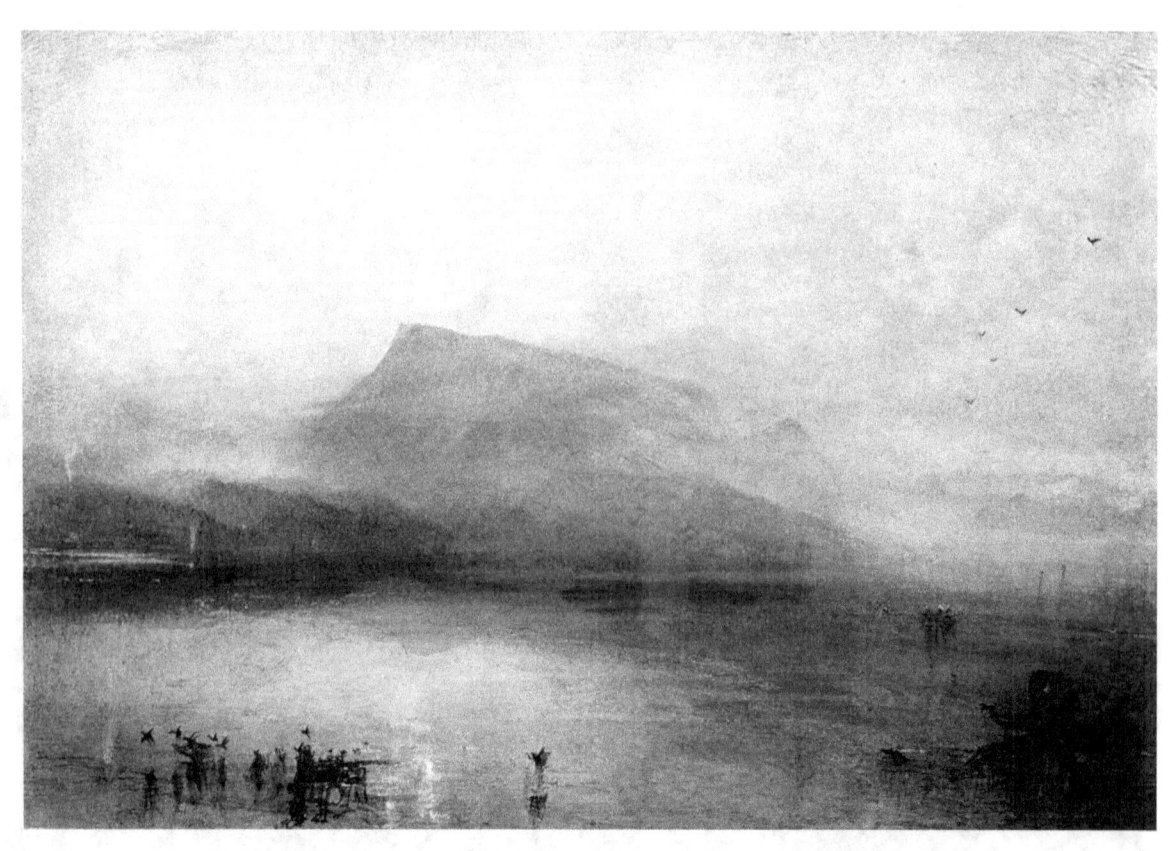

J.M.W. Turner, The Blue Rigi, Lake of Lucerne, Sunrise,
1842, Clore Gallery, London

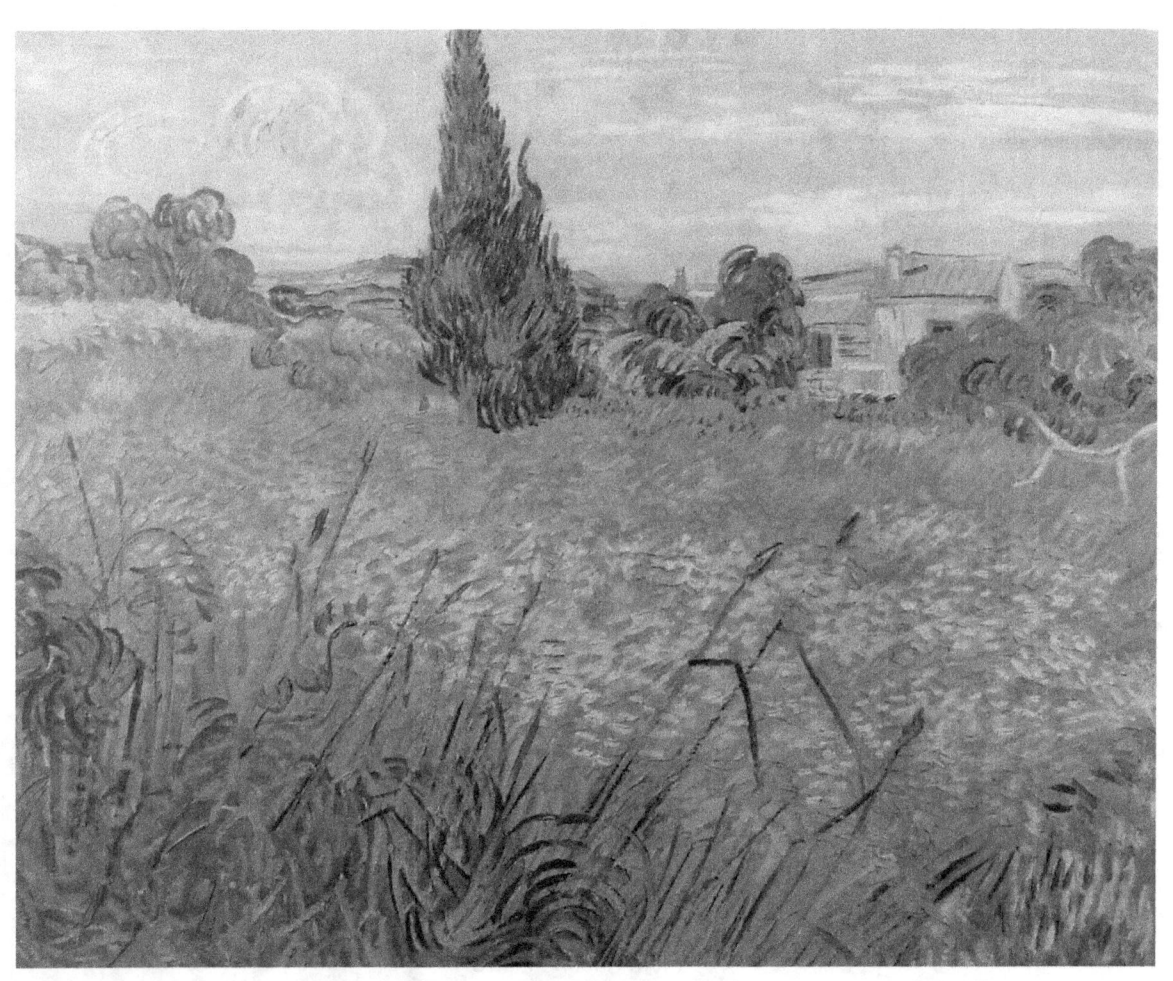

Vincent van Gogh, Wheatfield, Prague

From Robert Fludd's
Utriusque Cosmi maioris salicet et minoris metaphysica

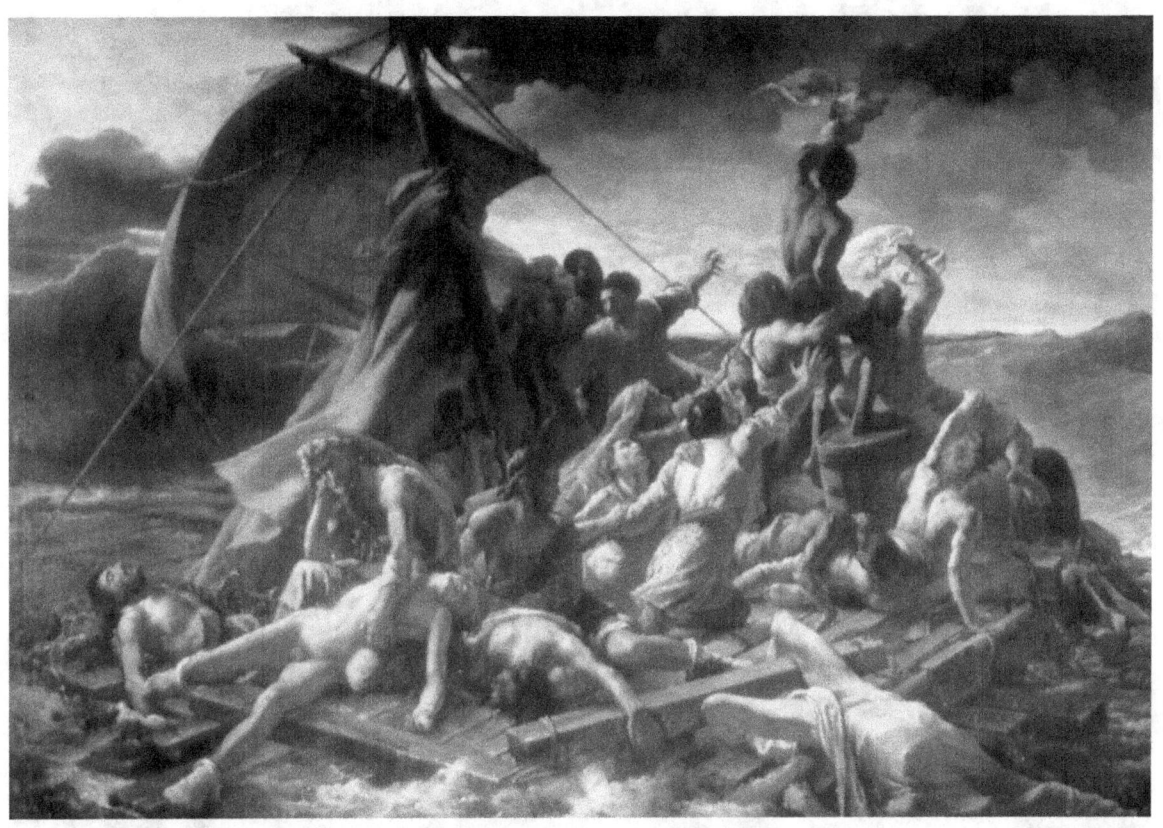

Théodore Géricault, The Raft of the Medusa, 1818-19, Louvre, Paris

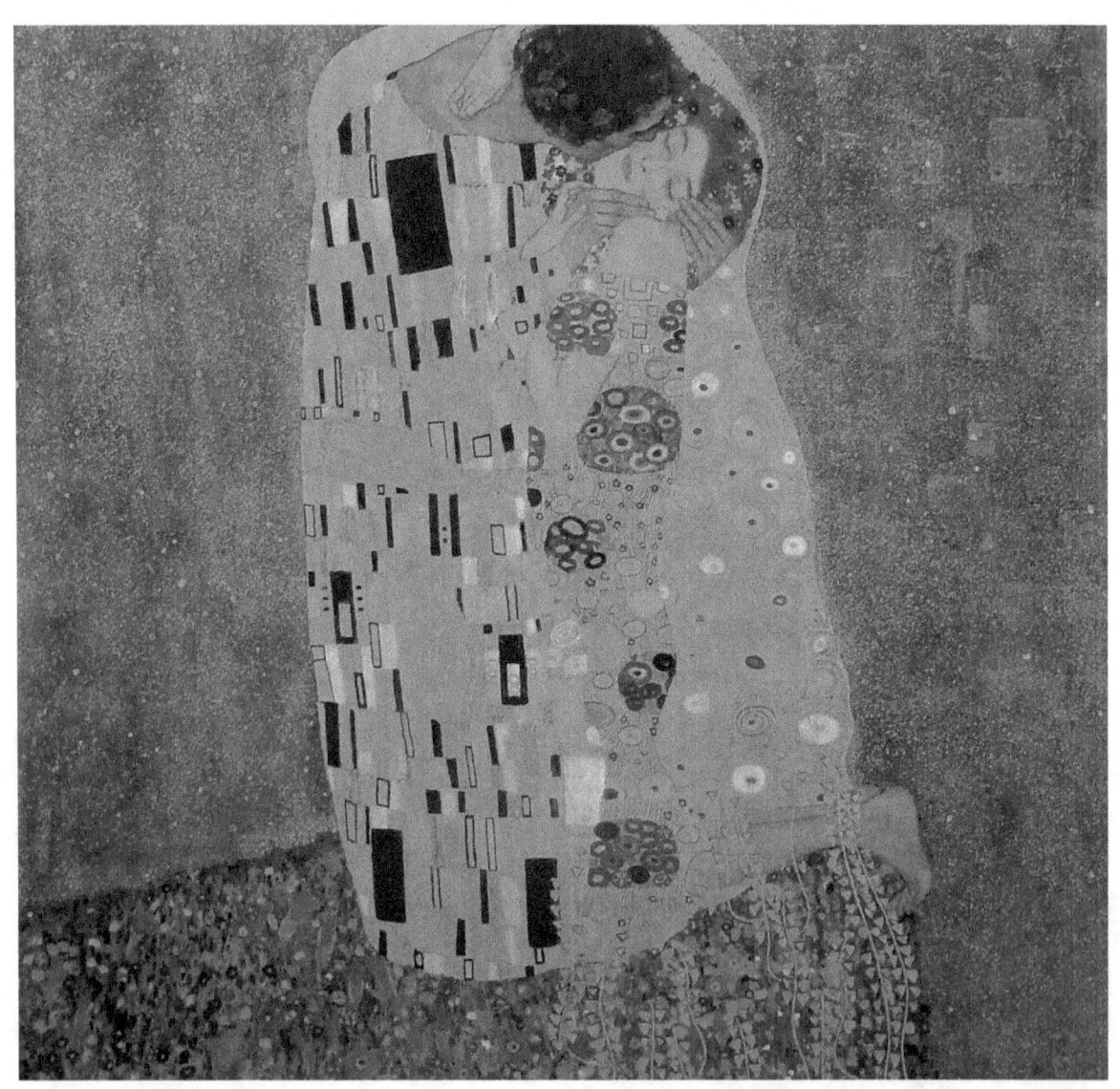

Gustav Klimt, The Kiss

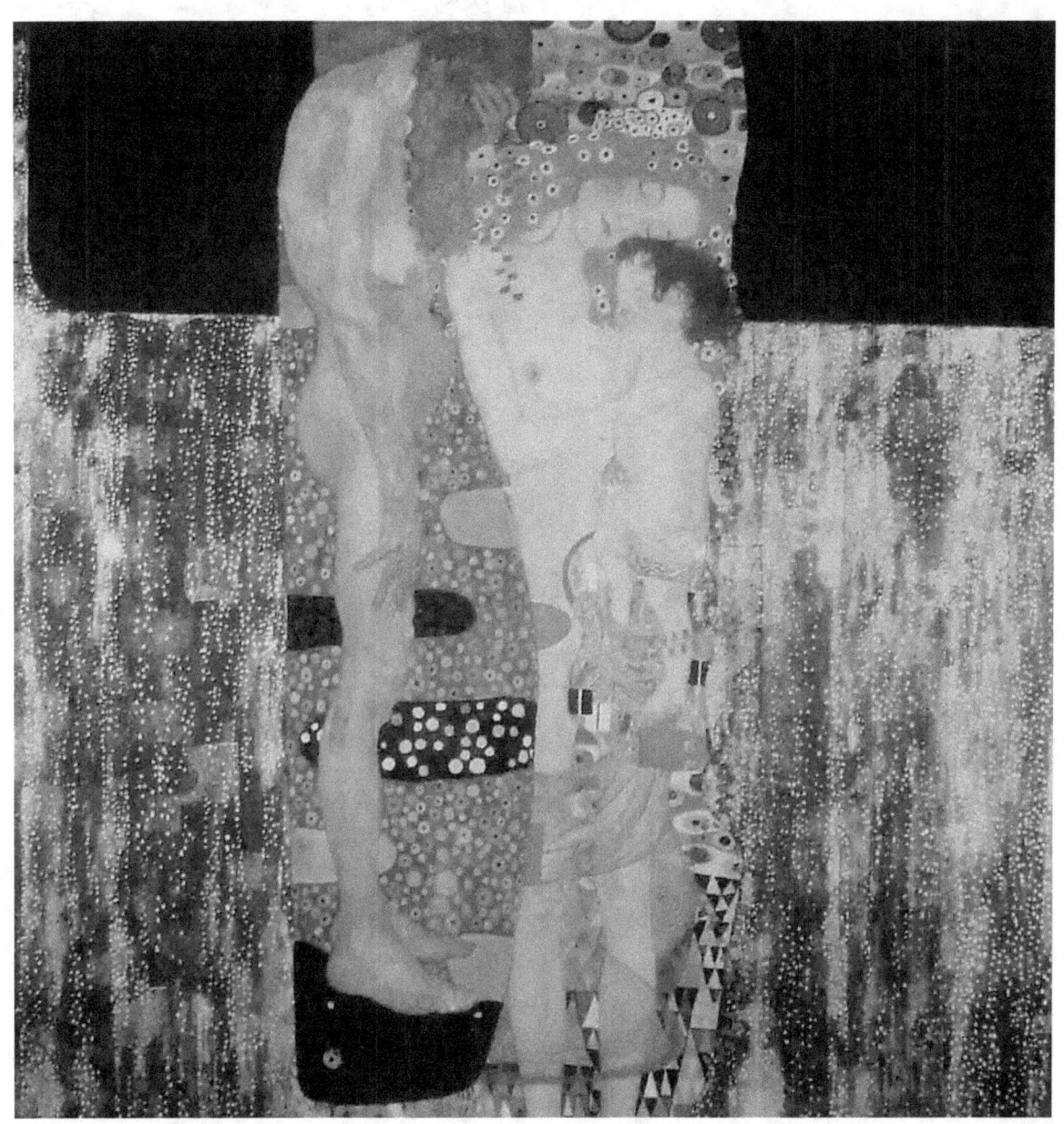

Gustav Klimt, The Three Ages of Woman, 1905

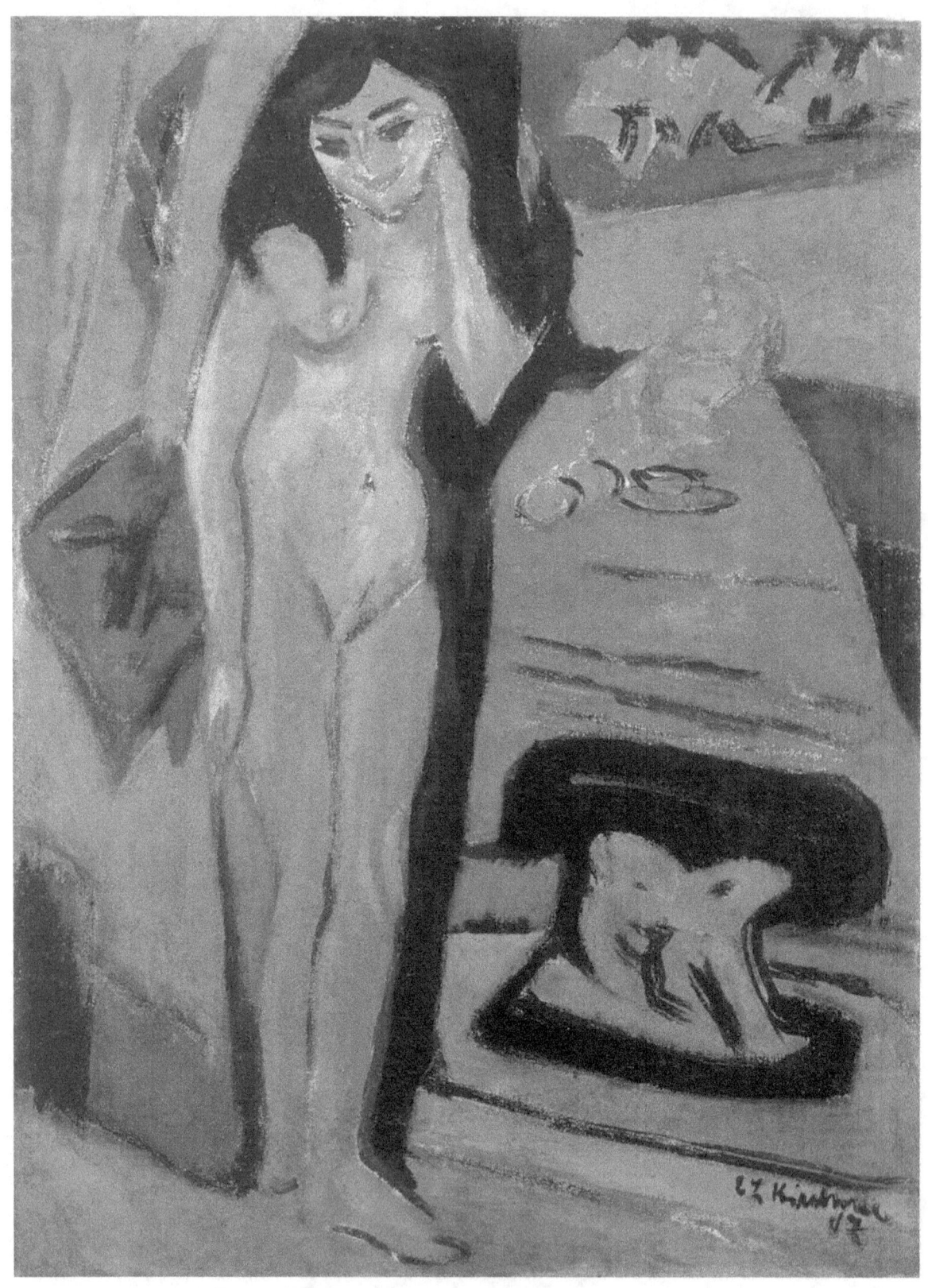

Ernst Ludwig Kirchner, Naked Woman, 1910/ 26, Amsterdam

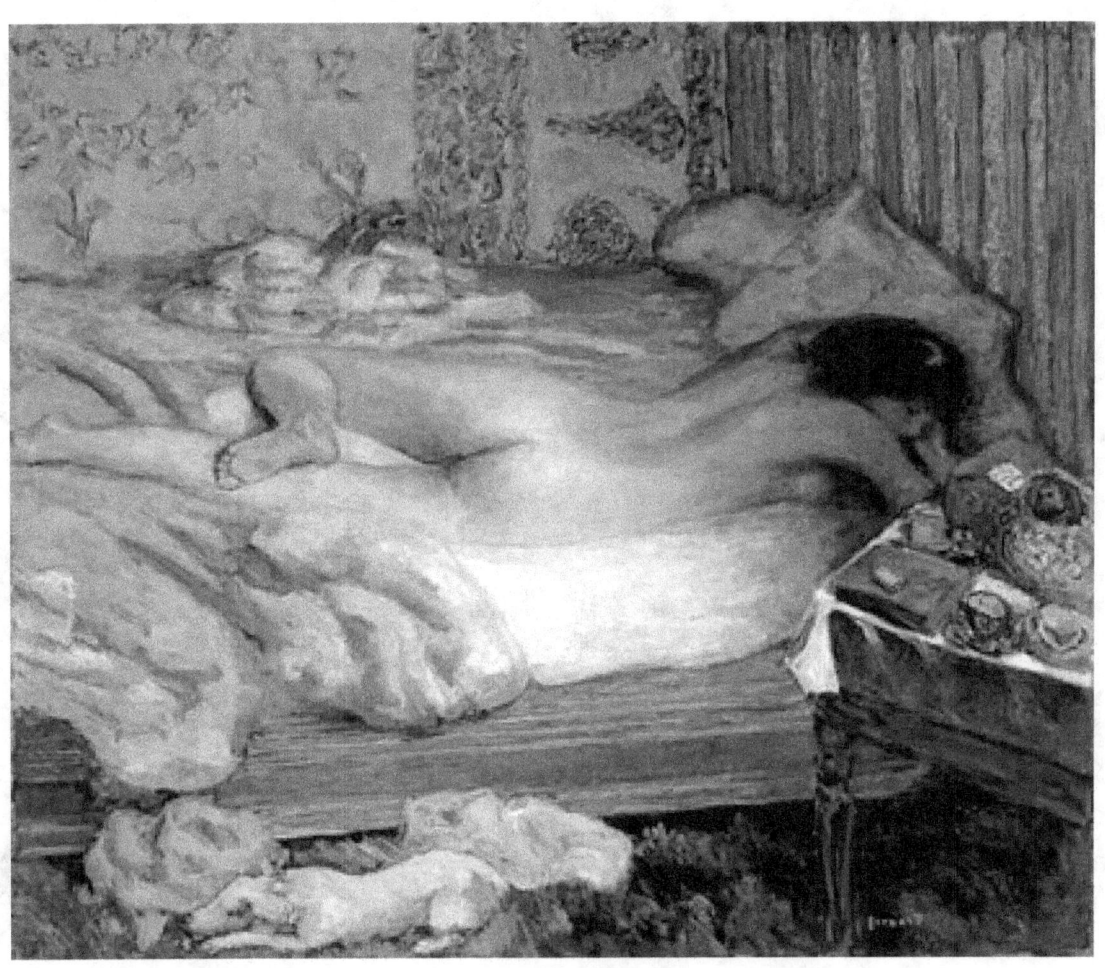

Pierre Bonnard

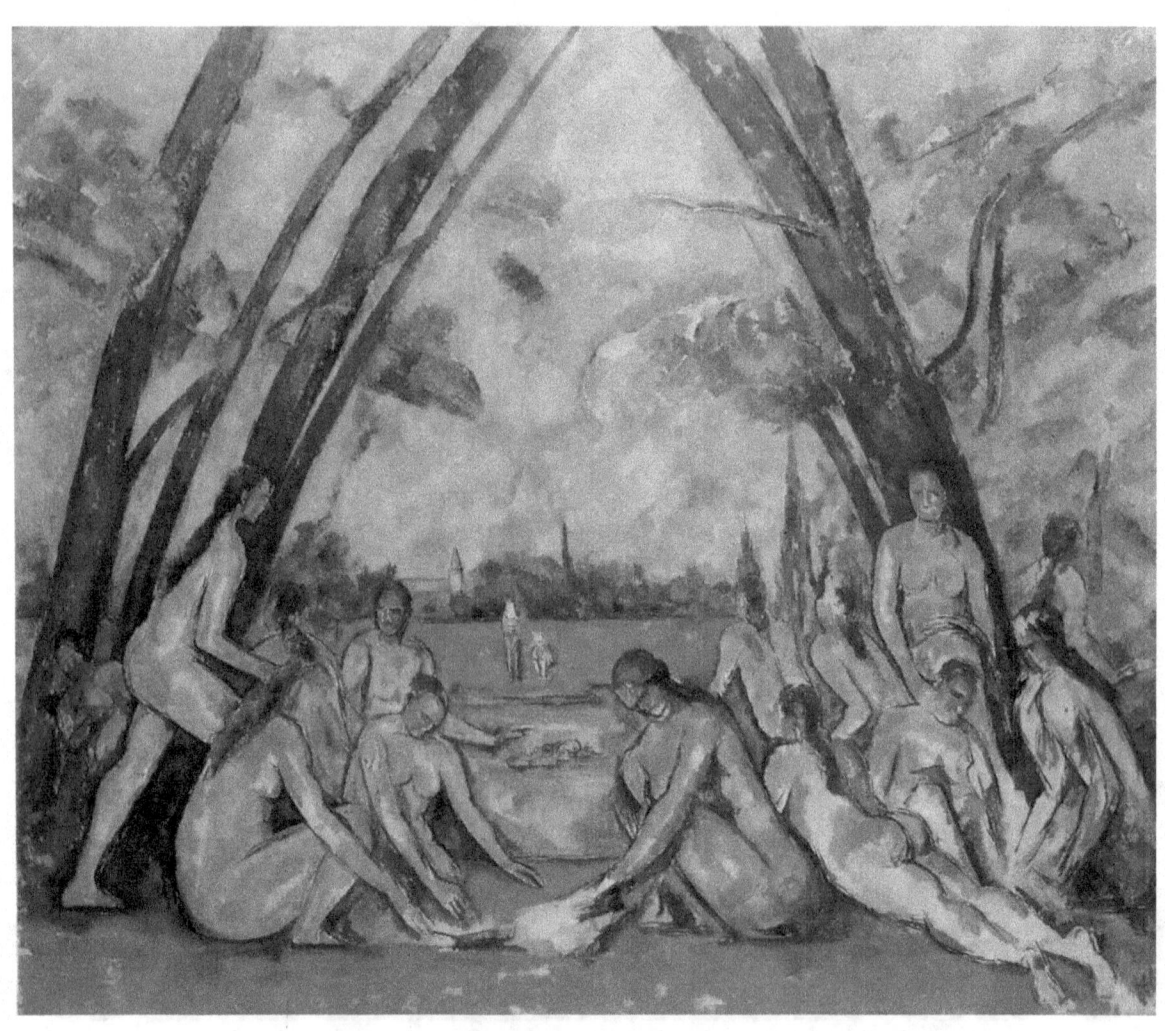

Paul Cézanne, Large Bathers, 1906,
Philadelphia Museum of Art

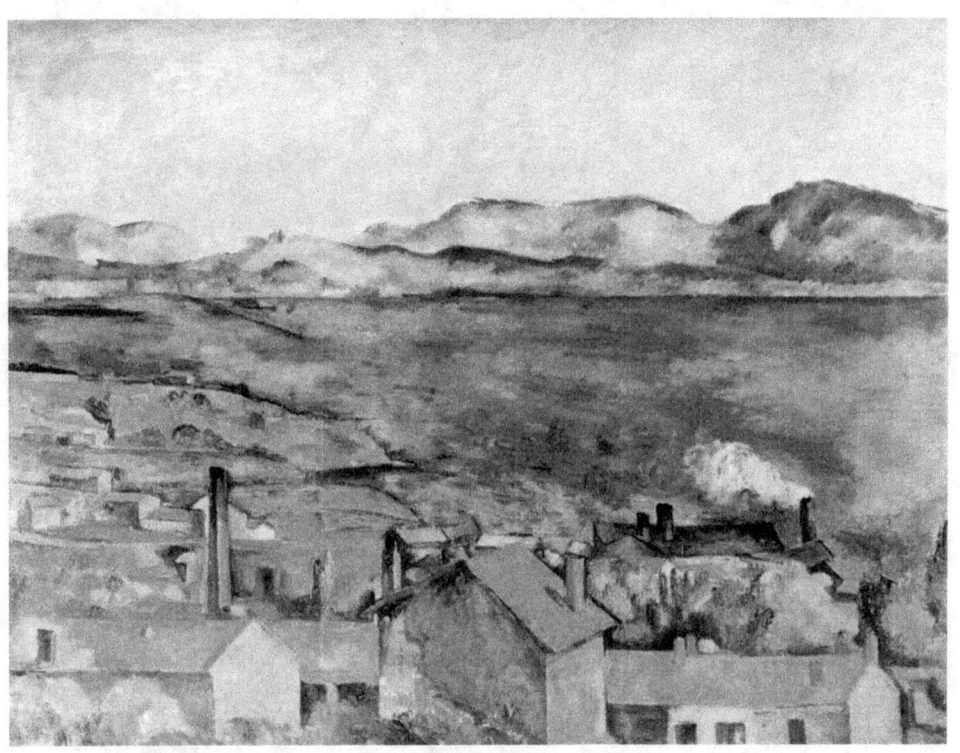

Paul Cézanne, The Bay From L'Estaque, c. 1886, Chicago

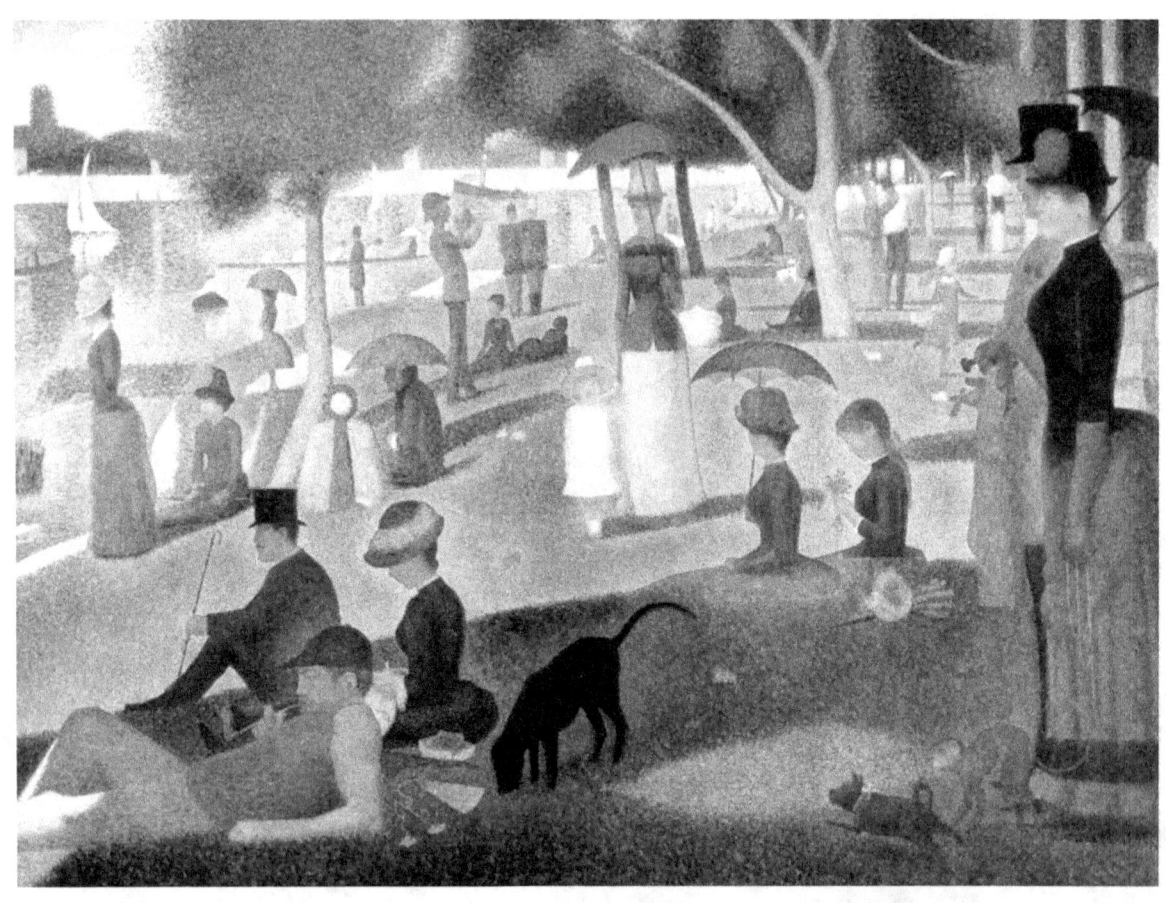

Georges Seurat, Sunday Afternoon On the Island of Grand Jatte, 1884-86
Art Institute, Chicago

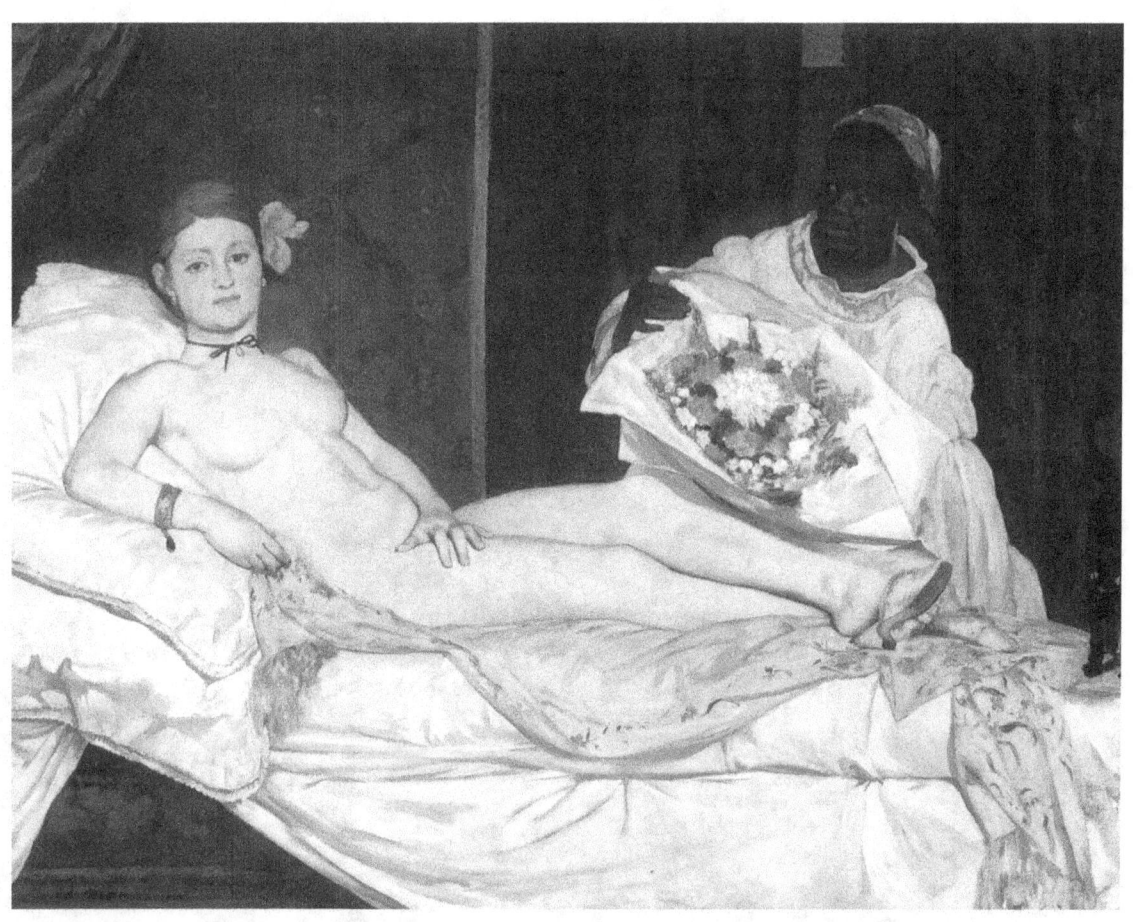

Edouard Manet, Olympia, Musée d'Orsay, Paris

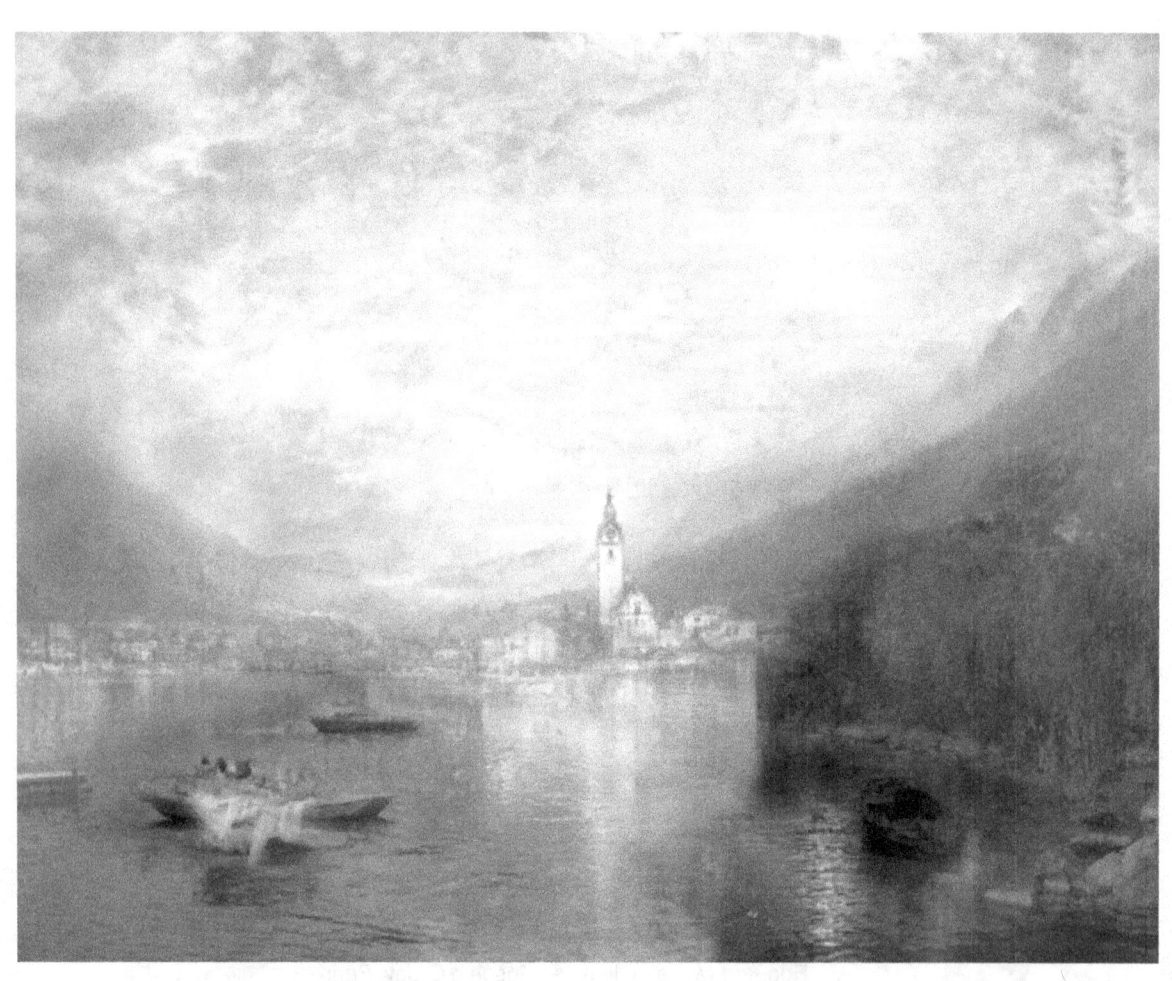

J.M.W. Turner, Lake of Lucerne, Clore Gallery, London

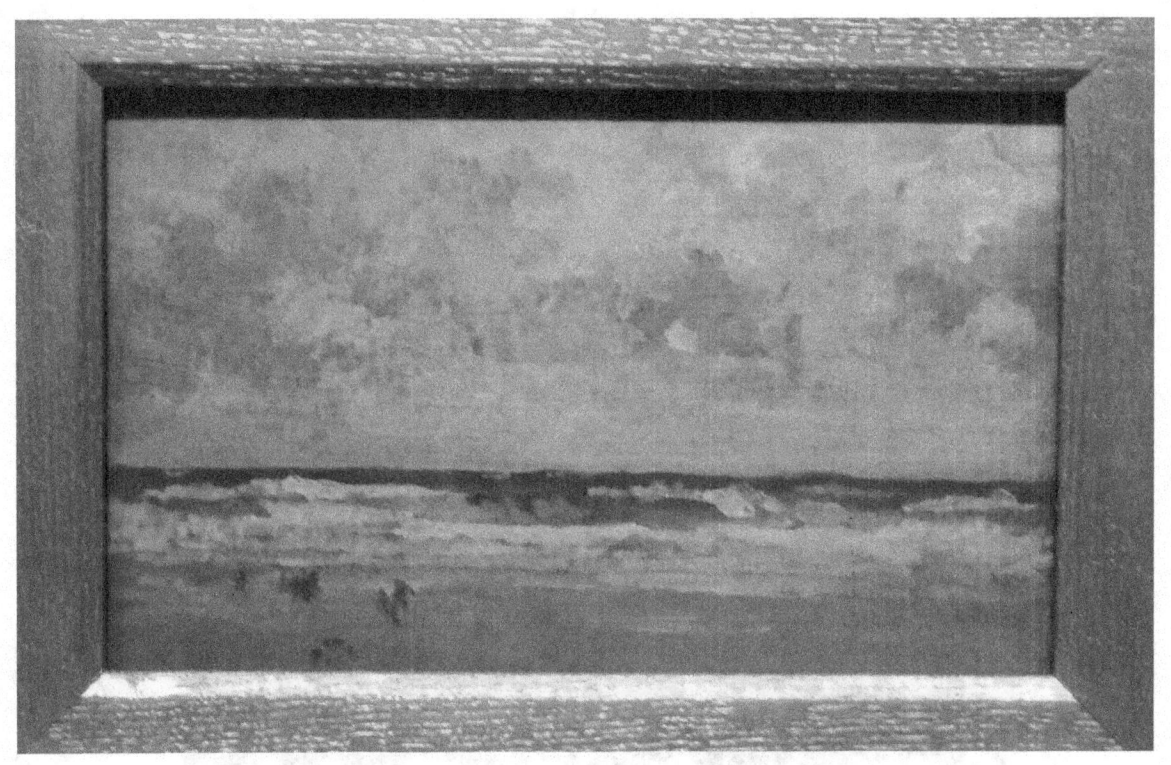

James Whistler, St Ives, Freer Gallery of Art, Washington, DC

Kasimir Malevich, Black Painting, St Petersburg

Kasimir Malevich, Suprematist Composition: White On White, 1918,
Museum of Modern Art, New York

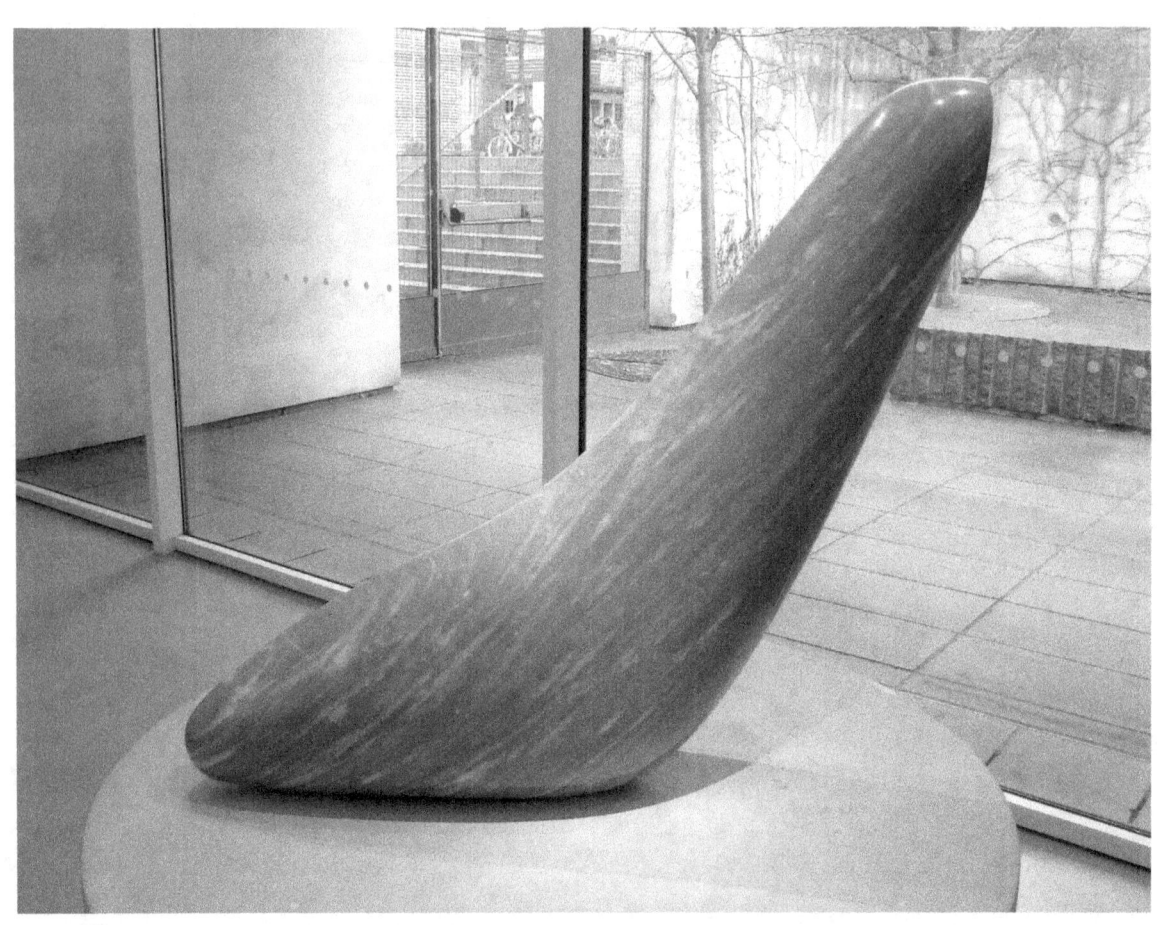

Constantin Brancusi

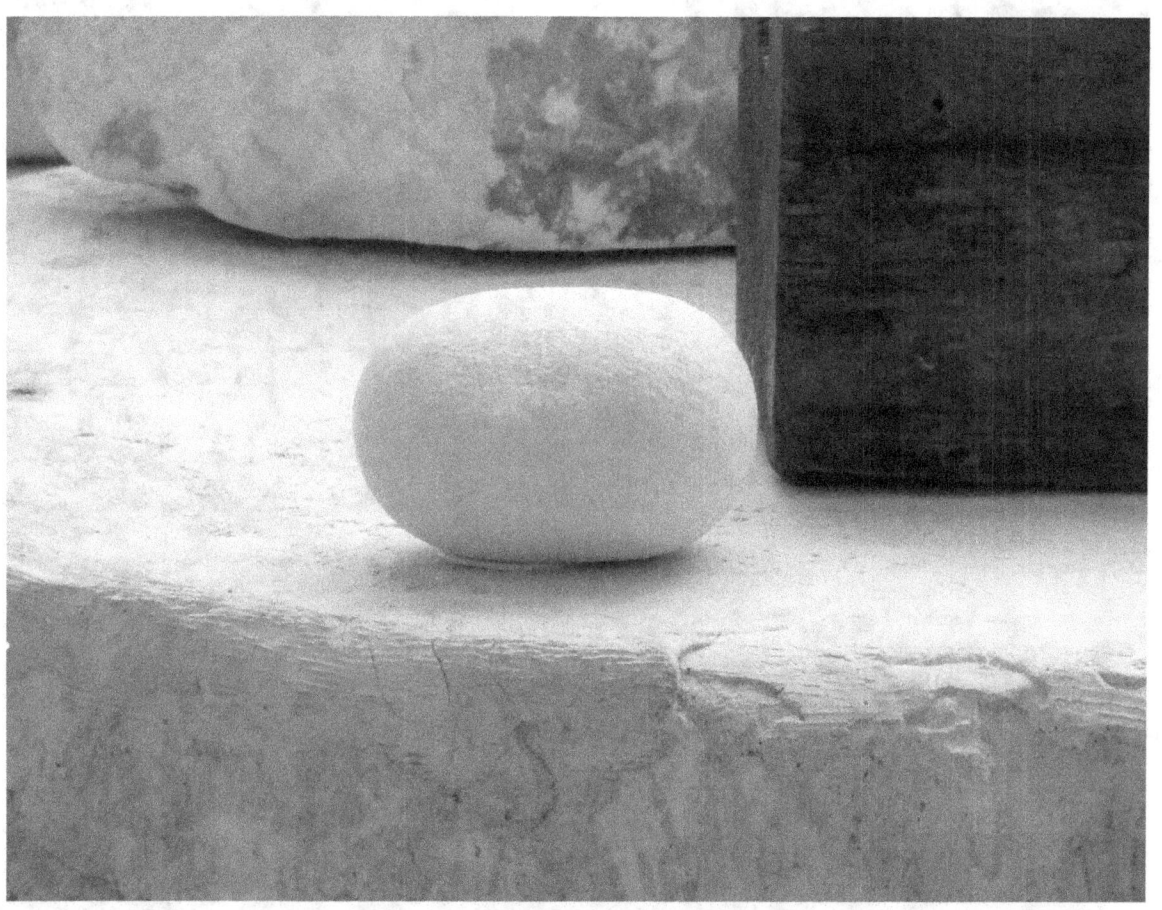

Constantin Brancusi, at the Brancusi Studio in Paris. This page and over.

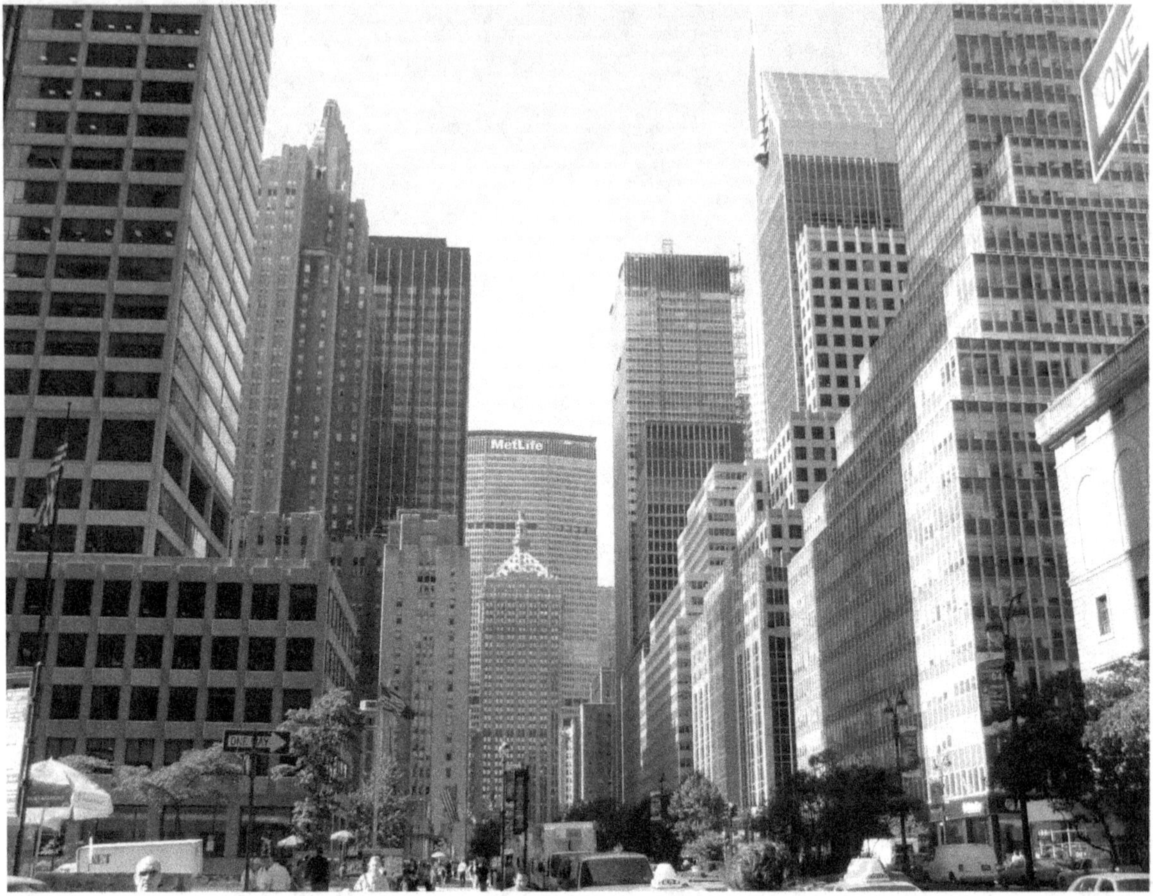

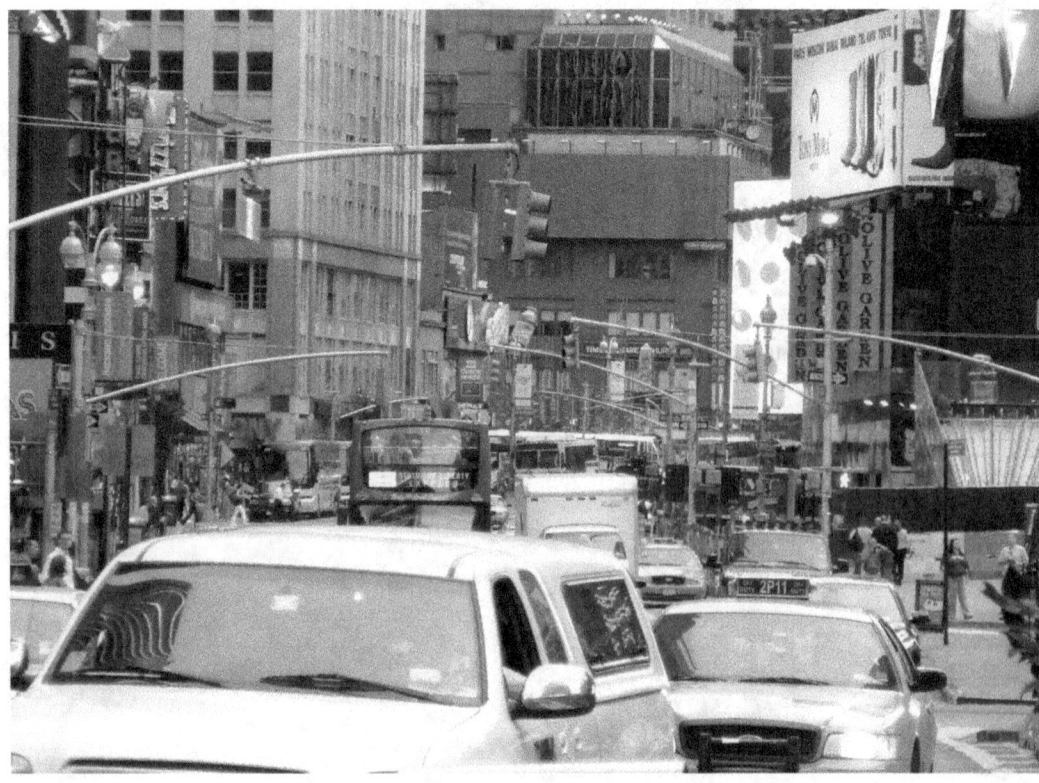

The centre of the art world, New York City,
where many Colorfield artists have lived and exhibitied.

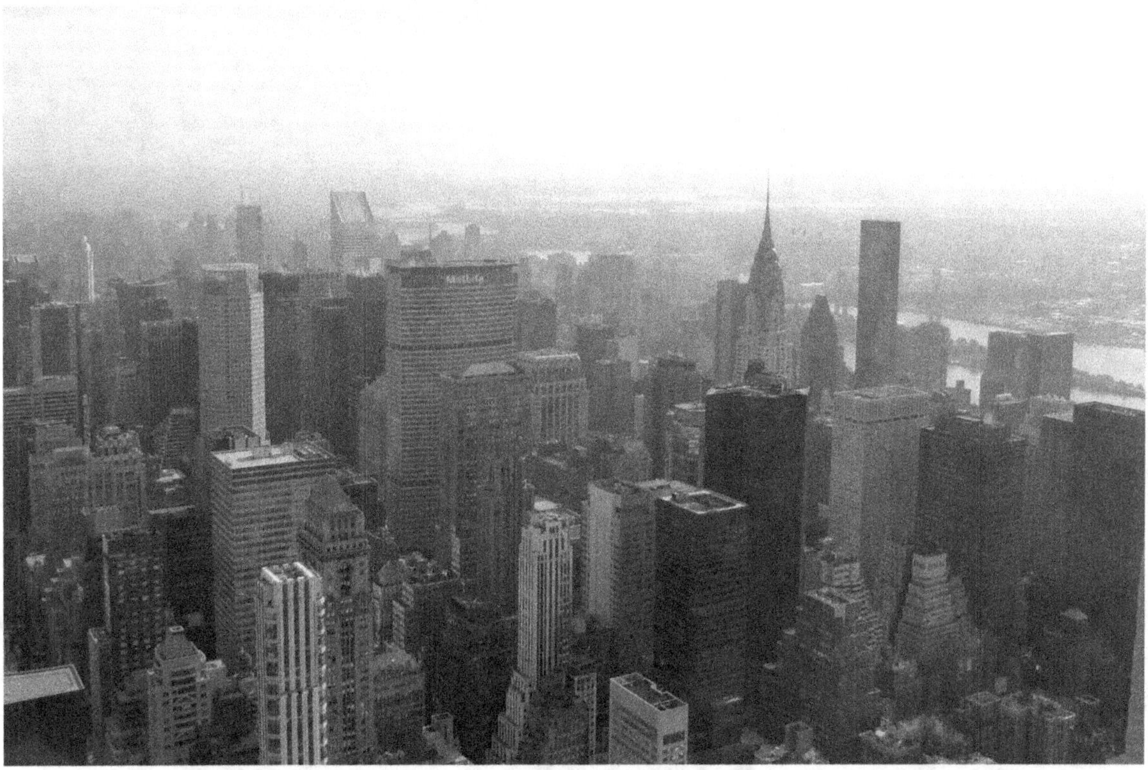

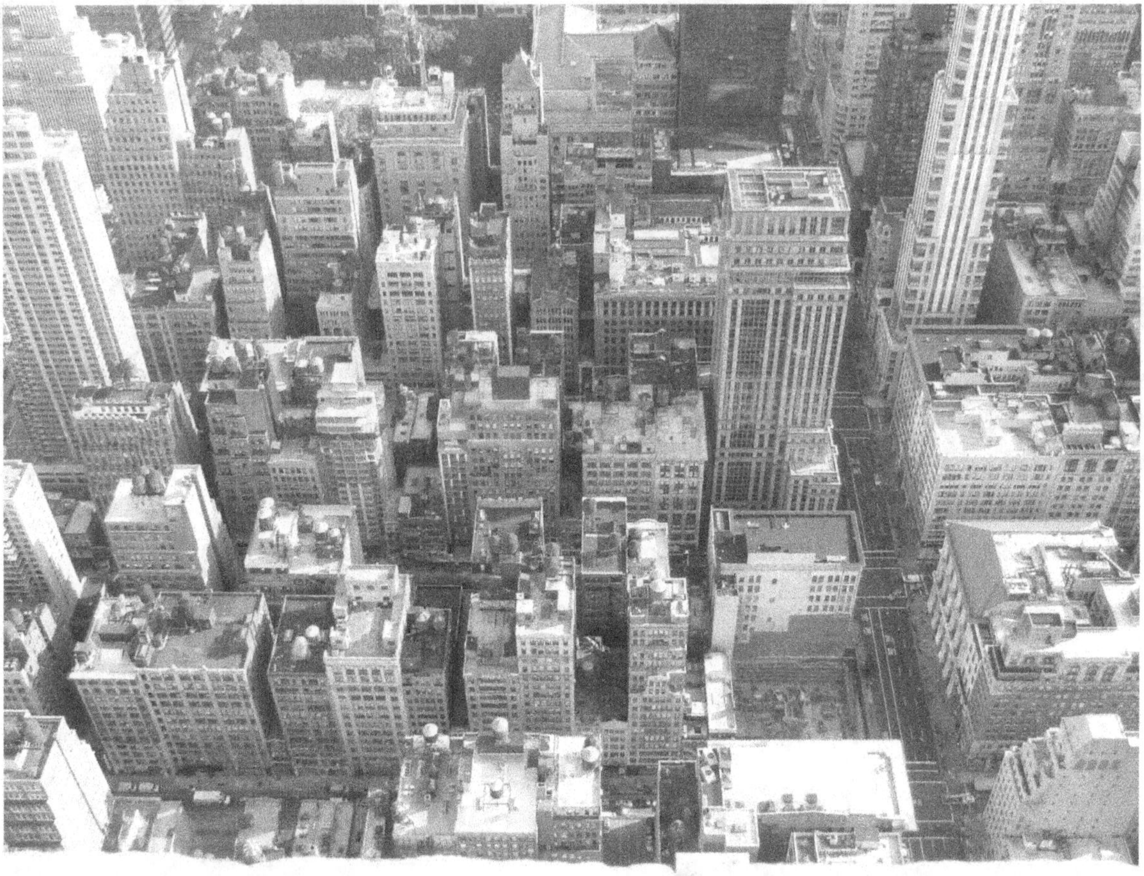

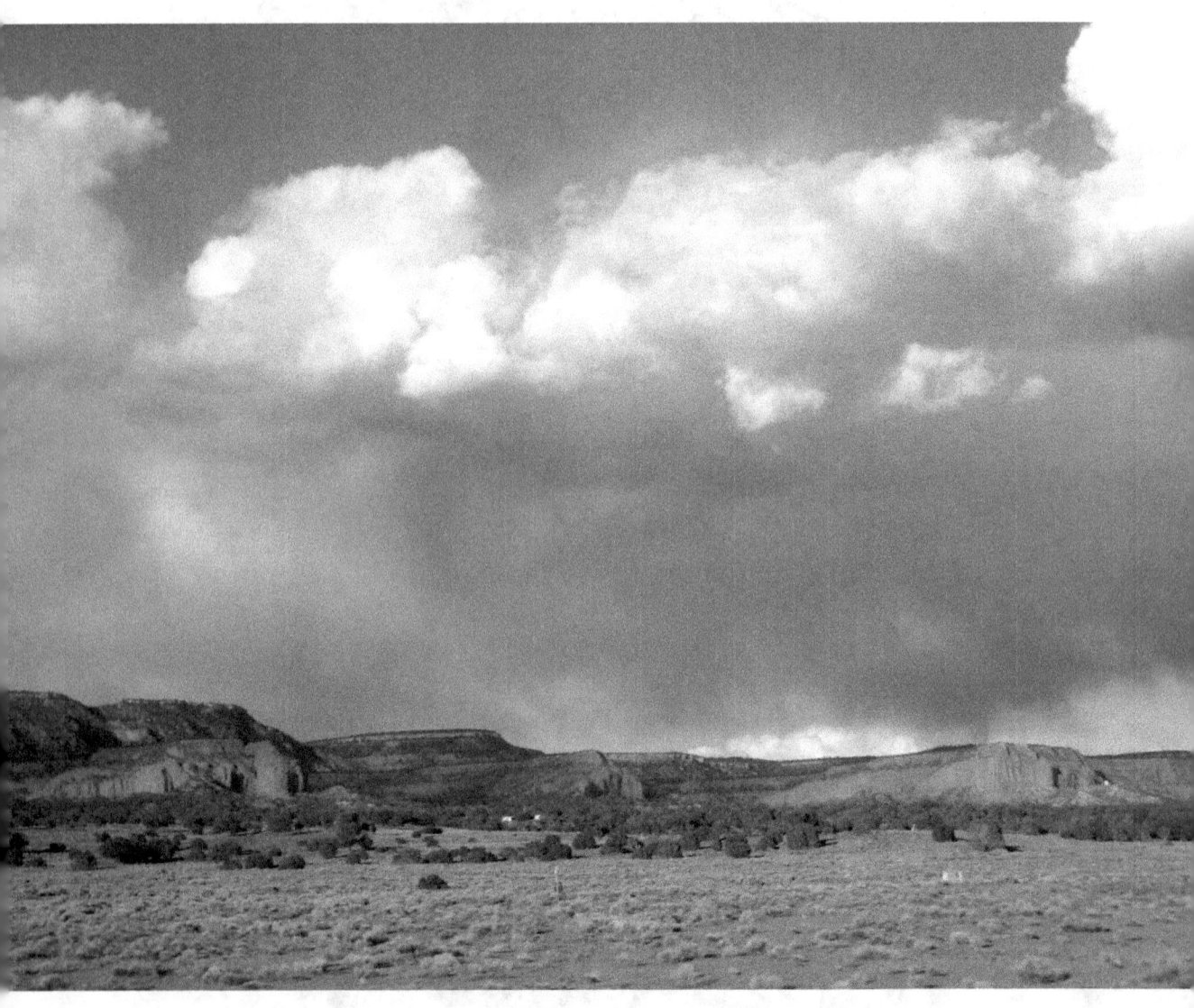

The light in New Mexico, an influence on Agnes Martin, and many other artists

NOTES

INTRODUCTION

1. In G. Battock, 1995, 150, 154.
2. R. Hughes, 1991, 156.
3. C. Riley, 1995, 70.

1 THE AESTHETICS OF COLORFIELD PAINTING

1. L. Alloway, 1966.
2. J. Pollock, in F.V. O'Connor & E. Thaw, eds. *Pollock*, Yale University Press, New Haven, CT, 1978, 248
3. In R. Hughes, 1991, 141.
4. See M. Fried, 1965, 14-15.
5. See W. Johnston, *The Still Point: Reflections on Zen and Christian Mysticism*, Fordham University Press, New York, NY, 1982, 50f.
6. A. Watts, *The Way of Zen*, Penguin, London, 1980, 198.
7. See H. Brinker, *The Zen in the Art of Painting*, Routledge, London, 1987, 141.

2 ABSTRACT EXPRESSIONISM AND SIXTIES COLORFIELD PAINTING

ABSTRACT EXPRESSIONIST PAINTING

1. C. Greenberg, "The Crisis of the Easel Picture", in 1961, 155.

BARNETT NEWMAN

1. More recent pieces on Barnett Newman include J. Ferrier & Y. le Pichon, "The Faraway Light of Barnett Newman", in *Art of Our Century*, Prentice-Hall, New York, NY, 1989; K. Baker; Y.-A. Bois, "Perceiving Newman", *Painting as Model*, MIT Press, Cambridge, MA, 1990; A. Gibson; M. Kimmelman, "Newman's Quest for a Vocabulary", *The New York Times*, Apl 15, 1988; J.B. Klaster, "Red Alert", *Artnews*, 91, 2, Feb, 1992. On Barnett Newman and the 'Abstract Sublime', see M. Zakian, "Barnett Newman and the Sublime", *Arts Magazine*, 62, 6, Feb, 1988, and "Barnett Newman: Painting a Sense of Place", *Arts Magazine*, 62, 7, Mch, 1988; I. Dunlop; P. Crowther, 1984; R. Nikas, "The Sublime Was Then (Search for Tomorrow)", *Arts Magazine*, 60, 7, Mch, 1986; P. Taaffe, "Sublimity, Now and Forever, Amen", *Arts Magazine*, 60, 7, Mch, 1986; H. Rosenberg, *Art on the Edge*, Macmillan, London, 1975.
2. In T. Hess, 1971, 24.
3. In F. Frascina, 101.
4. See D. Davis, "The Red, the Yellow, the Blue", *Newsweek*, Oct 18, 1971; T. de Duve, "Who's Afraid of Red, Yellow, and Blue?", *Artforum*, 22, 1, Sept, 1983; M. Imdahl, *Barnett Newman: Who's Afraid of Red, Yellow and Blue III*, Werkmonographien zur Bildenden Kunst, 147, 1971.

MARK ROTHKO

1. D. Aston, 1958; A. Brookner, "The New New York Scene", *Burlington Magazine*, 103, Nov, 1963; B. Robertson, 1961; M. Kozloff, 1961; R. Hobbs, 1978; D. Waldman, 1978, 69; P. Selz, in R. Goldwater; R. Goldwater, 1961; C. Greenberg, 1955, 193; D. Sylvester, 1961; I. Sandler, 1983; W. de Kooning, 1958, 176.
2. C. Greenberg, 1955, in F. Frascina, 101.
3. J. Ashbery, "Gray Eminence", *Art News*, 71, 1, Mch, 1972.
4. T. Matthews, "Religious Content In Contemporary Art", lecture, Congress on Religion, Architecture and the Visual Arts, New York, 1967.

5. Robert Hughes reckons Rothko may have been a religious painter, but in another era (1978b, 16).
6. See L. Alloway, 1963.
7. M. Rothko, in D. Ashton, 1983, 188.
8. C. McMahon, "The Sublime is How", in P. Crowther, 1995, 26.

3   MONOCHROME AND MONOTONOUS

1. See I. Sandler, 1970, 245f, L. Lippard, 1966, 62; R. Morris, 1966; K. McShine, 1966; R. Lund, 1986, 195-7.
2. I. Sandler, 1965, 97.
3. D. Judd, in G. Battock, 1995, 159.
4. J. Perreault, 1995, 260.
5. D. Judd, in K. McShine, 1966.
6. R. Mangold, quoted in F. Colpitt, 121.
7. S. LeWitt, quoted in F. Colpitt, 121.
8. A. Wooster, 1980, 143-7.
9. S. LeWitt, 1969, 1970; L. Lippard, 1967; R. Smith, 1975; A. Wooster, 1980.
10. Jasper Johns, "Sketchbook Notes", in *Art and Literature*, 4, Lausanne, Spring, 1965, 192.
11. Quoted in L. Steinberg, "Jasper Johns: The First Seven Years of His Art", in *Other Criteria: Confrontations with Twentieth-Century Art*, Oxford University Press, New York, NY, 1972, 31.
12. L. Alloway, "Serial Forms", in M. Tuchman, 1967, 14.
13. D. Judd, "Specific Objects", 1965, 82.
14. R. Rauschenberg, in B. Diamonstein, ed. *Inside New York's Art World*, New York, NY, 1977.
15. C. Robins, 1976, 19.

4   SIXTIES COLORFIELD PAINTERS

FRANK STELLA

1. D. Judd, 1962, 51.
2. S. Nodelman, 1967, 77.
3. W. Domingo, 44-45.
4. W. Rubin, quoted in E. de Antonio, 138.
5. J. Johns, in D. Sylvester, 1974, 14.
6. P. Fuller, "American Painting Since Last Year", *Art Monthly*, June, 1979, in D. Shapiro, 178.
7. W. Rubin, in E. de Antonio, 138-9.
8. K. Schwitters, quoted in F. Roh *German Art in the Twentieth Century: Painting, Sculpture, Architecture*, Thames & Hudson, London, 1968, 133.
9. J. Coplans, "Serial Imagery", 37.
10. B. Rose, "ABC Art", 59.
11. F. Stella: "The Pratt Lecture", 1960, in B. Richardson, 78
12. M. Kozloff, "Pop Culture, Metaphysical Designs and the New Vulgarians", *Art International*, Mch, 1962, 34-36.
13. B. O'Doherty, 21.
14. F. Stella, in E. de Antonio, 144.
15. D. Judd, in G. Battock, 1995, 161.
16. F. Stella, in quoted in B. Glaser, 59.
17. M. Kozloff, 1964, 64; B. O'Doherty, 21.
18. F. Colpitt, 54.
19. F. Stella, quoted in G. Battock, 1995, 160.
20. F. Stella, quoted in D. Wheeler, 1991. 204.

MORRIS LOUIS

1. R. Hughes, 1990, 200.
2. In R. Hughes, 1990, 201.
3. C. Greenberg, in D. Wheeler, 192.
4. J. Elderfield, 1986, 27.
5 J. Elderfield, ibid.
6. A. Kagan, 138.
7. In D. Wheeler, 193.
8. M. Louis, in J. Gage, 267.
9. R. Hughes, 1990, 201.

10 F. Stella, in E. de Antonio, 139.
11. In N. Stangos, 262.
12. A.J. Carmean, 1974, 9-15.
13. P. Fuller, "St Ives", 1985.
14. P. Fuller, 1993, 217.

HELEN FRANKENTHALER

1. H. Frankenthaler, quoted in E. de Antonio, 77.
2. In E. de Antonio, 85.

KENNETH NOLAND

1. K. Noland, quoted in D. Waldman, 1977.
2. F. Stella, in B. Glaser, 55.
3. K. Noland, in R. Hughes, 1997, 548.
4. K. Noland, in E. Johnson, 1982.

ROBERT RYMAN

1. R. Ryman, in R. Storr, 16.
2. See B. Richardson, 1976, 3; F. Colpitt, 29.
3. See C. Huber; N. Grimes, 1968, 86-92; C. Ratcliff, 1986, 92-97.
4. L. Nead, "Getting down to basics: art, obscenity and the female nude", in I. Armstrong, ed. *New Feminist Discourses: Critical Essays on Theories and Texts,* Routledge, London, 1992, 206.
5. R. Ryman, in R. Storr, 48.
6. R. Ryman, in D. Wheeler, 207.
7. A. Danto, 1997, 154; R. Storr, 1993.

AGNES MARTIN

1. B. Rose, 1986, 138.
2. A. Martin, 1973, 23.

AD REINHARDT

1. A. Reinhardt, "Art-as-Art", *Art International*, 6, 10, Dec 20, 1960, in 1991, 56
2. A. Reinhardt, *Art as Art*, 1991, 205-6.

Further extracts from *Art as Art* are cited in the text as 1991.
3. R. Hughes, 1997, 558.
4. R. Stankiewicz, *Sixteen Americans*, Museum of Modern Art, New York, NY, 1959
5. B. Newman, in H. Rosenberg, 1994, 59.
6. M. Benedikt, "New York Letter", in G. Battock, 1995, 91.
7. C. Greenberg, in G. Battock, 1995, 184.
8. M. Rothko, in D. Ashton, 1983, 179. Reinhardt was less generous about Rothko. In some undated notes, Reinhardt wrote:

What's wrong with the art world is not Andy Warhol or Andy Wyeth but Mark Rothko. The corruption of the best is the worst. Motherwell said someone said, "Rothko is the best Jewish artist in the world." ... How about Christians making synagogue murals? (Motherwell). How about Jews decorating Catholic churches? (Rothko). (1991, 190)

9. T. Merton, *Seeds of Contemplation*, Burns & Oates, London, 1962, 196.
10. P. Tillich, "Art", *Newsweek*, Feb, 1959, 54.
11. H. Frankenthaler, in E. de Antonio, 161.
12. A. Reinhardt, "Art-as-Art", *Environment*, 1962, 53.
13. A. Reinhardt, in *Art News*, May, 1957, and in G. Battock, 1995, 285.
14. A. Reinhardt, 1991, 108.
15. F. Stella, in G. Battock, 1995, 159.
16. M. Eliade, "The Sacred and the Modern Artist", in D. Apostolos-Cappadona, ed. *Art, Creativity and the Sacred*, New York, NY, 1984, 180f.
17. A. Reinhardt, 1991, 86-97, 108.
18. A. Reinhardt, interview, *Art International*, Dec, 1966, 18f
19. Robert Fludd, *Utriusque cosmi maiores et minors historia*, 1617, Frankfurt, Philosophical Research Library, Manley P. Hall

Collection, Los Angeles, CA.

20. *Heart Sutra*, in E. Conze, *Buddhist Scriptures*, Penguin, London, 1959, 163.

21. S. Tillim, "Ad Reinhardt", *Arts*, Feb, 1959, 54.

22. P. Colt, 32f.

23. N. & E. Calas, 212f.

24. W. Kandinsky, *Concerning the Spiritual in Art*, Dover, New York, NY, 1977.

25. L. Alloway, 1960, 50.

26. A. Reinhardt in a lecture, Nov 5, 1965, in L. Lippard, 1966, 168.

27. L. Lippard, 1966, 154.

BRICE MARDEN

1. S. Burton, "Reviews and Previews" *Art News*, Feb, 1968.

2. J. Taylor, 1976, 66.

3. C. Greenberg, 1961, 134.

4. L. Fontana, quoted in J. Van der Marck, *Lucas Fontana*, catalogue, Walker Art Center, Minneapolis, MN, 1966.

5. C. Robins, 1984, 182.

6. L. Shearer, 1975, 19-20.

7. B. Marden, 1991a, 26-27.

8. C. Ratcliffe, 1975, 85; C. Robins, 1984, 183.

ELLSWORTH KELLY

1. D. Ashton, 1982, 89.

2. E. Kelly, 1980, 31.

5   OTHER COLORFIELD, MINIMAL, HARD EDGE, SERIAL AND POST-PAINTERLY ABSTRACT PAINTERS

OTHER COLORFIELD PAINTERS

1. See P. Gardner, 1984, 47-55; R. Smith, 1987.

PAINTERS AFTER COLORFIELD PAINTING

1. S. Scully, in J. Higgins, "Sean Scully and the Metamorphosis of the Stripe", *Art News*, Nov, 1985; see also C. Ratcliff, *Sean Scully*, Modern Museum of Fort Worth, TX, 1993.

2. Jeff Koons: "Full Fathom Five", *Parkett*, 19, 1989.

BIBLIOGRAPHY

W.C. Agee. *Don Judd*, Whitney Museum of American Art, New York, NY, 1968

—. "Unit, Series, Site: A Judd Lexicon", *Art in America*, May, 1975

—. *The Sculpture of Donald Judd*, Art Museum of South Texas, Corpus Christi, TX, 1977

L. Aldrich. *Cool Art: 1967*, Museum of Contemporary Art, 1968

L. Alloway. "Signs and Surface: Notes on Black and White Paintings in New York", *Quadrum*, 9, New York, NY, 1960,

—. "The American Sublime", *Living Arts*, 1, 2, June, 1963

—. *Morris Louis*, Guggenheim, New York, NY, 1963

—. *Systematic Painting*, New York, NY, 1966

—. "Residual Sign Systems in Abstract Expressionism", *Artforum*, Nov, 1973

W. Andersen. *American Sculpture in Process, 1930/ 1970*, New York Graphics Society, Boston, MA, 1975

C. Andre. "Frank Stella: Preface to Stripe Painting", in D. Miller, 1959

—. "Brice Marden Paintings", *57th Street Review*, Nov 15, 1966

—. *Carl Andre, Sculpture, 1958-1974*, Kunsthalle, Bern, 1975

D. Anfam. *Abstract Expressionism*, Thames & Hudson, London, 1990

D. Antin. "Differences – Sames: NY, 1966-1967", *Metro*, 13, Feb, 1968

E. de Antonio & M. Tuchman. *Painters Painting,* Abbeville Press, New York, NY, 1984

M. Archer. *Art Since 1960*, Thames & Hudson, London, 1997

H.H. Arnason. *Robert Motherwell*, Abrams, New York, NY, 1982

J. Ashbery. "Gray Eminence", *ARTnews*, 71, 1, Mch, 1972

D. Ashton. "Art: Mark Rothko", *Art & Architecture*, 75, 1958

—. "Young Abstract Painters: Right On!", *Arts Magazine*, Feb, 1970

—. *The Life and Times of the School*, Adams & Dart, Bath, 1972

—. & A. Martin. *Agnes Martin*, Hayward Gallery, London, 1977

—. "Rothko's Passion", *Art International*, Feb, 1979

—. *American Art Since 1945*, Thames & Hudson, London, 1982

—. *About Rothko*, Oxford University Press, New York, NY, 1983

M. Auping, ed. *Abstract Expressionism*, New York, NY, 1987

—. *Abstraction, Geometry, Painting: Selected Geometric Abstract Painting in America Since 1945,* Abrams, New York, NY, 1989

R. Ayers. "Color and Motion", *Artscribe*, 33, Feb, 1982

J. Baer. "Letters", *Artforum*, 6, 1, Sept, 1967

E. Baker. "Judd the Obscure", *Art News*, 67, 2, 1968

K. Baker. "Reckoning with Notation: The Drawings of Pollock, Newman, and Louis", *Artforum*, 18, 10, Summer, 1980b

—. *Minimalism: Art of Circumstance*, Abbeville, New York, NY, 1988

S. Bann. *Brice Marden: Paintings, Drawings, Etchings, 1975-80*, Stedelijk Museum, Amsterdam, 1981

—. & W. Allen, eds. *Interpreting Contemporary Art*, Reaktion Books, London, 1991

S. Barnes. *The Rothko Chapel*, Rothko Chapel, Houston, TX. 1989

G. Baro. "Toward Speculation in Pure Form", *Art International*, Summer, 1967

D. Batchelor *et al. Sol LeWitt*, Museum of Modern Art, Oxford, 1993

—. *Minimalism*, Tate Publishing, London

C. Battaglia. "Tre Artisti: Ryman, Marden, Bell", *QUI Arte Contemporanea*, June, 1973

G. Battock. "The Moral Integrity of Smudges", *New York Times*, Jan 25, 1968

—. *Idea Art*, Dutton, New York, NY, 1973

—. "Art in America: Confusions", *Domus*, Mch, 1975

—. ed. *Minimal Art: A Critical Anthology*, Dutton, New York, NY, 1968/ 1995

J. Beardsley. *Earthworks and Beyond: Contemporary Art in the Landscape*, Abbeville Press, New York, NY, 1984

D. Belgrad. *The Culture of Spontaneity: Improvisation and the Arts in Postwar America*, University of Chicago Press, Chicago, IL, 1998

J. Bell. "Positive and Negative", *Arts Magazine*, Nov, 1974

A. Benjamin, ed. *Installation Art, Art & Design*, 30, 1993

N. Bennett, ed. *The British Art Show: Old Allegiances and New Directions, 1979-1984*, Arts Council/ Orbis, London, 1984

M. Berger. *Labyrinths: Robert Morris, Minimalism, and the 1960s*, Harper & Row, New York, NY, 1989

M. Bochner. "Art in Process – Structures", *Arts Magazine*, 40, 9, 1966

—. "Primary Structures", *Arts*, June, 1966

—. "Systematic", *Arts Magazine*, 41, 1, Nov, 1966

—. "Serial Art Systems: Solipsism", *Arts Magazine*, 41, 8, Summer, 1967

—. "Mel Bochner on Malevich", interview with John Coplans, *Artforum*, June, 1974

D. Bourdon. "The Mini-Conceptual Age", *Village Voice*, Oct 17, 1974

—. "You Can't Tell a Painter By His Colors", *Village Voice*, Mch 24, 1975

—. *Carl Andre: Sculpture, 1959-1977*, Jaap Rietman, New York, NY, 1978

M. Bourel & S. Coudere. *Art Minimal II, De la Surface au Plan*, CAPC Musée d'Art contemporain de Bordeaux, 1986

J. Burnham. *Beyond Modern Sculpture*, Braziller, New York, NY, 1968

—. "A Dan Flavin Retrospective in Ottawa", *Artforum*, 8, 4, Dec, 1969

—. "Robert Morris", *Artforum*, 8, 7, 1970

—. "Haacke's Cancelled Show at the Guggenheim", *Artforum*, June, 1971

N. & E. Calas. *Icons and Image of the Sixties*, Dutton, New York, NY, 1971

J. Campbell. *The Power of Myth*, with B. Moyers, ed. B. Flowers, Doubleday, New York, NY, 1988

P. Carlson. "Donald Judd's Equivocal Objects", *Art in America*, Jan, 1984

A.J. Carmean. "Modernist Art: 1960-1970", *Studio International*, July, 1974

—. *Morris Louis*, National Gallery of Art, Washington DC, 1976

—. "Morris Louis and the Modern Tradition", *Arts Magazine*, 51, Sept, 1976

B. Cavaliere. "Notes on Rothko", *Flash Art*, nos. 86-87, Jan, 1979

J.N. Chandler. "Tony Smith and Sol LeWitt", *Art International*, 12, 7, 1968

—. "The Colours of Monochrome", *Artscanada*, 28, 160/1, Nov, 1971

A. Chave. "Minimalism and the Rhetoric of Power", *Arts*, Jan, 1990

H.B. Chipp, ed. *Theories of Modern Art*, University Press of California, Los Angeles, CA, 1968

B. Clearwater. *Mark Rothko: Works on Paper*, National Gallery of Art, Washington, DC, 1984

R. Cohen. "Frank Stella", *ART News*, May, 1985

F. Colpitt. *Minimal Art: The Critical Perspective*, University of Washington Press, Seattle, WA, 1990

P. Colt. "Notes on Ad Reinhardt", *Art International*, Lugano, 8, 8, Oct, 1964

M. Compton & D. Sylvester. *Robert Morris*, Tate Gallery, London, 1971

J.C. Cooper. *An Illustrated Dictionary of Traditional Symbols*, Thames & Hudson, London, 1978

J. Coplans. "Post-Painterly Abstraction", *Artforum*, 2, 12, Summer, 1964

—. "Serial Imagery", *Artforum*, 7, 2, Oct, 1968

—. *Donald Judd*, Pasadena Art Museum, CA, 1971

J. Cornell. *Theatre of the Mind: Selected Diaries, Letters and Files*, Thames & Hudson, London, 1994

M. Craig-Martin. *Minimalism*, Tate Gallery, Liverpool, 1989

M. Crichton. *Jasper Johns*, Thames & Hudson, London, 1977

T. Crow. *Modern Art in the Common Culture*, Yale University Press New Haven, CT, 1996

P. Crowther. "Barnett Newman and the Sublime", *Oxford Art Journal*, 7, 2, 1984

–. ed. *The Contemporary Sublime, Art & Design*, 40, 1995

A. Danto. *After the End of Art*, Princeton University Press, NJ, 1997

E. de Kooning. "Kline and Rothko: Two Americans in Action", *Art News Annual*, 27, 1958

A. Dempsey. *Styles, Schools, Movements*, Thames & Hudson, London, 2002

J. De Mul. *Romantic Desire in (Post)Modern Art and Philosophy*, State University of New York Press, Albany, NY, 1999

N. de Oliveira *et al. Installation Art*, Thames & Hudson, London, 1994

–. *et al*, eds. *Installation Art in the New Millennium*, Thames & Hudson,London, 2003

E. Develing. *Carl Andre*, Gemeentenmeuseum, The Hague, 1969

–. & Lucy Lippard. *Minimal Art*, Stadtische Kunsthalle, Dusseldorf, 1969

W. Domingo. "Brice Marden", *Arts Magazine*, Jan, 1971

–. "Color Abstraction", *Arts Magazine*, Jan, 1971

I. Dunlop. "Edvard Munch, Barnett Newman and Mark Rothko: The Search For the Sublime", *Arts Magazine*, 53, 6, Feb, 1979

L. Durrell. *Collected Poems 1931-1974*, ed. James A. Brigham, Faber 1980

–. *The Mediterranean Shore: Travels in Lawrence Durrell Country*, introduction & commentary by Durrell, Pavilion/ Michael Joseph, 1988

J. Elderfield. *Morris Louis*, Arts Council, London, 1974

–. *Contrasts of Form: Geometric Abstract Art, 1910-1980*, New York, NY, 1985

–. *Morris Louis*, Museum of Modern Art, New York, NY, 1986

–. *Helen Frankenthaler*, New York, NY, 1989

M. Eliade. *Ordeal by Labyrinth,* University of Chicago Press, Chicago, IL, 1984

–. *Symbolism, the Sacred and the Arts*, Crossroad, New York, NY, 1985

D. Factor. "Los Angeles", *Artforum*, 4, 9, May, 1966

J. Fineberg. "Robert Morris Looking Back", *Arts Magazine*, 55, 1, 1980

–. *Art Since 1940: Strategies of Being*, Laurence King, London, 2000

P. Fingesten. *The Eclipse of Symbolism*, Columbia, 1970

E. Firestone. "Color in Abstract Expressionism: Sources and Background For Meaning", *Arts Magazine*, Mch, 1981

J. Flam. "Old Artists, New Styles", *Wall Street Journal*, Mch 25, 1987

S. Foley. *Unitary Forms: Minimal Structures by Carl Andre, Donald Judd, John McCracken, Tony Smith*, Museum of Modern Art, San Francisco, CA, 1970

S. Foster. *The Critics of Abstract Expressionism*, UMI Research Press, Ann Arbor, MI, 1980

R. Francis. *Jasper Johns,* New York, NY, 1984

H. Frankenthaler. "Interview with Helen Frankenthaler", *Artforum*, 4, 2, Oct 1965

E. Franz. *Jackson Pollock*, Abbeville, New York, NY, 1983

F. Frascina *et al*, eds. *Modern Art and Modernism: A Critical Anthology*, Paul Chapman, 1988

M. Fried. "New York Letter", *Art International*, 8, 3, Apl, 1964

–. *Three American Painters: Kenneth Noland, Jules Olitski, Frank Stella*, Fogg Art Museum, Harvard University, Cambridge,

MA, 1965

—. "Shape as Form: Frank Stella's New Paintings", *Artforum*, 5, 3, Nov, 1966

—. "Art and Objecthood", *Artforum*, 5, Summer, 1967

—. *Morris Louis*, Museum of Fine Arts, Boston, MA, 1967

—. *Morris Louis*, Abrams, New York, NY, 1970

M. Friedman. "Robert Morris: Polemics and Cubes", *Art International*, 10, 10, Dec, 1966

—. *14 Sculptors*, Walker Art Center, Minneapolis, MN, 1969

P. Fuller. "The Legacy of Mark Rothko", *Art Monthly*, 20, Oct, 1978

—. "St Ives", *Artscribe*, 53, June, 1985

—. *Peter Fuller's Modern Painters: Reflections on British Art*, ed. J. McDonald, Methuen, London, 1993

J. Gage. *Colour And Culture*, Thames & Hudson, London, 1993

—. *Colour and Meaning: Art, Science and Symbolism*, Thames & Hudson, London, 1999

P. Gardner. "Elizabeth Murray Shapes Up", *Art News*, Sept, 1984

C. Geelhaar. *Frank Stella Workings Drawings, 1956-1970*, tr. C. Hamlin, Kunstmuseum, Basel, 1980

A. Gibson. "Regression and Color in Abstract Expressionism: Barnett Newman, Mark Rothko and Clyfford Still", *Arts Magazine*, Mch, 1981

J. Gilbert-Rolfe. "Brice Marden, David Novros, Bykert Gallery", *Artforum*, May, 1974

—. "Appreciating Ryman", *Arts Magazine*, 50, 4, Dec, 1975

E. Gillen, ed. *German Art From Beckmann To Richter*, Dumont Buchverlag, Cologne, 1997

B. Glaser. "Questions to Stella and Judd", ed. L. Lippard, *Art News*, 65, 5, Sept, 1966

A. Glimcher. *Mark Rothko: The 1958-1959 Murals*, Pace Gallery, New York, NY, 1978

—. *The Art of Mark Rothko*, Barrie & Jenkins, London, 1992

T. Godfrey. "The Human Presence in Recent Abstract Painting", *Aspects*, Fall, 1979

—. *The New Image: Painting in the 1980s*, Phaidon, London, 1986

—. *Conceptual Art*, Phaidon, London, 1998

R. Goldberg. *Performance: Live Art Since the 60s*, Thames & Hudson, London, 1998

J. Goldman. *Frank Stella*, Princeton University Museum of Art, Princeton, NJ, 1983

A. Goldsworthy. *Hand to Earth: Andy Goldsworthy, Sculpture, 1976-1990*, Henry Moore Centre for Sculpture, Leeds, Yorkshire, 1990

C. Greenberg. "American-Type Painting", *Partisan Review*, Spring, 1955

—. "Modernist Painting", *Arts Yearbook*, 4, Art Digest, New York, NY, 1961

—. *Art and Culture*, Beacon Press, Boston, MA, 1961

—. *Post-Painterly Abstraction*, Los Angeles County Museum, Los Angeles, CA, 1964

—. *Three American Painters: Louis, Noland, Olitski*, Norman Mackenzie Art Gallery, Saskatchewan, 1965

N. Grimes. "Robert Ryman's White Magic", *Art News*, Summer, 1968

S. Guberman. *Frank Stella: An Illustrated Biography*, Rizzoli, New York, NY, 1995

S. Guilbaut. *How New York Stole the Idea of Modern Art: Abstract Expressionism, Freedom and the Cold War*, University of Chicago Press, Chicago IL, 1983

A. Haden-Guest. "The King of Wrap", *The Sunday Times Magazine*, Jan, 1994

K. Halbreich. *Affinities: Myron Stout, Bill Jensen, Brice Marden, Terry Winters*, Hayden Gallery, MIT, Cambridge, MA, 1983

B. Haskell. *Jo Baer*, Whitney Museum of American Art, New York, NY, 1975

—. *Donald Judd*, Whitney Museum of American Art, New York, NY, 1988

A. Henri. *Environments and Happenings*, Thames & Hudson, London, 1974a

—. *Total Art*, Praeger, New York, NY, 1974b

T. Hess. *Barnett Newman*, Walker, New York,

NY, 1969

—. "Rules of the Game: Part II: Marden and Rockburne", *New York Magazine*, Nov 11, 1974

Galerie Max Hetzler. *Carl Andre, Gunther Forg, Hubert Kiecol, Richard Long, Meuser, Reinhard Mucha, Bruce Nauman and Ulrich Ruckreim*, Cologne, 1985

R. Hobbs & G. Levin. *Abstract Expressionism: The Formative Years*, Whitney Museum of American Art, New York, NY, 1978

—. *Robert Smithson: Sculpture,* Cornell University Press, Ithaca, NY, 1981

N. Hodges, ed. *The Contemporary Sublime, Art & Design*, 40, 1995

R. Hooker. "Sublimity as Process: Hegel, Newman and Shave", in P. Crowther, 1995

D. Hopkins. *After Modern Art*, Oxford University Press, Oxford, 2000

C. Huber. *Robert Ryman*, Kunsthalle, Basel, 1975

R. Hughes. "Mark Rothko in Babylon", *The New York Review of Books*, 1978a

—. "Blue Chip Sublime", *The New York Review*, Dec 21, 1978b

—. "Morris Louis", *Time*, 1982

—. *Nothing If Not Critical: Selected Essays on Art and Artists*, Collins Harvill, London, 1990

—. *The Shock of the New*, Thames & Hudson, London, 1991

—. *American Visions: The Epic History of Art In America*, Knopf, New York, NY, 1997

S. Hunter, ed. *American Art of the 20th Century*, Thames & Hudson, London, 1973

—. *Tony Smith*, Pace Gallery, New York, NY, 1979

—. *An American Renaissance: Painting and Sculpture Since 1940*, Abbeville Press, New York, NY, 1986

E.H. Johnson, ed. *American Artists on Art*, Harper & Row, New York, NY, 1982

D. Joselit. *American Art Since 1945*, Thames & Hudson, London, 2003

D. Judd. "Frank Stella", *Arts Magazine,* 36, Sept, 1962

—. "In the Galleries", *Arts Magazine*, 37, 10, Sept, 1963

—. "Local History", *Arts Yearbook 7*, 1964

—. "Black, White and Gray", *Arts Magazine*, 38, 6, Mch, 1964

—. "Specific Objects", *Arts Yearbook*, 8, Art Digest, New York, NY, 1965

—. "Barnett Newman", *Studio International*, 179, 919, Feb, 1970

—. *Complete Writings, 1959-1975*, Nova Scotia College of Art and Design, Halifax, Canada, 1975

—. *Complete Writings, 1975-1986*, Van Abbemuseum, Netherlands, 1987

A. Kagan. *Absolute Art*, W.H. Green, St Louis, 1995

J. Kastner, ed. *Land and Environmental Art*, Phaidon, London, 1998

E. Kelly. *Ellsworth Kelly*, Stedelijk Museum, Amsterdam, 1980

—. *Line Form Color,* Chicago University Press, Chicago, IL, 1999

—. *The Early Drawings, 1948-1955,* Chicago University Press, Chicago, IL, 1999

C. Knight. *Art of the Sixties and Seventies*, Rizzoli, New York, NY, 1987

M. Kozloff. "Mark Rothko's New Retrospective", *Art Journal*, 20, 3, 1961

—. "New York Letter", *Art International*, 8, 3, Apl, 1964

—. *Jasper Johns*, New York, NY, 1969

R.E. Kraus. *Passages in Modern Sculpture,* Thames & Hudson, London, 1977

J. Kristeva. *The Kristeva Reader*, ed. T. Moi, Blackwell, Oxford, 1986

—. *Desire in Language: A Semiotic Approach to Literature and Art*, ed. Leon Roudiez, tr. T. Gora *et al*, Blackwell, Oxford, 1982

D. Kuspit. "Sol LeWitt", *Art in America*, 63, 5, 1975

—. "Authoritarian Abstraction", *Journal of Aesthetics and Art Criticism*, 36, 1, Autumn,

1977

—. "Symbolic Pregnance in Mark Rothko and Clyfford Still", *Arts Magazine*, 52, 7, Mch, 1978

—. *The Critic as Artist*, University of Michigan Press, Ann Arbor, MI, 1984

—. "Donald Judd", *Artforum*, 23, 5, Feb, 1985

J. Kutner. "Brice Marden, David Novros, Mark Rothko: The Urge to Communicate through Non-Imagistic Painting", *Arts Magazine*, 50, 1, Sept, 1975

I. Lamaitre. "Interview with Tony Cragg", *Artefactum*, 2, Dec, 1985

D. Lee. "Serial Rights", *Art News*, 66, 8, Dec, 1967

A. Legg, ed. *Sol LeWitt*, Museum of Modern Art, New York, NY, 1978

P. Leider. "Literalism and Abstraction: Frank Stella's Retrospective at the Modern", *Artforum*, 8, Apl, 1970

—. *Stella Since 1970*, Fort Worth Art Museum, Texas, TX, 1978

—. "Shakespeare's Fish", *Art in America*, Oct, 1990

G. Levin. *20th Century American Painting*, Sotheby's Publications, London, 1987

S. LeWitt. "Paragraphs on Conceptual Art", *Art Language*, May, 1969

—. *Sol LeWitt*, Gemeentemuseum, The Hague, 1970

I. Licht. "Dan Flavin", *Artscanada*, Dec, 1968

L. Lippard. "New York Letter: April-June, 1965", *Art International*, 9, 6, 1965

—. *Ad Reinhardt*, Jewish Museum, New York, NY, 1966

—. "An Impure Situation", *Art International*, May 20, 1966

—. "The Silent Art", *Art in America*, 55, 1, Jan-Feb, 1967

—. "Sol LeWitt: Non-Visual Structures", *Artforum*, Apl, 1967

—. "Rebelliously Romantic?", *New York Times*, June 4, 1967

—. "Escalation in Washington", *Art Inter-national*, 12, 1, Jan, 1968

—. *Tony Smith*, Thames & Hudson, London, 1972

—. *Grids*, Philadelphia Institute of Contemporary Art, PA, 1972

—. *Six Years: The Dematerialization of the Art Object From 1966 to 1972*, Praeger, New York, NY, 1973

—. *From the Center: feminist essays on women's art*, Dutton, New York, NY, 1976

—. *Ad Reinhardt*, Abrams, New York, NY, 1981

M. Louis. *Bronze Veils*, Andre Emmerich Gallery, New York, NY, 1969

E. Lucie-Smith. *Art of the Seventies*, Phaidon, London, 1980

—. *Lives of the 20th Century Artists*, Weidenfeld & Nicolson, London, 1986

—. *Sculpture Since 1945*, Phaidon, London, 1987

—. *Art Today,* Phaidon, London, 1989

—. *Sexuality in Western Art*, Thames & Hudson, London, 1991

—. *Movements In Art Since 1945*, Thames & Hudson, London, 1995

R. Lund. "Why Isn't Minimal Art Boring?", *Journal of Aesthetics and Art Criticism*, 45, 2, Winter, 1986

N. Lynton. *The Story of Modern Art*, Phaidon, London, 1989

S.H. Madoff. "The Return of Abstraction", *Arts News*, Jan, 1986

B. Marden. *Paintings, Drawings and Prints, 1975-1980*, ed. N. Serota, Whitechapel Art Gallery, London, 1981

—. "The '60s in Abstract Painting: 13 Statements... Brice Marden", *Art in America*, Oct, 1983

—. *Brice Marden: The Grove Group*, text: R. Witten, Gagosian Gallery, New York, NY, 1991

—. *Brice Marden: Recent Drawings and Etchings*, Matthew Marks Gallery, New York, NY, 1991

—. *Paintings and Drawings*, ed. D. Whitney,

Harry N. Abrams, New York, NY, 1992a

—. *Brice Marden: Prints, 1961-1991: A Catalogue Raisonné*, text: J. Lewison, Tate Gallery, London, 1992b

—. *Cold Mountain*, Houston Fine Arts, TX, 1992

—. *Brice Marden: Paintings, Drawings, Etchings*, Matthew Marks Gallery, New York, NY, 1993

—. *Work Books*, Richter, 1997

A. Martin. *Agnes Martin*, Institute of Contemporary Art, Philadelphia, PA, 1973

H. Matisse. *Matisse on Art*, Dutton, New York, NY, 1978

D. Mayall. *The Minimal Tradition*, Aldrich Museum of Contemporary Art, Ridgefield, CT, 1979

D. McKinney. *Mark Rothko*, Kunsthaus Zürich, 1971

—. *Yves Klein, Brice Marden, Sigmar Polke*, Hirschl & Alder Modern, New York, NY, 1989

K. McShine. *Primary Structures*, Jewish Museum, New York, NY, 1966

J. Mellow. "New York Letter", *Art International*, 20 Apl, 1966

F. Meyer. *Frank Stella*, Kunsthalle, Basel, 1976

J. Meyer, ed. *Minimalism*, Phaidon, London, 2000

U. Meyer. *Conceptual Art*, Dutton, New York, NY, 1972

D. Miller, ed. *Sixteen Americans*, Museum of Modern Art, New York, NY, 1959

C. Millett. "De Kooning, Newman, Rothko: des bâtards", *Art Press International*, 26, Mch, 1979

M. Miss. *Mary Miss: Interior Works*, Bell Gallery, University of Rhode Island, Autumn, 1981

K. Moffet. *Morris Louis*, Museum of Fine Arts, Boston, MA, 1979

—. *Kenneth Noland*, New York, NY, 1977

—. *Jules Olitski*, New York, NY, 1981

R. Morris. "Notes on Sculpture", *Artforum*, Feb, 1966, Oct, 1966, June, 1967, Apl, 1969

—. "Aligned with Nazca", *Artforum*, Oct, 1975

—. *Robert Morris: Mirror Works, 1961-1978*, Leo Castelli Gallery, New York, NY, 1979

R. Murdoch. *Modular Painting*, Albright-Knox Art Gallery, Buffalo, 1970

L. Nead. *Female Nude: Art, Obscenity and Sexuality*, Routledge, London, 1992

T. Neff, ed. *A Quiet Revolution: British Sculpture Since 1965*, Thames & Hudson, London, 1987

B. Nemitz. *Trans Plant: Living Vegetation in Contemporary Art*, Hatje Cantz, 2000

B. Newman. *The Stations of the Cross*, Guggenheim, New York, NY, 1966

—. *Selected Writings and Interviews*, ed. J.P. O'Neill, Knopf, New York, NY, 1990

S. Nodelman. "Sixties Art: Some Philosophical Perspectives", *Perspecta. The Yale Architectural Journal*, 11, 1967

—. *Marden, Novros, Rothko: Painting in the Age of Actuality*, Institute for the Arts, Rice University, Houston, TX, 1978

G. Nordland. *Fourteen Abstract Painters*, Frederick S. Wright Art Gallery, University of California, Los Angeles, CA, 1979

—. *Richard Diebenkorn*, New York, NY, 1987

B. O'Doherty. "Frank Stella and a Crisis of Nothingness", *New York Times*, 19 Jan, 1964, section 2, 21

F. Orton. *Jasper Johns: The Sculptures*, Henry Moore Institute, Leeds, Yorkshire, 1996

P. Osborne, ed. *Conceptual Art*, Phaidon, London, 2002

A. C. Papadakis, ed. *British and American Art: The Uneasy Dialectic*, Art & Design, 3, 9/10, Academy Group, London, 1987

—. ed. *Abstract Art and the Rediscovery of the Spiritual*, Art & Design, 3, 5/6, Academy Group, London, 1987

—. ed. *The New Romantics*, Art & Design, vol 4, 11/12, Academy Group, London, 1988

P. Patton. "Robert Morris and the Fire Next Time", *Art News*, 82, 10, Dec, 1983

J. Perreault. "A Minimal Future? Union-Made: Report on a Phenomenon", *Arts Magazine*,

41, Mch, 1967

J. Perrone. "Seeing Through Boxes", *Artforum*, 15, Nov, 1976

—. "Review", *Artforum*, Dec, 1976

R. Pincus-Witten. "Systematic Painting", *Artforum*, 5, 3, Nov, 1966

—. "Ryman, Marden, Manzoni: Theory, Sensibility, Mediation", *Artforum*, 10, 10, June, 1972

—. "Sol LeWitt", *Artforum*, 11, 6, Feb, 1973

—. *Postminimalism*, Out of London, New York, NY, 1977

L. Ponti. "Tony Cragg", *Domus*, 611, Nov, 1980

M. Poirier & J. Necol. "The '60s in Abstract Painting: 13 Statements... Brice Marden", *Art in America*, Oct, 1983

—. "Color-coded Mysteries", *ARTnews*, Jan, 1985

C. Ratcliff. "Robert Ryman's Double Positive", *Art News*, Mch, 1971

—. "Once More With Feeling", *Art News*, 71, 4, Summer, 1972

—. "Abstract Painting, Specific Spaces: Novros and Marden in Houston", *Art in America*, 63, 5, Nov, 1975

—. *In the Realm of the Monochrome*, Renaissance Society, University of Chicago, Chicago, IL, 1979

—. "The Compleat Smithson", *Art in America*, Jan, 1980

—. "Mostly Monochrome", *Art in America*, 69, 4, Apl, 1981

—. "Robert Ryman Making Distinctions", *Art in America*, June, 1986

—. *Out of the Box*, Allworth Press, 2001

A. Reinhardt. *Art as Art: The Selected Writings of Ad Reinhardt*, University of California Press, Berkeley, CA, 1991

B. Reise. "Untitled, 1969: A Footnote on Art and Minimal Stylehood", *Studio International*, 177, 910, Apl, 1969

—. "The Stance of Barnett Newman", *Studio International* 179, 920, Mch, 1970

B. Richardson. *Frank Stella: The Black Paintings*, Baltimore Museum of Art, Baltimore, MD, 1976

C.A. Riley II. *Color Codes: Modern Theories in Color in Philosophy, Painting and Architecture, Literature, Music and Psychology*, University Press of New England, Hanover, NH, 1995

A.C. Ritche. *Salute to Mark Rothko*, Yale University Art Gallery, New Haven, CT, 1971

B. Robertson, ed. *Mark Rothko: A Retrospective Exhibition, Paintings, 1945-1960*, Whitechapel, London, 1961

C. Robins. "Object, Structure or Sculpture: Where Are We?", *Arts Magazine*, 40, 9, 1966

—. "Empty Paintings", *SoHo Weekly News*, 22 Apl, 1976

—. *The Pluralist Era: American Art, 1968-1981*, Harper & Row, New York, NY, 1984

S. Rodman. *Conversations With Artists*, Devin-Adair, New York, NY, 1957

A. Rorimer. *New Art in the 60s and 70s*, Thames & Hudson, London, 2001

B. Rose. "ABC Art", *Art in America*, 53, 5, Nov, 1965

—. *American Art Since 1900*, Thames & Hudson, London, 1967

—. *A New Aesthetic*, Washington Gallery of Modern Art, Washington DC, 1967

—. *American Painting*, Skira/ Rizzoli International, New York, NY, 1986

H. Rosenberg. *The De-Definition of Art*, Horizon Press, New York, NY, 1972

—. *Barnett Newman*, Abrams, New York, NY, 1978/ 1994

—. *The Tradition of the New*, Da Capo Press, New York, NY, 1994

R. Rosenblum. "The Abstract Sublime", *Art News*, 59, 10, Feb, 1961

—. "Frank Stella: Five Years of Variations on an Irreducible Theme", *Artforum*, 3, 6, Mch, 1965

—. *Frank Stella*, Penguin, London, 1971

—. "Notes on Sol LeWitt", in Legg, 1978

—. *Modern Painting and the Northern*

Romantic Tradition, Thames & Hudson, London, 1978

—. *Mark Rothko*, Pace Gallery, New York, NY, 1981

—. *Jasper Johns' Paintings and Sculptures, 1954-1974*, Ann Arbor, MI, 1985

—. "Romanticism and Retrospective: An Interview with Robert Rosenblum", in Papadakis, 1988

M. Rothko. *Mark Rothko, 1903-1970: A Retrospective*, Guggenheim, New York, NY, 1979

—. *Mark Rothko, 1903-1970*, Tate Gallery, London, 1987

—. *Mark Rothko in New York*, Guggenheim, New York, NY, 1994

L. Rubin. *Frank Stella Paintings: 1958-1965*, New York, NY, 1986

W.S. Rubin. *Frank Stella*, New York Graphic Society, Greenwich, CT, 1970

—. *Frank Stella: 1970-1987*, Museum of Modern Art, New York, NY, 1987

R. Ryman. "An Interview with Robert Ryman", Phyllis Tuchman, *Artforum*, 9, 9, May, 1971

—. "The 60's in Abstract", *Art in America*, 71, 9, Oct, 1983

I. Sandler. *Concrete Expressionism*, Loeb Student Center, New York University, NY, 1965

—. "The New Cool-Art", *Art in America*, 53, 1, Feb, 1967

—. *The Triumph of American Painting*, Harper & Row, New York, NY, 1970

—. *American Art of the 1960s*, Harper & Row, New York, NY, 1988

—. *Art of the Postmodern Era: From the 1960s to the Early 1990s*, HarperCollins, London, 1997

P. Schjeldahl. "Rothko and Belief", *Art in America*, Mch, 1979

—. *Art in Our Time: The Saatchi Collection*, Lund Humphries, London, 1984

B. Schwabsky. "The Real Situation: Philip Guston and Mark Rothko at the End of the Sixties", *Arts Magazine*, 61, 4, Dec, 1986

W. Seitz. *Abstract Expressionist Painting in America*, Harvard University Press, Cambridge, MA, 1983

L. Seldes. *The Legacy of Mark Rothko*, Secker & Warburg, London, 1978

P. Selz. *Mark Rothko*, Museum of Modern Art, New York, NY, 1961

—. *Art in a Turbulent Era*, UMI Research Press, Ann Arbor, MI, 1985

E. Shanes. *Constantin Brancusi*, Abbeville, New York, NY, 1989

D. Shapiro & C. Shapiro, eds. *Abstraction Expressionism: A Critical Record*, Cambridge University Press, Cambridge, 1990

L. Shearer. *Brice Marden*, Guggenheim, New York, NY, 1975

P. Sims. *From Minimalism to Expressionism*, New York, NY, 1963

H. Singerman, ed. *Individuals: A Selected History of Contemporary Art, 1945-1986*, Museum of Contemporary Art, Los Angeles, CA, 1986

H.J. Smagula. *Currents: Contemporary Directions in the Visual Arts*, Prentice-Hall, Englewood Cliffs, NJ, 1983

B. Smith. *Fluorescent Light, etc, from Dan Flavin*, National Gallery of Canada, Ottawa, 1969

—. *Donald Judd*, National Gallery of Canada, Ottawa, 1975

R. Smith. "Sol LeWitt", *Artforum*, Jan, 1975

—. "Review", *Artforum*, Dec, 1975

—. *Elisabeth Murray*, Abrams, New York, NY, 1987

R. Smithson. *The Writings of Robert Smithson*, ed. N. Holt, New York University Press, New York, NY, 1979

A. Solomon & C. Greenberg. *Morris Louis*, Whitechapel Art Gallery, London, 1965

E.M. Solomon. *Recent Drawings: William Allan, James Bishop, Vija Celmins, Brice Marden, Jim Nutt, Alan Saret, Pat Steir, Richard Tuttle*, American Foundation of Art,

New York, NY, 1975

N. Spector. *Robert Ryman*, Whitechapel Art Gallery, London, 1977

N. Stangos, ed. *Concepts of Modern Art*, Thames & Hudson, London, 1981

F. Stella. *Moby Dick*, Cantz, 1983

–. *Works and New Graphics*, ICA, London, 1985

–. *Working Space*, Harvard University Press, Cambridge, MA, 1986

–. *Frank Stella*, Madrid, 1995

K. Stiles & P. Selz, eds. *Theories & Documents of Contemporary Art: A Sourcebook of Artists' Writings*, University of California Press, Berkeley, CA, 1996

–. *Out of Actions: Between Performance and the Object, 1949-1979*, Thames & Hudson, London, 1998

R. Storr. *Robert Ryman*, Abrams, New York, NY, 1993

D. Swanson. *Morris Louis*, Walker Art Center, Minneapolis, MN, 1977

D. Sylvester. "Interview", *Jasper Johns Drawings*, Museum of Modern Art, Oxford, 1974

–. *About Modern Art*, Chatto & Windus, London, 1996

J. Taylor *et al. Robert Rauschenberg*, Smithsonian Institute, Washington, DC, 1976

M. Tuchman. *American Sculpture of the Sixties*, Los Angeles County Museum of Art, LA, CA, 1967

–. *The New York School*, Thames & Hudson, London, 1971

–. *The Spiritual in Art: Abstract Painting 1880-1985*, Los Angeles County Museum of Art/ Abbeville Press, New York, NY, 1986

P. Tuchman. "Minimalism and Critical Response", *Artforum*, 15, 9, May, 1977

M. Tucker. *Robert Morris*, New York, NY, 1970

D. Upright. *Morris Louis*, Abrams, New York, NY, 1985

G. de Vries, ed. *On Art: Artists' Writings on the Changed Notion of Art After 1965*, Cologne, 1974

S. Wagstaff. "Paintings to Think About", *Art News*, 62, 9, Jan, 1964

D. Waldman. *Carl Andre*, Guggenheim, New York, NY, 1970

–. *Robert Mangold*, New York, NY, 1971

–. *Robert Ryman*, New York, NY, 1972

–. "Color, Format and Abstract Art: An Interview with Kenneth Noland", *Art in America*, 65, 3, May, 1977

–. *Mark Rothko*, Thames & Hudson, London, 1978

L. Weintraub. *The Maximal Implications of the Minimalist Line*, Edith C. Blum Art Institute, New York, NY, 1985

D. Wheeler. *Art Since Mid-Century: 1945 to the Present*, Thames & Hudson, London, 1991

J. White. *The Birth and Rebirth of Pictorial Space*, Faber, London, 1981

R. Williams. *After Modern Sculpture: Art in the United States and Europe 1965-70*, Manchester University Press, Manchester, 2000

W. Wilson. "Dan Flavin: Fiat Lux", *Art News*, Jan, 1970

A. Sargent Wooster. "Sol LeWitt's Expanding Grid", *Art in America*, 68, 5, May, 1980

WEBSITES

Donald Judd <chinati.org>
Richard Diebenkorn <diebenkorn.org>
Kenneth Noland <kennethnoland.com>
DIA <diacenter.org> and <diaart.org>
Female Artists <female-artists.net>
Gerhard Richter <gerhard-richter.com>
The Artists <the-artists.org>
Crescent Moon Publishing <crmoon>

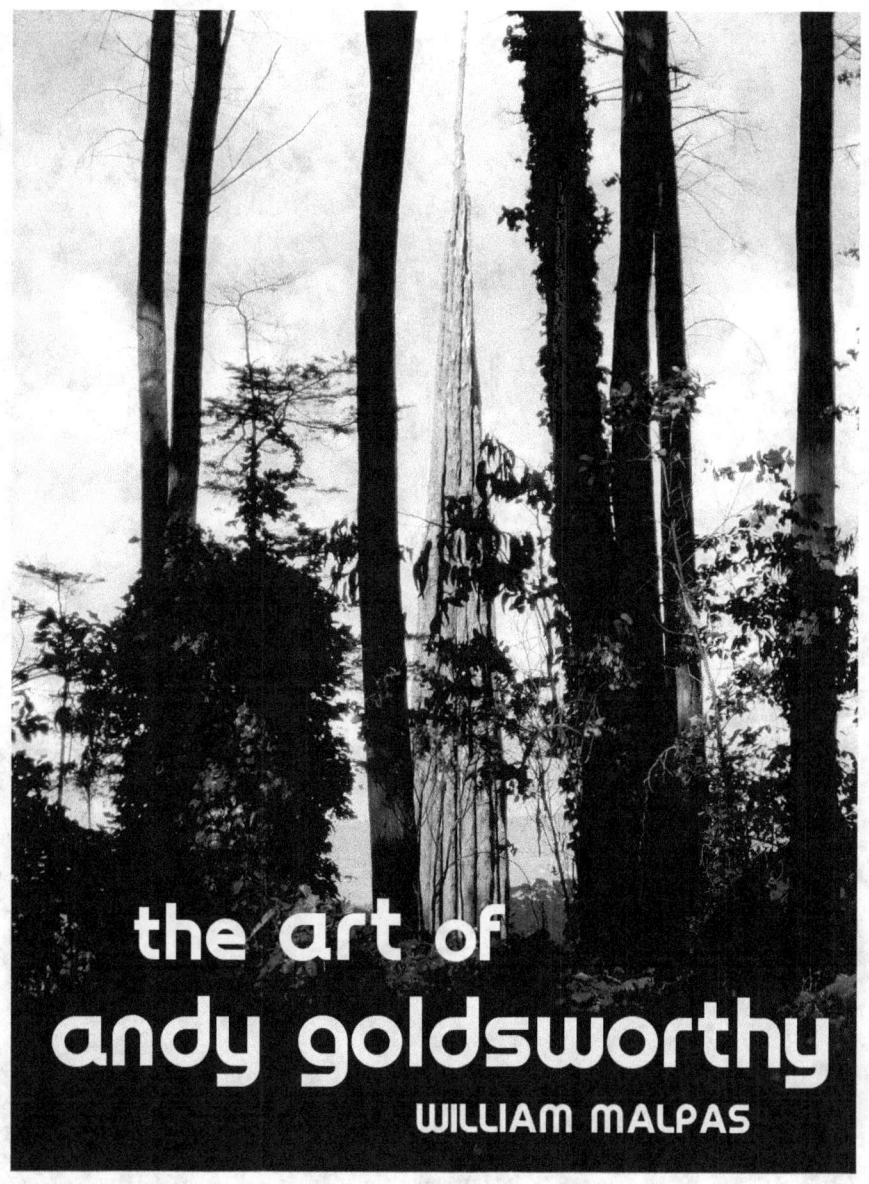

the art of
andy goldsworthy
WILLIAM MALPAS

This is the most comprehensive and detailed account of the art of Andy Goldsworthy available.

This study of Andy Goldsworthy discusses all of Goldsworthy's major exhibitions, books and projects, including the *Sheepfolds* project; *Garden of Stones* in New York; TV and dance collaborations; and the books *Wood, Stone, Time* and *Passage*. William Malpas surveys all of Goldsworthy's output, and analyzes his relation with other land artists such as Robert Smithson, the Christos, Walter de Maria, Chris Drury, Richard Long and David Nash; women sculptors; sculpture in the modern era; and Goldsworthy's place in the contemporary British art scene.

Beauties, Beasts, and Enchantment

CLASSIC FRENCH FAIRY TALES

Translated and with an Introduction
by Jack Zipes

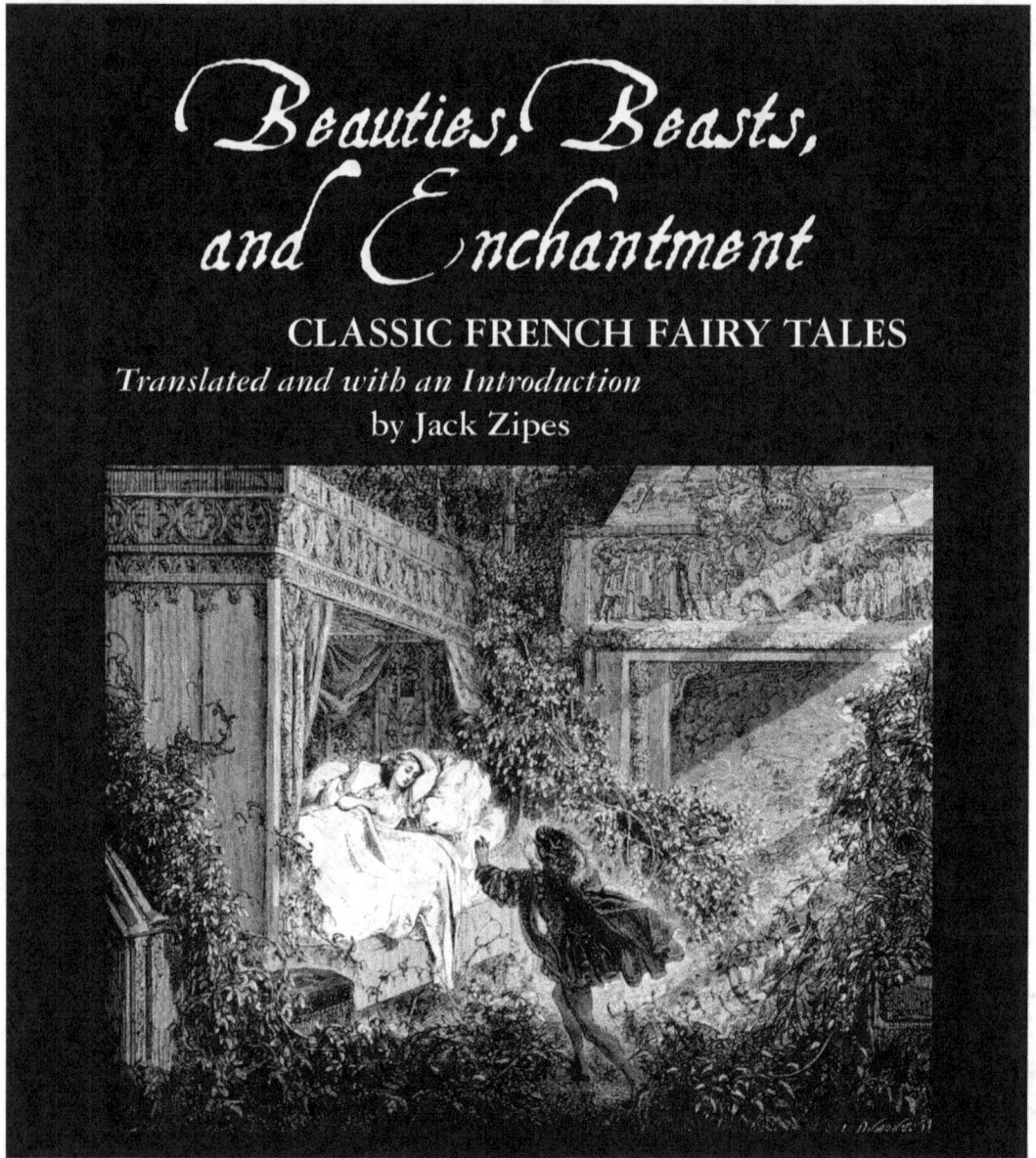

A collection of 36 classic French fairy tales translated by renowned writer Jack Zipes. *Cinderella, Beauty and the Beast, Sleeping Beauty* and *Little Red Riding Hood* are among the classic fairy tales in this amazing book.
Includes illustrations from fairy tale collections.
Jack Zipes has written and published widely on fairy tales.

'Terrific... a succulent array of 17th and 18th century 'salon' fairy tales'
- *The New York Times Book Review*

'These tales are adventurous, thrilling in a way fairy tales are meant to be... The translation from the French is modern, happily free of archaic and hyperbolic language... a fine and sophisticated collection' - *New York Tribune*

'Enjoyable to read... a unique collection of French regional folklore' - *Library Journal*

'Charming stories accompanied by attractive pen-and-ink drawings' - *Chattanooga Times*

Introduction and illustrations   612pp.   ISBN 9781861712510 Pbk   ISBN 9781861713193 Hbk

MAURICE SENDAK

& the art of children's book illustration

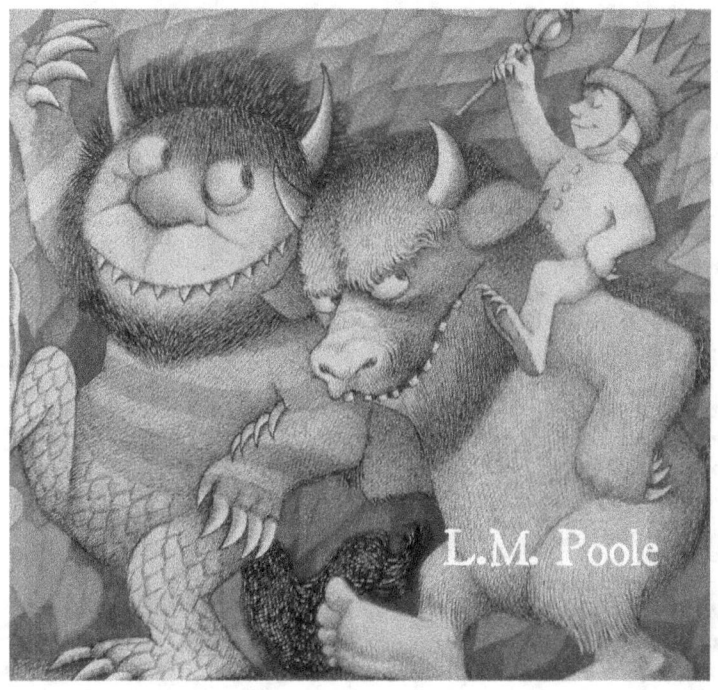

L.M. Poole

Maurice Sendak is the widely acclaimed American children's book author and illustrator. This critical study focuses on his famous trilogy, *Where the Wild Things Are*, *In the Night Kitchen* and *Outside Over There*, as well as the early works and Sendak's superb depictions of the Grimm Brothers' fairy tales in *The Juniper Tree*. L.M. Poole begins with a chapter on children's book illustration, in particular the treatment of fairy tales. Sendak's work is situated within the history of children's book illustration, and he is compared with many contemporary authors.

Fully illustrated. The book has been revised and updated for this edition.
ISBN 9781861714282 Pbk   ISBN 9781861713469 Hbk

CRESCENT MOON PUBLISHING

ARTS, PAINTING, SCULPTURE

The Art of Andy Goldsworthy
Andy Goldsworthy: Touching Nature
Andy Goldsworthy in Close-Up
Andy Goldsworthy: Pocket Guide
Andy Goldsworthy In America
Land Art: A Complete Guide
The Art of Richard Long
Richard Long: Pocket Guide
Land Art In the UK
Land Art in Close-Up
Land Art In the U.S.A.
Land Art: Pocket Guide
Installation Art in Close-Up
Minimal Art and Artists In the 1960s and After
Colourfield Painting
Land Art DVD, TV documentary
Andy Goldsworthy DVD, TV documentary
The Erotic Object: Sexuality in Sculpture From Prehistory to the Present Day
Sex in Art: Pornography and Pleasure in Painting and Sculpture
Postwar Art
Sacred Gardens: The Garden in Myth, Religion and Art
Glorification: Religious Abstraction in Renaissance and 20th Century Art
Early Netherlandish Painting
Leonardo da Vinci
Piero della Francesca
Giovanni Bellini
Fra Angelico: Art and Religion in the Renaissance
Mark Rothko: The Art of Transcendence
Frank Stella: American Abstract Artist
Jasper Johns
Brice Marden
Alison Wilding: The Embrace of Sculpture
Vincent van Gogh: Visionary Landscapes
Eric Gill: Nuptials of God
Constantin Brancusi: Sculpting the Essence of Things
Max Beckmann
Caravaggio
Gustave Moreau
Egon Schiele: Sex and Death In Purple Stockings
Delizioso Fotografico Fervore: Works In Process 1
Sacro Cuore: Works In Process 2
The Light Eternal: J.M.W. Turner
The Madonna Glorified: Karen Arthurs

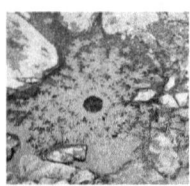
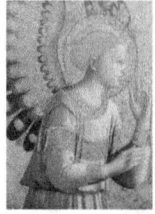
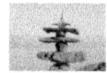
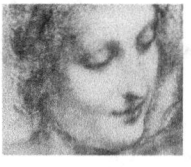
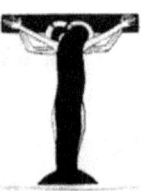
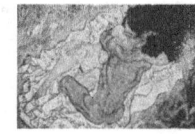

LITERATURE

J.R.R. Tolkien: The Books, The Films, The Whole Cultural Phenomenon
J.R.R. Tolkien: Pocket Guide
Tolkien's Heroic Quest
The *Earthsea* Books of Ursula Le Guin
Beauties, Beasts and Enchantment: Classic French Fairy Tales
German Popular Stories by the Brothers Grimm
Philip Pullman and *His Dark Materials*
Sexing Hardy: Thomas Hardy and Feminism
Thomas Hardy's *Tess of the d'Urbervilles*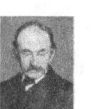
Thomas Hardy's *Jude the Obscure*
Thomas Hardy: The Tragic Novels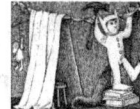
Love and Tragedy: Thomas Hardy
The Poetry of Landscape in Hardy
Wessex Revisited: Thomas Hardy and John Cowper Powys
Wolfgang Iser: Essays and Interviews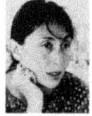
Petrarch, Dante and the Troubadours
Maurice Sendak and the Art of Children's Book Illustration
Andrea Dworkin
Cixous, Irigaray, Kristeva: The *Jouissance* of French Feminism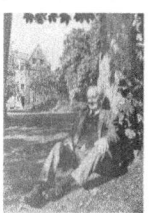
Julia Kristeva: Art, Love, Melancholy, Philosophy, Semiotics and Psychoanalysis
Hélene Cixous I Love You: The *Jouissance* of Writing
Luce Irigaray: Lips, Kissing, and the Politics of Sexual Difference
Peter Redgrove: Here Comes the Flood
Peter Redgrove: Sex-Magic-Poetry-Cornwall
Lawrence Durrell: Between Love and Death, East and West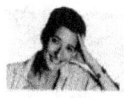
Love, Culture & Poetry: Lawrence Durrell
Cavafy: Anatomy of a Soul
German Romantic Poetry: Goethe, Novalis, Heine, Hölderlin
Feminism and Shakespeare
Shakespeare: Love, Poetry & Magic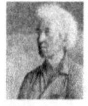
The Passion of D.H. Lawrence
D.H. Lawrence: Symbolic Landscapes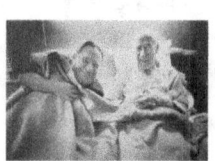
D.H. Lawrence: Infinite Sensual Violence
Rimbaud: Arthur Rimbaud and the Magic of Poetry
The Ecstasies of John Cowper Powys
Sensualism and Mythology: The Wessex Novels of John Cowper Powys
Amorous Life: John Cowper Powys and the Manifestation of Affectivity (H.W. Fawkner)
Postmodern Powys: New Essays on John Cowper Powys (Joe Boulter)
Rethinking Powys: Critical Essays on John Cowper Powys
Paul Bowles & Bernardo Bertolucci
Rainer Maria Rilke
Joseph Conrad: *Heart of Darkness*
In the Dim Void: Samuel Beckett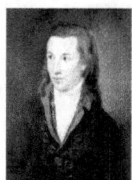
Samuel Beckett Goes into the Silence
André Gide: Fiction and Fervour
Jackie Collins and the Blockbuster Novel
Blinded By Her Light: The Love-Poetry of Robert Graves
The Passion of Colours: Travels In Mediterranean Lands
Poetic Forms

POETRY

Ursula Le Guin: Walking In Cornwall
Peter Redgrove: Here Comes The Flood
Peter Redgrove: Sex-Magic-Poetry-Cornwall
Dante: Selections From the Vita Nuova
Petrarch, Dante and the Troubadours
William Shakespeare: Sonnets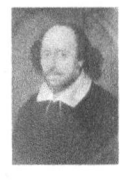
William Shakespeare: Complete Poems
Blinded By Her Light: The Love-Poetry of Robert Graves
Emily Dickinson: Selected Poems
Emily Brontë: Poems
Thomas Hardy: Selected Poems
Percy Bysshe Shelley: Poems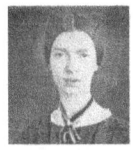
John Keats: Selected Poems
Joh n Keats: Poems of 1820
D.H. Lawrence: Selected Poems
Edmund Spenser: Poems
Edmund Spenser: Amoretti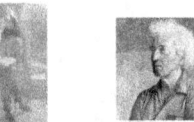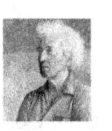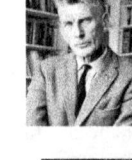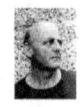
John Donne: Poems
Henry Vaughan: Poems
Sir Thomas Wyatt: Poems
Robert Herrick: Selected Poems
Rilke: Space, Essence and Angels in the Poetry of Rainer Maria Rilke
Rainer Maria Rilke: Selected Poems
Friedrich Hölderlin: Selected Poems
Arseny Tarkovsky: Selected Poems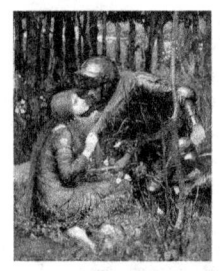
Arthur Rimbaud: Selected Poems
Arthur Rimbaud: A Season in Hell
Arthur Rimbaud and the Magic of Poetry
Novalis: Hymns To the Night
German Romantic Poetry
Paul Verlaine: Selected Poems
Elizaethan Sonnet Cycles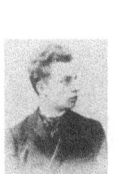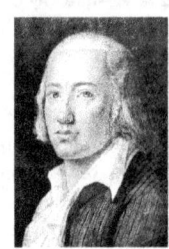
D.J. Enright: By-Blows
Jeremy Reed: Brigitte's Blue Heart
Jeremy Reed: Claudia Schiffer's Red Shoes
Gorgeous Little Orpheus
Radiance: New Poems
Crescent Moon Book of Nature Poetry
Crescent Moon Book of Love Poetry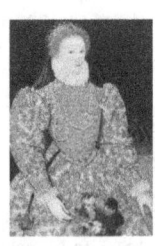
Crescent Moon Book of Mystical Poetry
Crescent Moon Book of Elizabethan Love Poetry
Crescent Moon Book of Metaphysical Poetry
Crescent Moon Book of Romantic Poetry
Pagan America: New American Poetry

MEDIA, CINEMA, FEMINISM and CULTURAL STUDIES

J.R.R. Tolkien: The Books, The Films, The Whole Cultural Phenomenon
J.R.R. Tolkien: Pocket Guide
The *Lord of the Rings* Movies: Pocket Guide
The Cinema of Hayao Miyazaki
Hayao Miyazaki: *Princess Mononoke*: Pocket Movie Guide
Hayao Miyazaki: *Spirited Away*: Pocket Movie Guide
Tim Burton
Ken Russell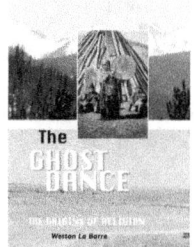
Ken Russell: *Tommy*: Pocket Movie Guide
The Ghost Dance: The Origins of Religion
The Peyote Cult
Cixous, Irigaray, Kristeva: The *Jouissance* of French Feminism
Julia Kristeva: Art, Love, Melancholy, Philosophy, Semiotics and Psychoanalysis
Luce Irigaray: Lips, Kissing, and the Politics of Sexual Difference
Hélene Cixous I Love You: The *Jouissance* of Writing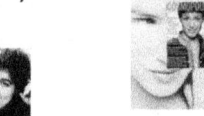
Andrea Dworkin
'Cosmo Woman': The World of Women's Magazines
Women in Pop Music
Discovering the Goddess (Geoffrey Ashe)
The Poetry of Cinema
The Sacred Cinema of Andrei Tarkovsky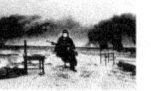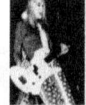
Andrei Tarkovsky: Pocket Guide
Andrei Tarkovsky: *Mirror*: Pocket Movie Guide
Andrei Tarkovsky: *The Sacrifice*: Pocket Movie Guide
Walerian Borowczyk: Cinema of Erotic Dreams
Jean-Luc Godard: The Passion of Cinema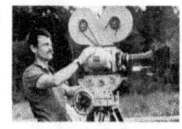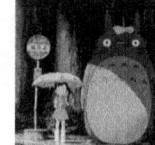
Jean-Luc Godard: *Hail Mary*: Pocket Movie Guide
Jean-Luc Godard: *Contempt*: Pocket Movie Guide
Jean-Luc Godard: *Pierrot le Fou*: Pocket Movie Guide
John Hughes and Eighties Cinema
Ferris Bueller's Day Off: Pocket Movie Guide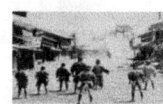
Jean-Luc Godard: Pocket Guide
The Cinema of Richard Linklater
Liv Tyler: Star In Ascendance
Blade Runner and the Films of Philip K. Dick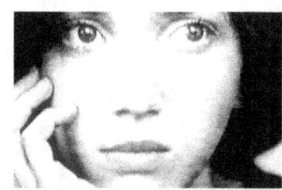
Paul Bowles and Bernardo Bertolucci
Media Hell: Radio, TV and the Press
An Open Letter to the BBC
Detonation Britain: Nuclear War in the UK
Feminism and Shakespeare
Wild Zones: Pornography, Art and Feminism
Sex in Art: Pornography and Pleasure in Painting and Sculpture
Sexing Hardy: Thomas Hardy and Feminism

In my view *The Light Eternal* is among the very best of all the material I read on Turner. (Douglas Graham, director of the Turner Museum, Denver, Colorado)

The Light Eternal is a model monograph, an exemplary job. The subject matter of the book is beautifully organised and dead on beam. (Lawrence Durrell)

It is amazing for me to see my work treated with such passion and respect. (Andrea Dworkin)

CRESCENT MOON PUBLISHING
P.O. Box 1312, Maidstone, Kent, ME14 5XU, Great Britain. www.crmoon.com